IRELAND
The Emerald Isle

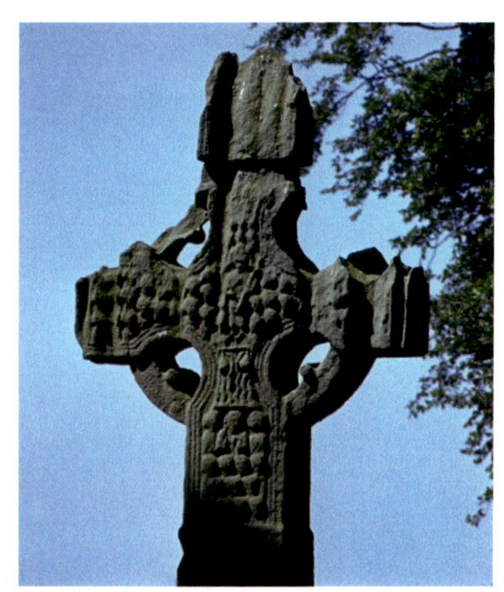

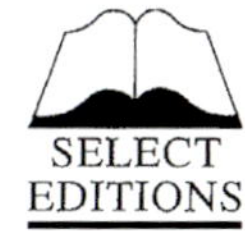

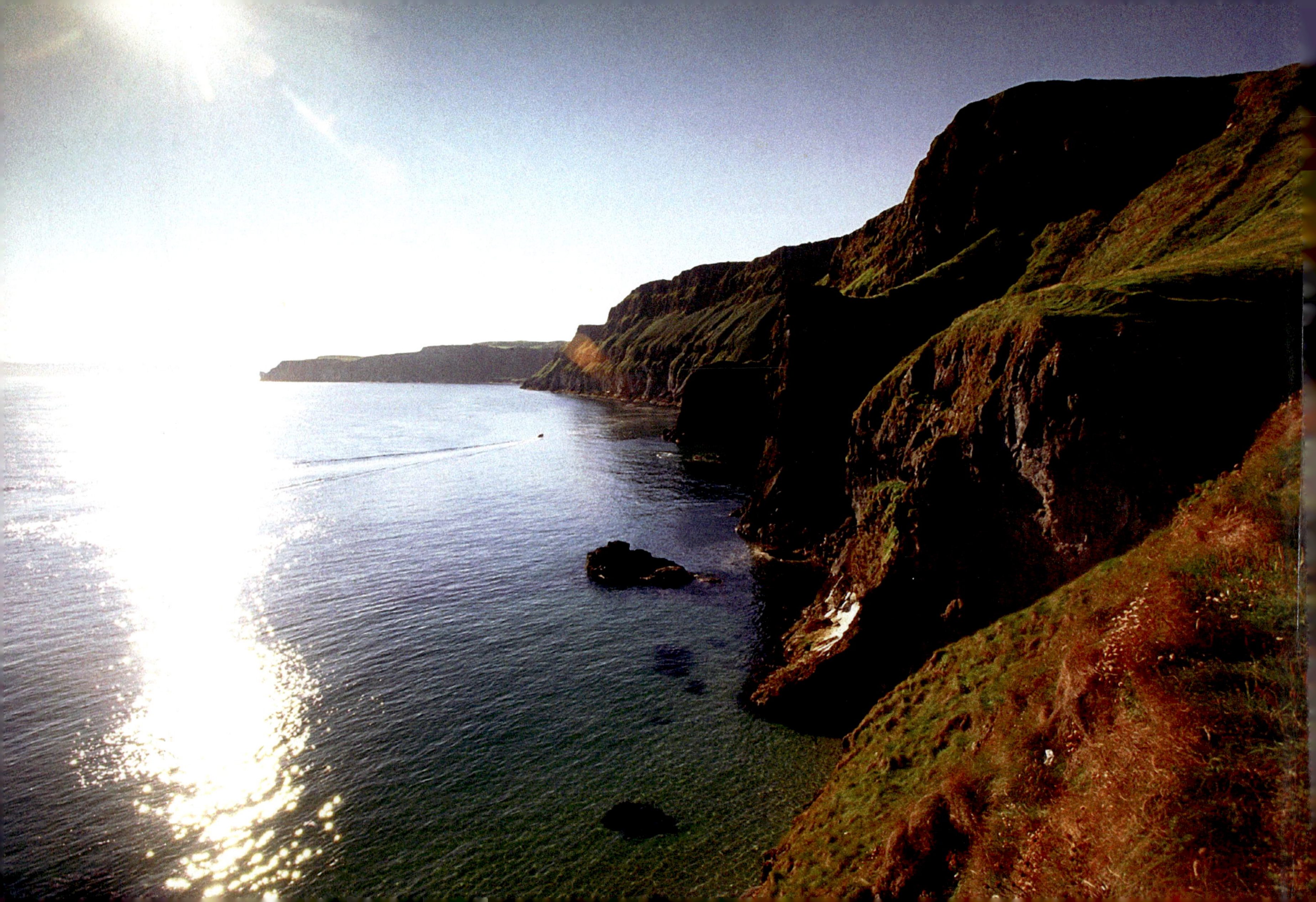

IRELAND
The Emerald Isle

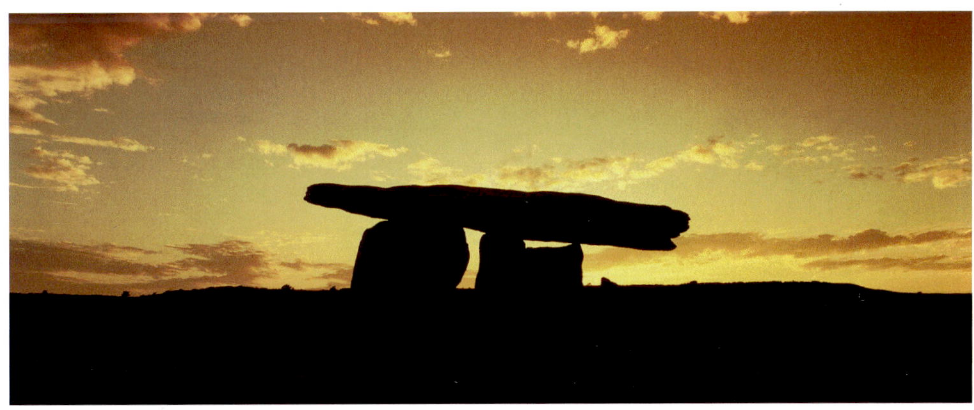

Alex Hook

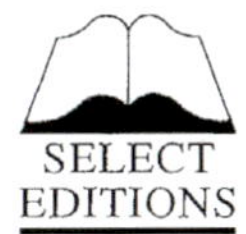

Published 2004 in the UK exclusively for

SELECTABOOK
Folly road,
Roundway,
Devises,
Wiltshire
SN10 2HT

All enquiries please email selectabookltd@tiscali.co.uk

All notations of errors or omissions (author inquiries, permissions) concerning the content of this book should be addressed to TAJ Books 27, Ferndown Gardens, Cobham, Surrey, UK, KT11 2BH, info@tajbooks.com.

ISBN 1-84406-034-9

Printed in China.
1 2 3 4 5 08 07 06 05 04

Northern Ireland 8

Western Ireland 48

Southern Ireland 74

East of Ireland 112

Introduction

At the heart of Ireland lies unspoilt naturalness, which encompasses a beautiful landscape, quality local produce, and people who are spontaneous in their humour, genuine, hospitable, and welcoming.

This book looks at the natural beauty and long history of the "Emerald Isle"—each as dramatic as the other. Today split into two by politics and religion—divisions that have caused rifts for centuries—as elsewhere this turbulence has led to much of the physical history of Ireland: castles and country houses; city walls and great cathedrals.

This book is divided into four general geographical sections. The first covers Northern Ireland, the six counties that were part of Ulster, one of Ireland's four traditional kingdoms (the others were Munster, Leinster, and Connaught). It is a prosperous area, the most prosperous part of Ireland before the EC stimulated growth in the south. Based on the city of Belfast—known for its shipbuilding—Northern Ireland has its fair share of Ireland's natural beauty—from the dramatic coastline of the Causeway Coast, with its many myths and legends, to the Mountains of Mourn to the southeast.

Granted World Heritage status for its unique splendour, the Giant's Causeway is a remarkable natural occurrence that seems it must be man-made. Further west, on the River Foyle stands Derry (or Londonderry), whose walls are among the best-preserved city fortifications in Europe. Crossing the Sperrins brings you to Belfast city and its surrounding hills.

A village in the 17th century, now it contains nearly half a million people—a third of Northern Ireland's population. Belfast was the engine-room that drove the whirring wheels of the Industrial Revolution in Ulster. The development of industries like linen, rope-making, and shipbuilding doubled the size of Belfast every ten years. The world's largest dry dock is here and the shipyard's giant cranes tower over the port. The doomed RMS Titanic was built in the Harland & Wolff shipyards, as were her sister ships.

To the south, "The Mountains o' Mourne sweep down to the sea"—at Newcastle. The sea itself invades the land, forming the great bird sanctuary and yachting paradise of Strangford Lough. St. Patrick sailed into the lough in 432AD and eventually died at Downpatrick. Armagh has been the spiritual capital of Ireland for over 1,500 years and is the seat of both Protestant and Catholic archbishops. St. Patrick called Armagh

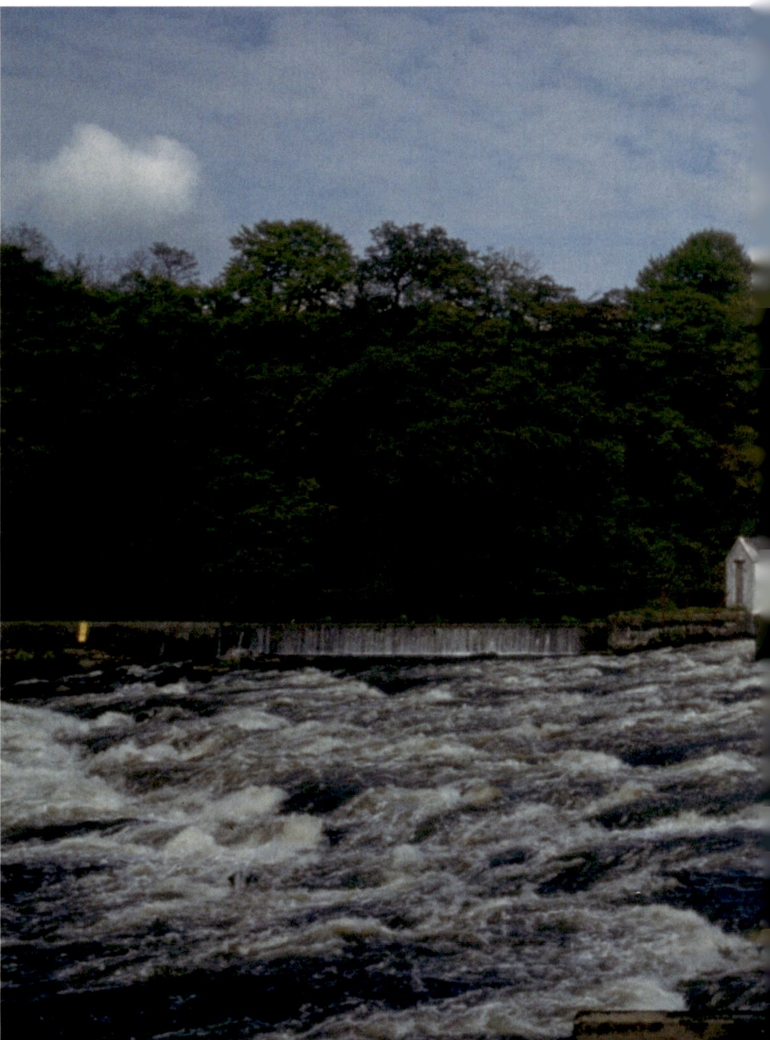

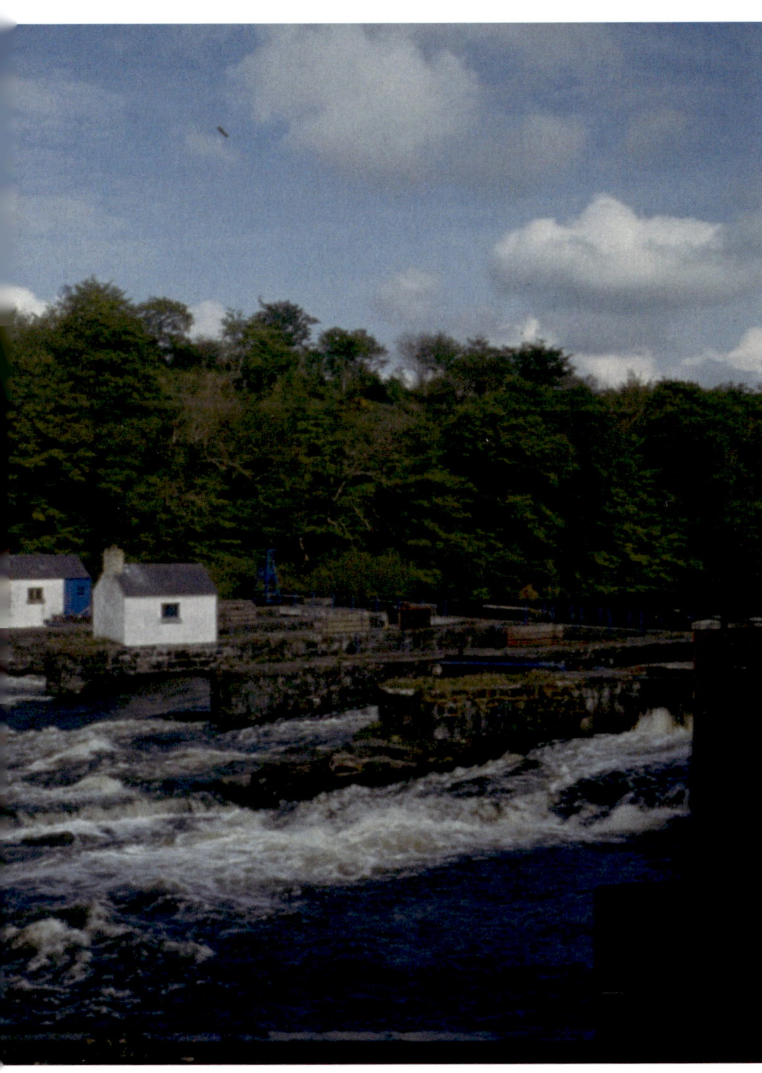

"my sweet hill" and built his stone church on the hill where the Anglican cathedral now stands.

The second geographical split provides the West of Ireland, constituting Donegal and the western counties from Sligo and Leitrim to Limerick and Clare. The three counties of Mayo, Galway, and Roscommon form the heart of Connaught, whose rugged Atlantic coast is still largely unspoilt. Partly this is due to the privations of the Great Famine of the mid-19th century that led to massive emigration and rural depopulation. Gaelic is spoken by almost half the population as a first language, and the area also boasts the wild Connemara peninsula, much of it a national park, as well as the lively city of Galway. Off the coast of Galway lie the Aran Islands, for so long bastions of Irish religious learning and traditions.

The lower counties in this section—Clare, Limerick and Tipperary—lie alongside the great River Shannon. This is an area of great natural beauty, but it is also home to remarkable examples of Ireland's past—from the neolithic burials of the Burren, a vast expanse of limestone pavement, to the 15th century Bunratty Castle and the great religious foundation at Cashel, based on the seat of the ancient kings of Munster.

The third section of the book looks at Kerry and Cork, probably the best-known area of Ireland for tourists. From the sandy Atlantic beaches of the Dingle peninsula, through Macgillycuddy's Reeks and the lakes of Killarney, the pretty town of Kinsale and on to Cork and the River Blackwater, this area is extremely popular for outdoor pursuits—and of course, it boasts the site of the Blarney Stone, guaranteed to keep you from ever being tongue-tied again!

Finally, the fourth section covers Dublin and the east of the country, such counties as Waterford, Kilkenny, Meath, Wicklow, and Kildare. As one of the best preserved Georgian cities in Britain, Dublin is a beautiful city with a nightlife and cultural institutions well worthy of a visit.

Northern Ireland

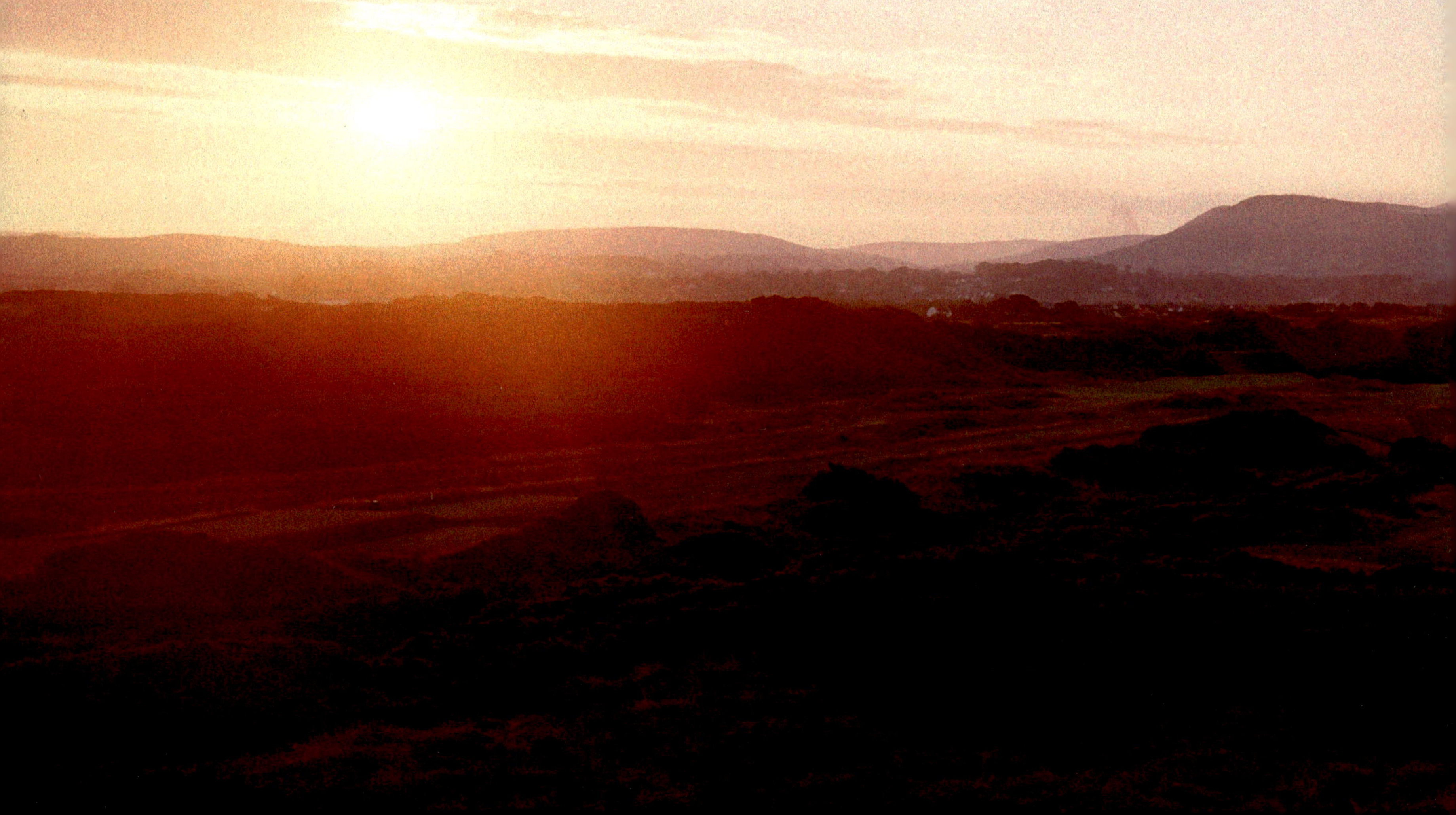

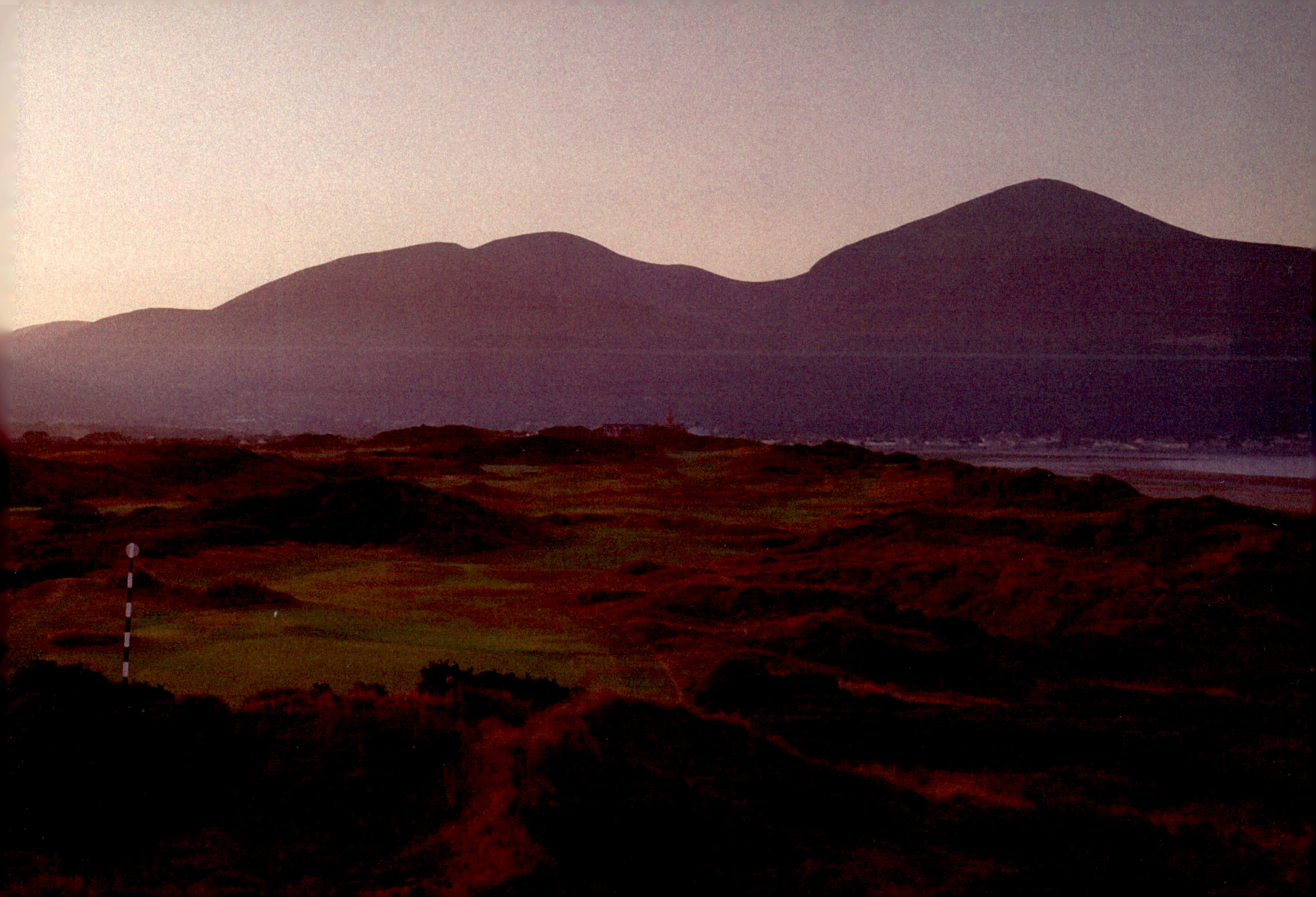

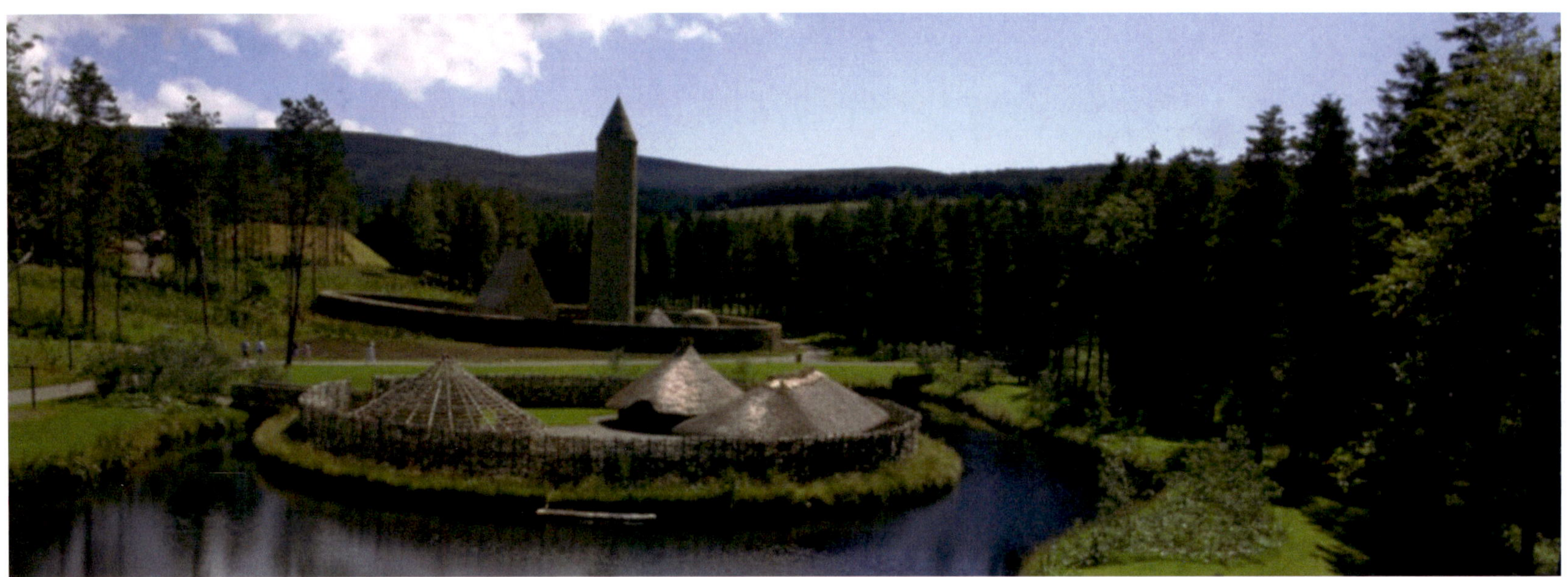

Ulster History Park
(above)

The Park focuses on the period from 8000BC to the 17th century, with fascinating reconstructions of buildings from the mesolithic era to Plantation times.

The outdoor area of the Ulstory History Park features replica megalithic tombs and houses from early Christian plus a mighty Round Tower on the 35-acre site.

Queen's University Belfast
(right)

Founded by Queen Victoria, the Queen's University in Ireland, was designed to be a non-denominational alternative to Trinity College Dublin which was controlled by the Anglican Church. The University was made up of three Queen's Colleges - in Cork, Galway and Belfast. Although it was the first University in the north of Ireland, Queen's drew on a tradition of learning which goes back to 1810 and the foundation of the Belfast Academical Institution.

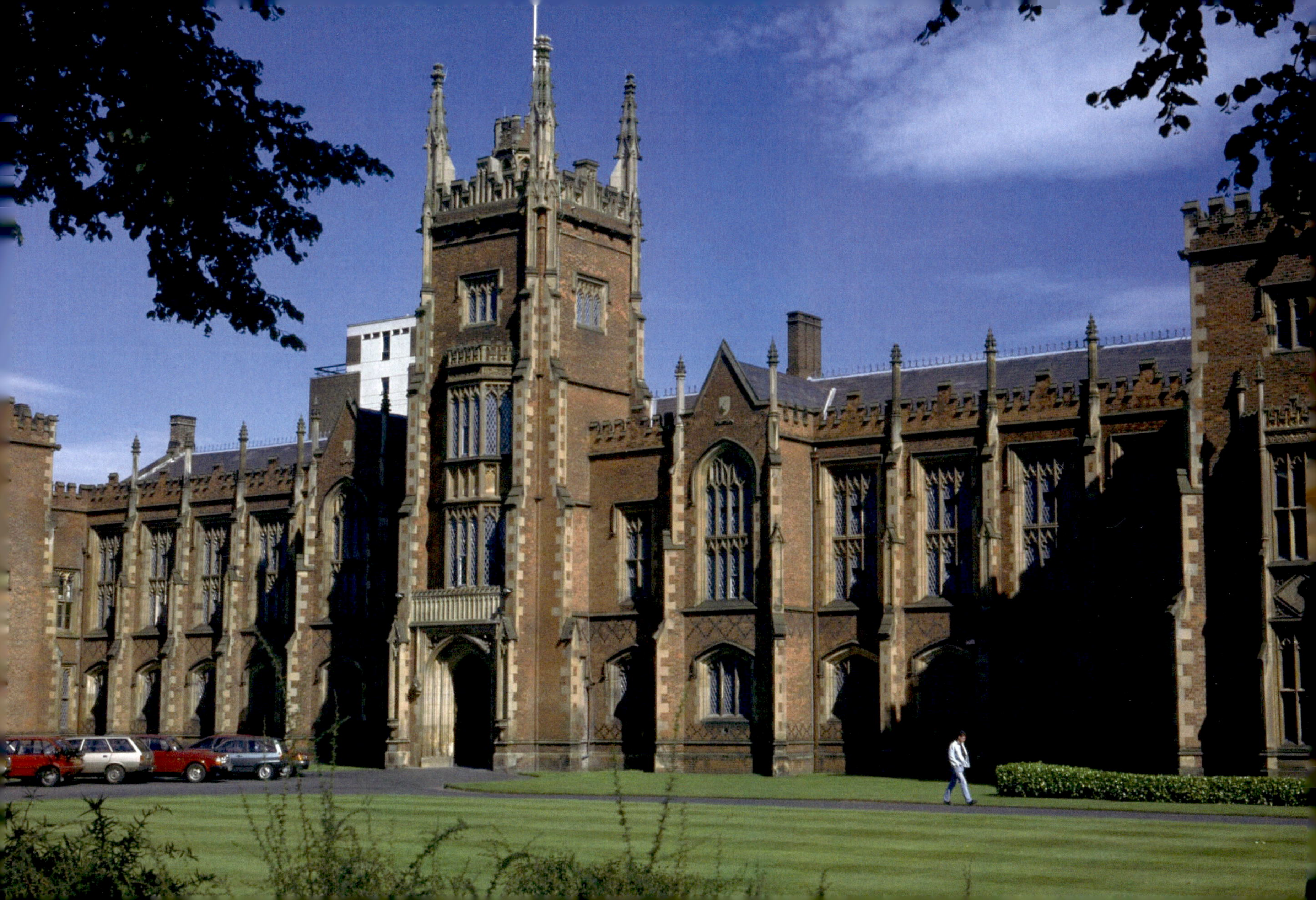

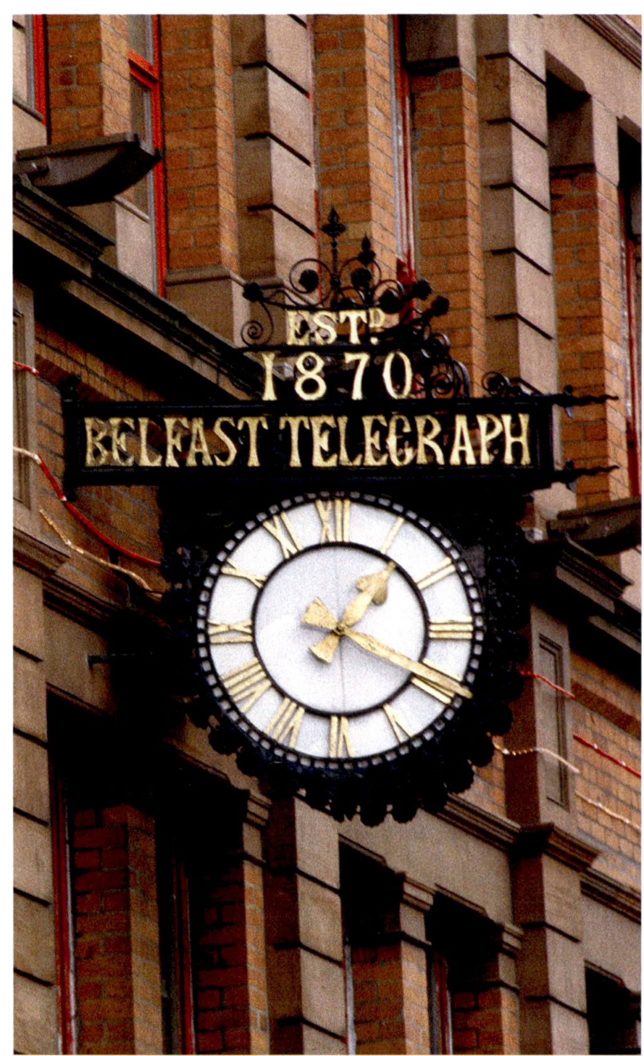

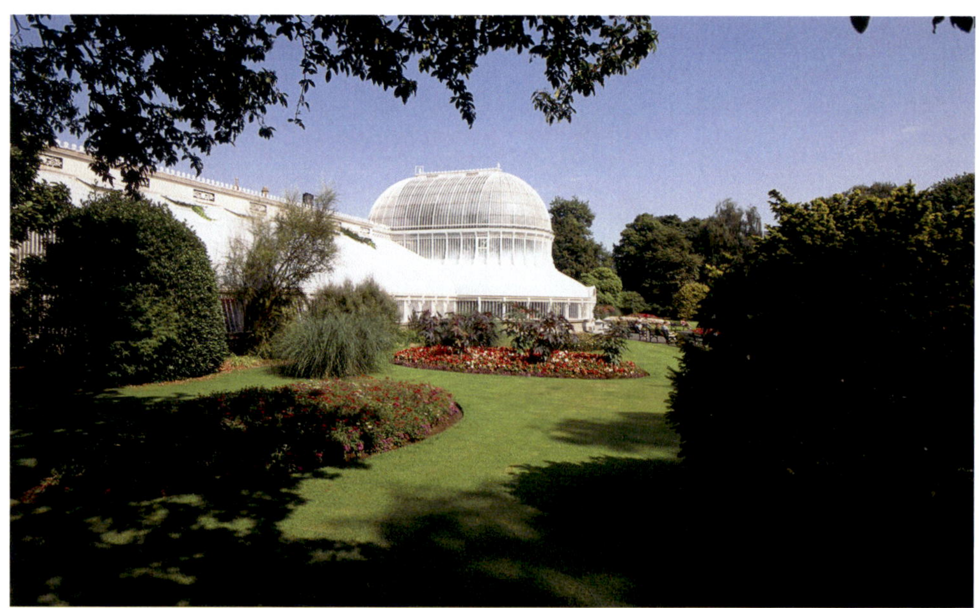

Belfast Telegraph (left)
In 1870 the first copies of the Belfast Telegraph appeared on the street. Northern Ireland's largest-selling newspaper was acquired by Trinity in 1996. The Belfast Telegraph titles were sold in 2000 as a condition of the merger.

Botanic Gardens (above)
An elegant structure of curved glass and cast iron, the Palm House (1839) was recently renovated. In the Tropical Ravine, plants grow in a sunken glen.

Grand Opera House (right)
Designed by Frank Matcham, Belfast's opera house opened in Great Victoria Street in 1894.

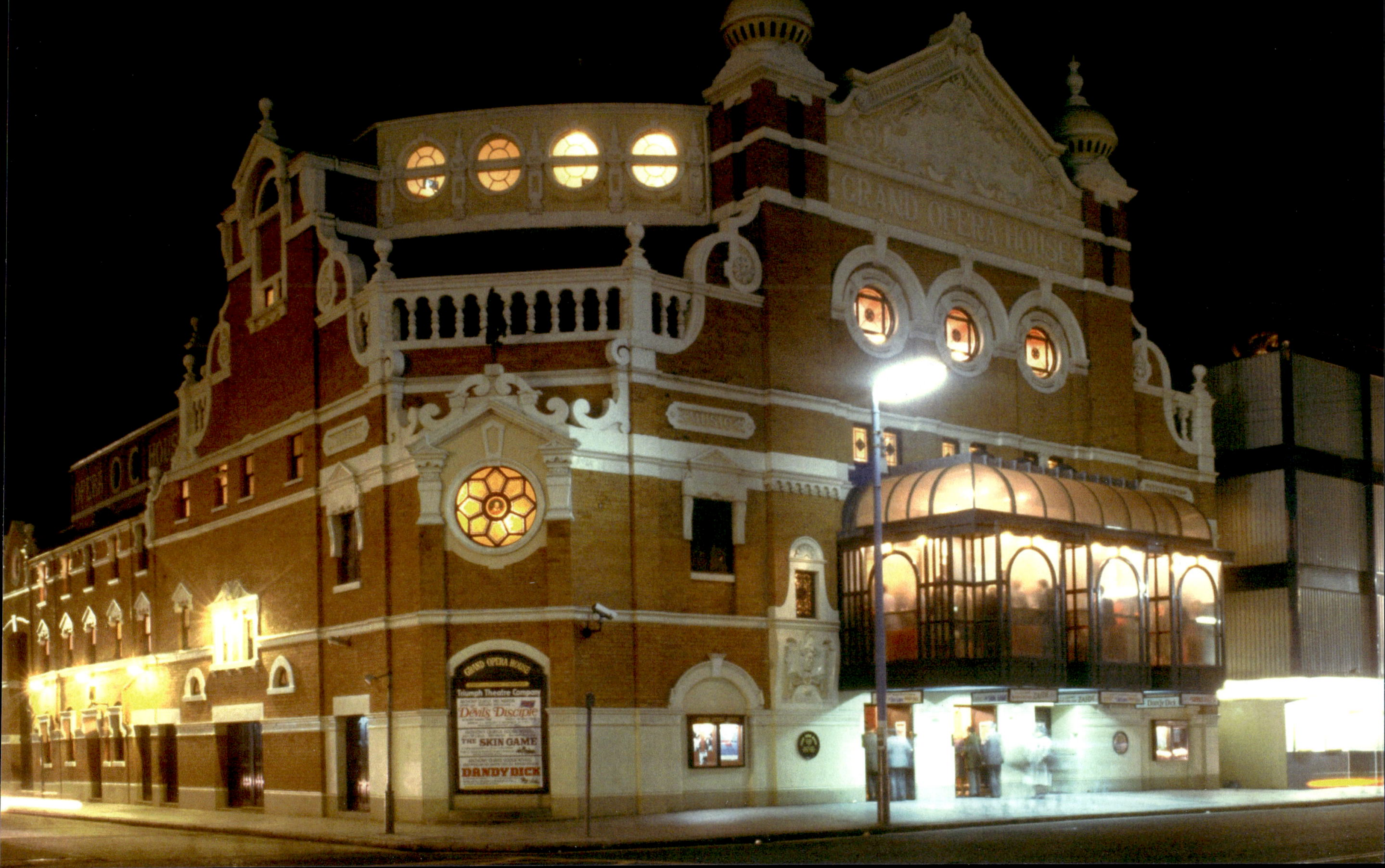
GRAND OPERA HOUSE
GRAND OPERA HOUSE
Triumph Theatre Company
Devils Disciple
THE SKIN GAME
DANDY DICK

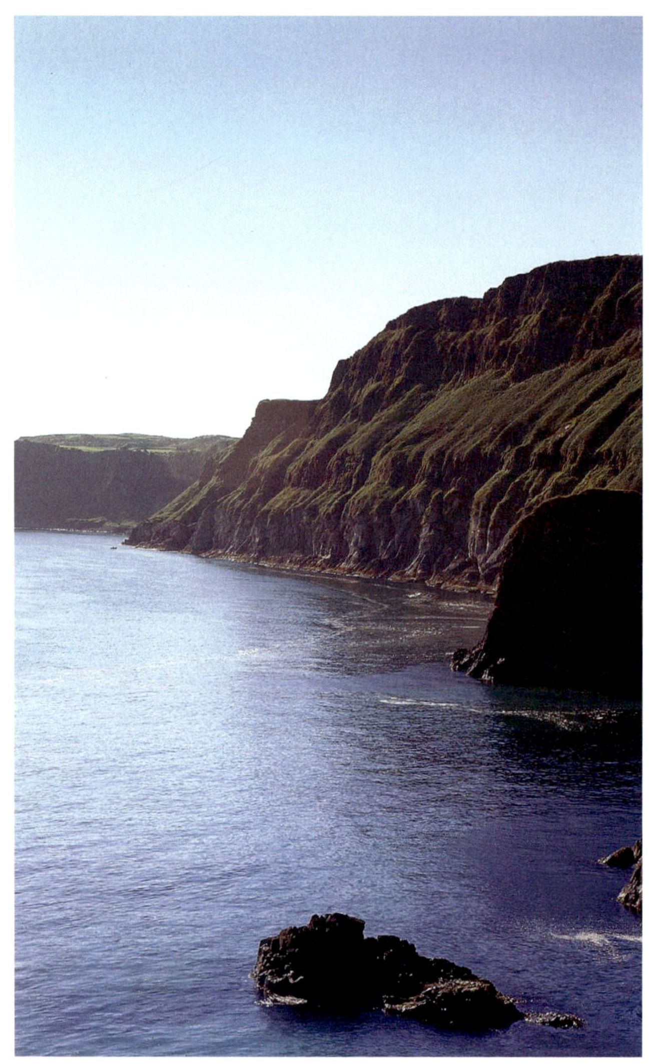

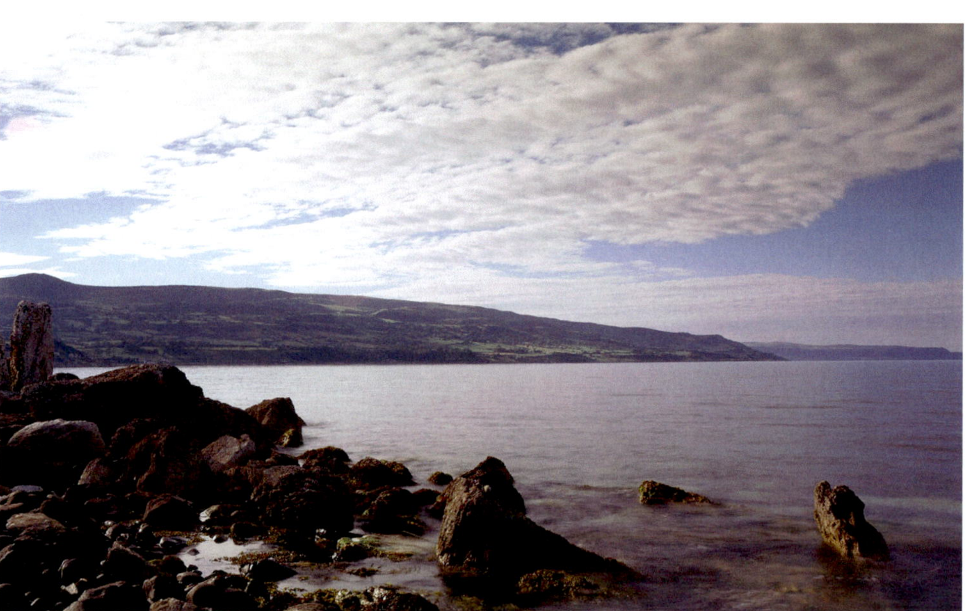

Carrick-a-Rede (left)
The North Antrim Coastal Path boasts many attractions—from the Giant's Causeway to Carrickfergus castle. This photograph was taken near Carrick-a-Rede a 50ft rope bridge over a 75ft chasm.

Ballygaley (above)
The Antrim coast some 20 miles from Belfast is close to Scotland and ferries run regularly from Larne and Ballycastle. Between the two is Ballygaley whose castle was built in 1625 by James Shaw in typical Scottish Baronial style.

Carnlough (right)
Carnlough harbour is the village's main focal point. Originally built by a local landowner and extended by the Marchioness of Londonderry, it is now run by Larne Borough Council.

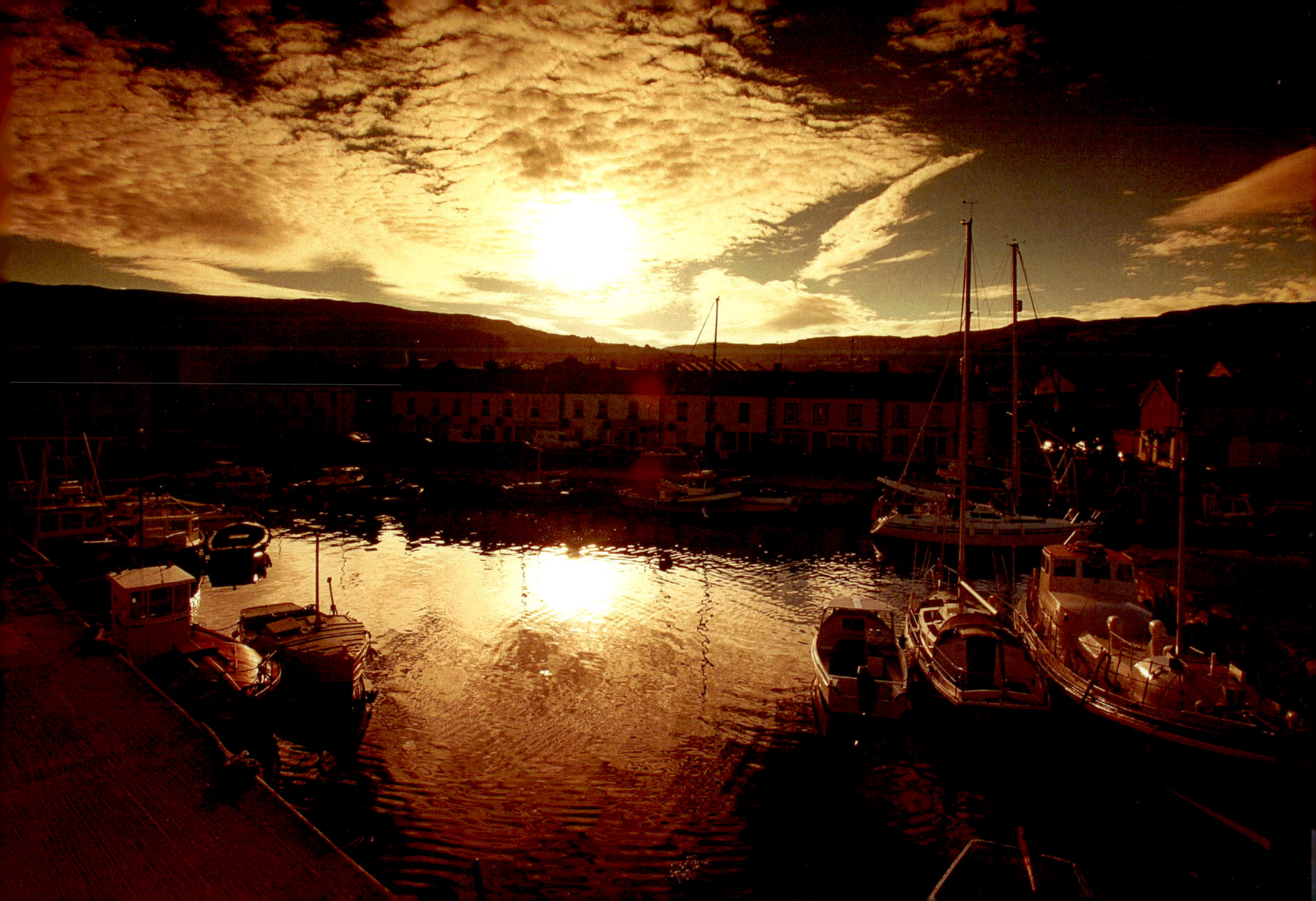

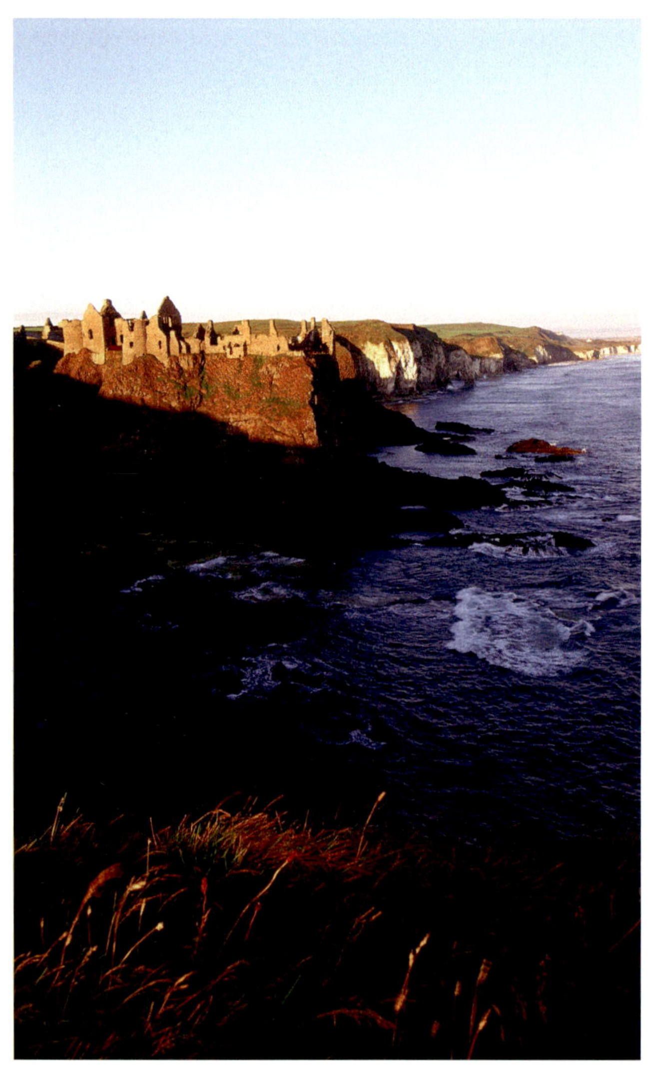

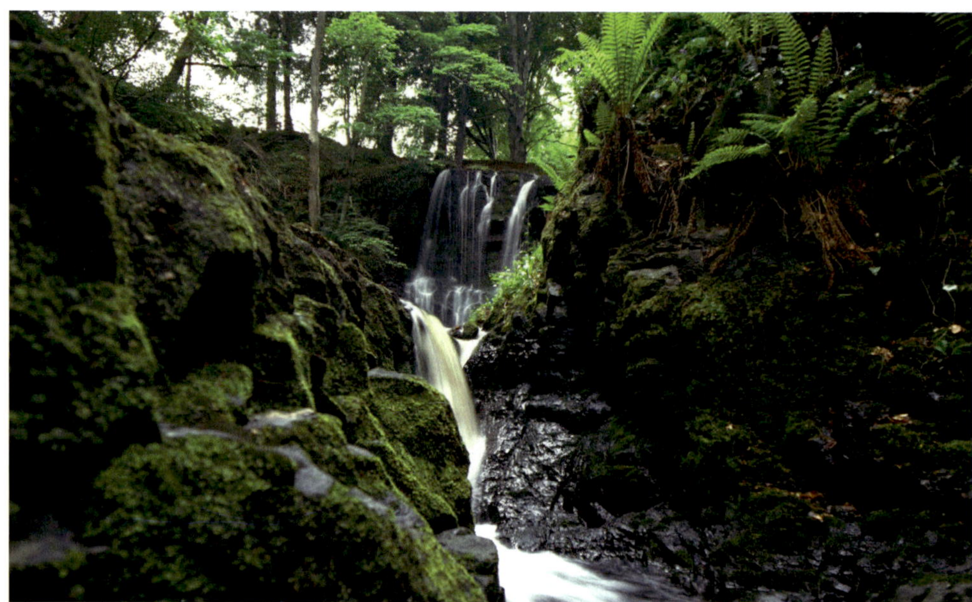

Dunluce Castle (left and right)

The castle as seen today dates largely from the 16th and 17th centuries but the outer walls with round towers are 14th century. In 1584 Sorley Boy MacDonnell captured it from the English when one of his men, employed in the castle, hauled his comrades up the cliff in a basket. Sorley Boy came into money in 1588 when the Spanish Armada treasure ship Girona was wrecked by storm off the Giant's Causeway. He used it to modernise the castle.

Glenariff (above)

The "queen of the glens" has a series of waterfalls plunging down through a gorge traversed by a path crossing rustic bridges.

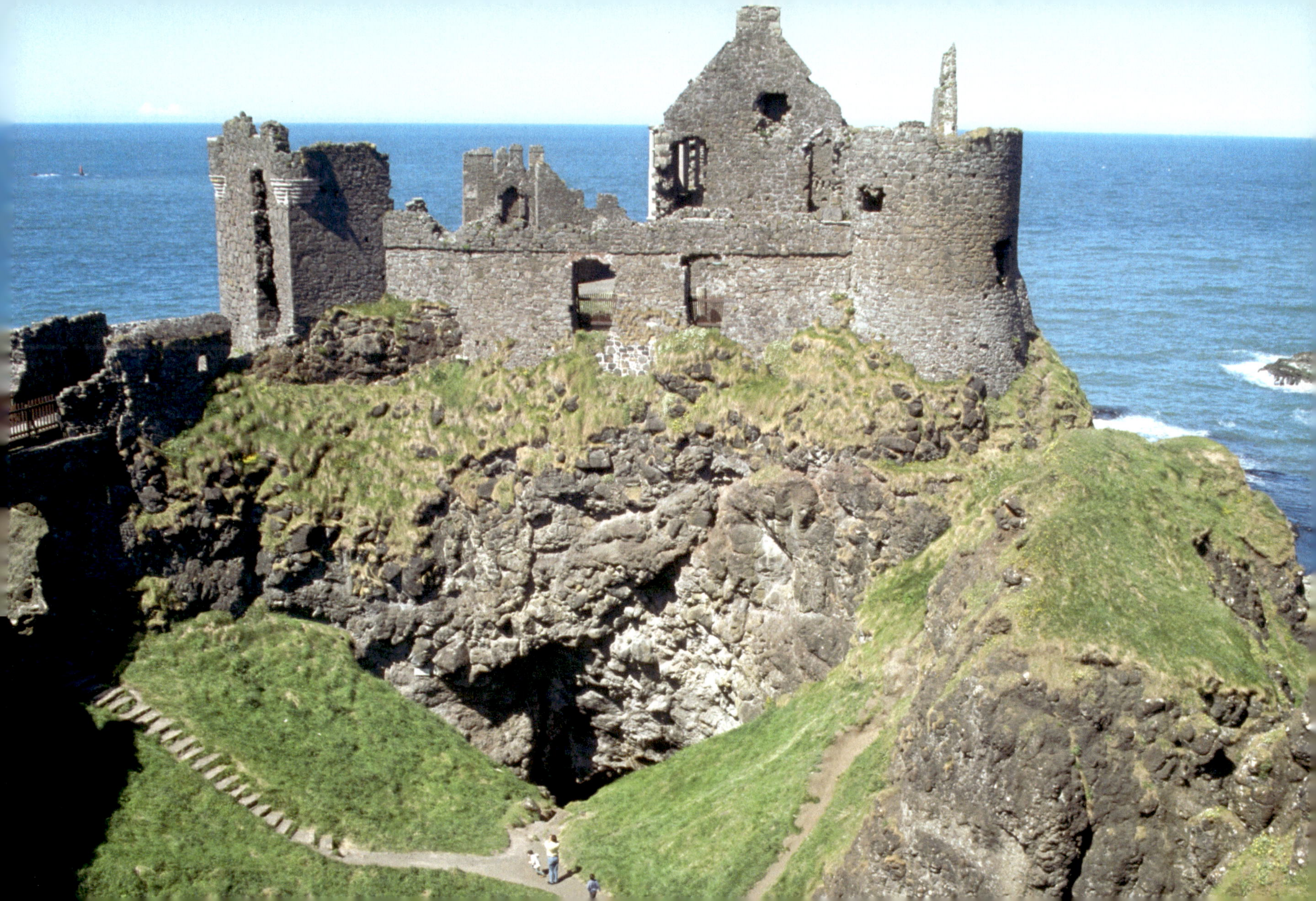

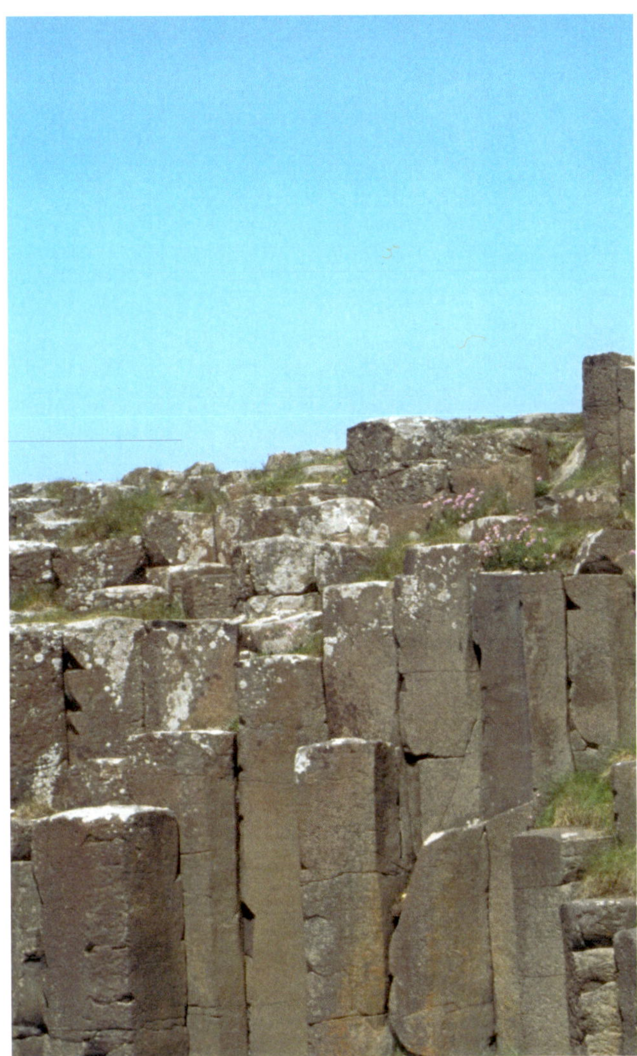

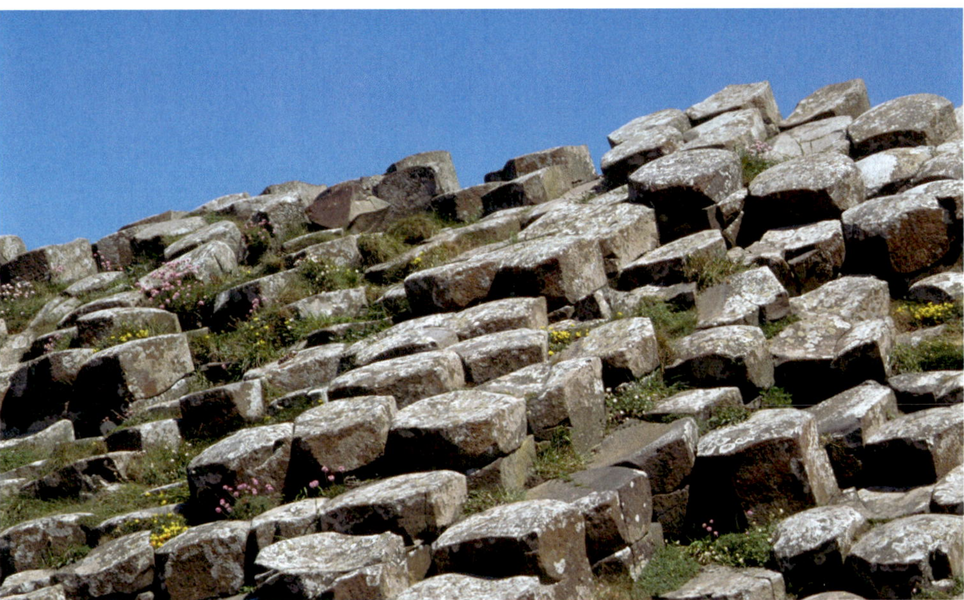

Giant's Causeway

The causeway is a mass of basalt columns packed tightly together, formed by quick cooling and shrinking lava that burst to the earth's surface about 70 million years ago. Altogether there are around 40,000 of these stone columns, mostly hexagonal but some with four, five, seven, and eight sides. That's what the geography books say: all Ireland knows, however, that the causeway is the work of the giant Finn McCool. After he fell in love with a lady giant on Staffa, an island in the Hebrides, he built it to bring her across the water.

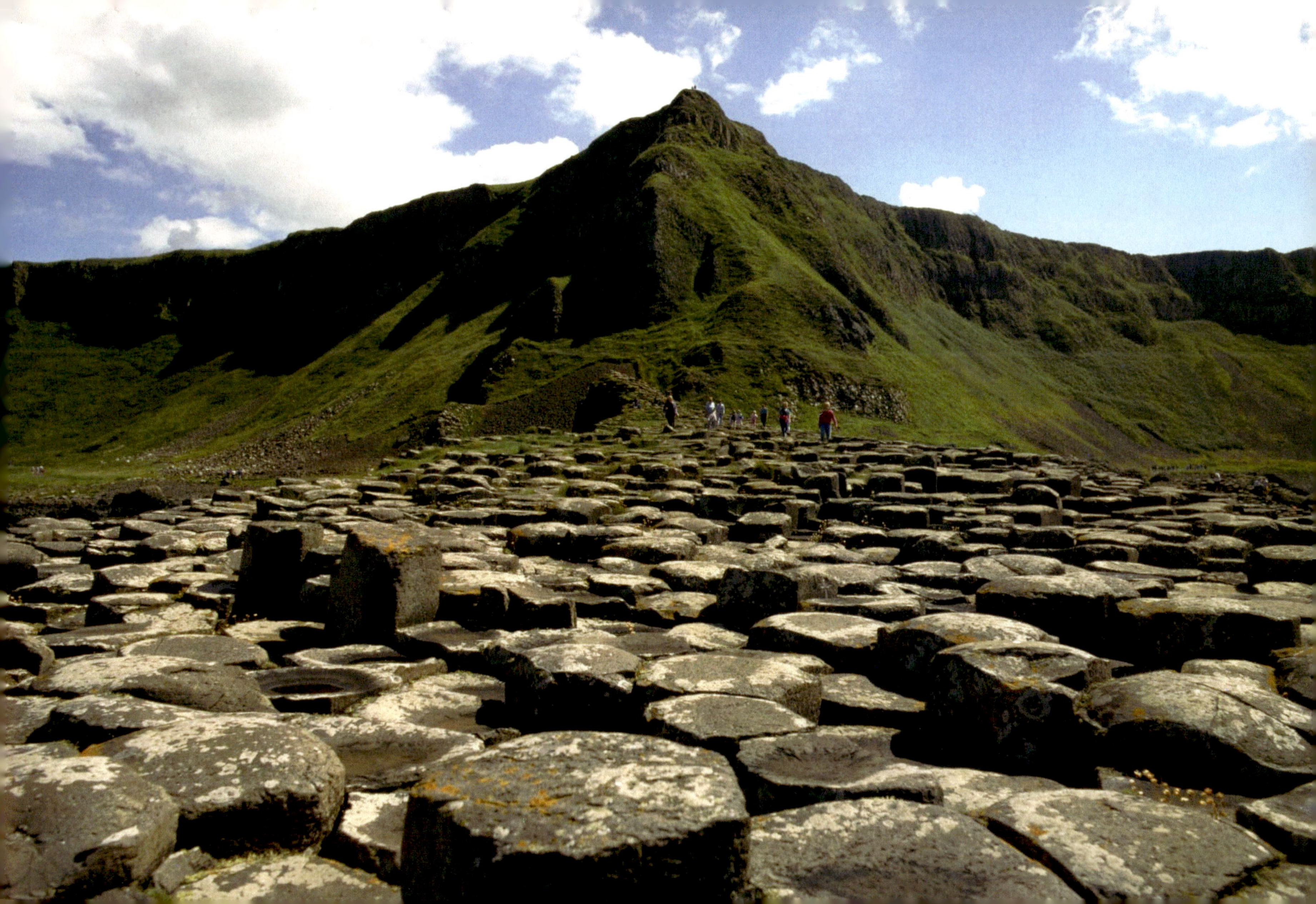

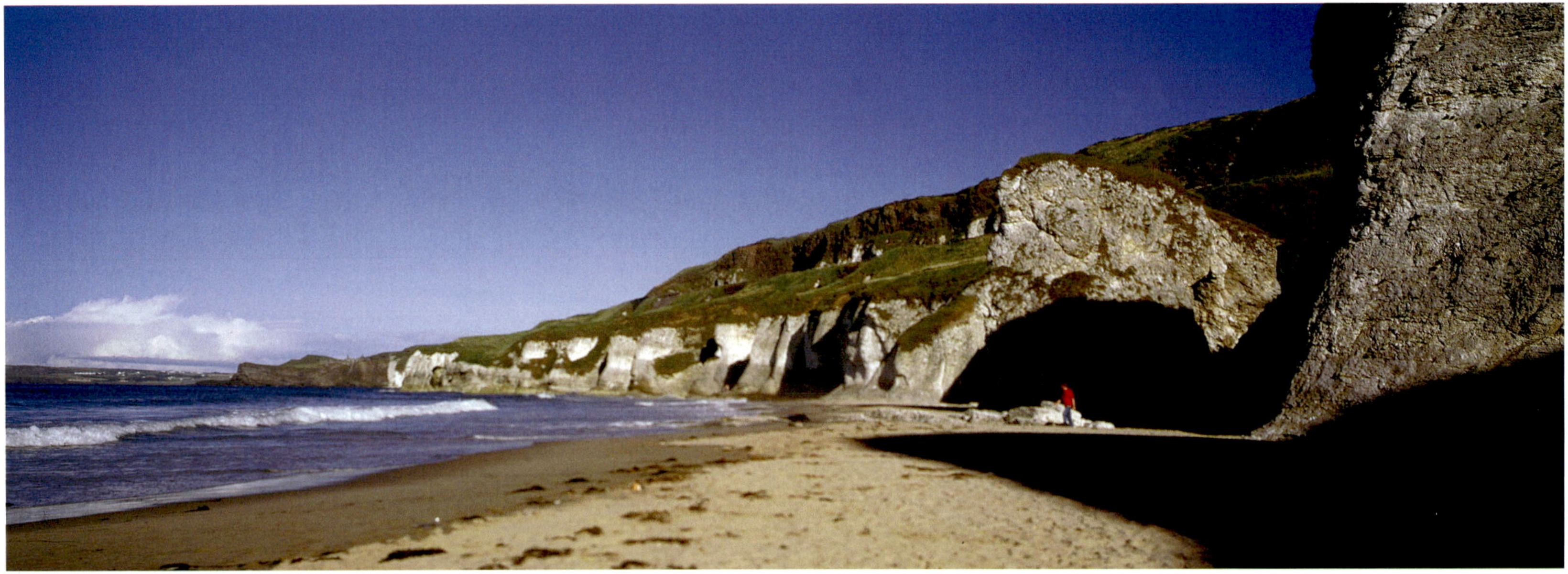

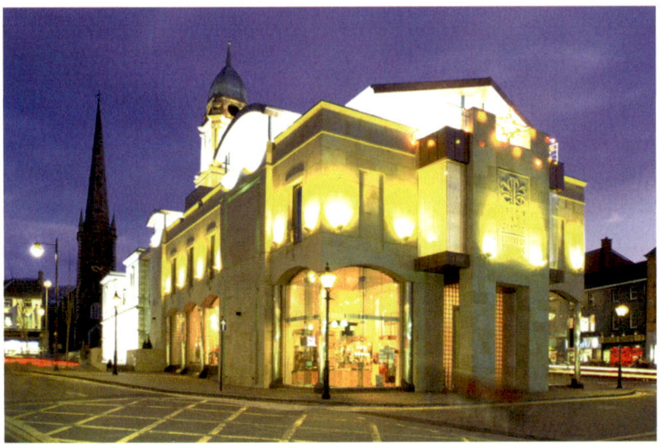

Irish Linen Centre (left)
The building houses the linen centre and Lisburn Museum. There is an audio-visual presentation on the lives of workers in a Victorian factory setting, and hand loom weavers producing linen on restored 19th century looms.

Whiterock Beach, Portrush (above)
The White Rocks are a famous landmark on the North Coast, the limestone formations containing many fossils from earlier times. The dunes are included in an ongoing conservation programme to safeguard their future.

Mourne (right)
The Mourne Mountains are among Ireland's tallest. Slieve Donard, the highest peak, is 2,796ft. There are ten summits over 2,000ft and the range covers some 80 square miles of unspoilt mountain and moorland grandeur.

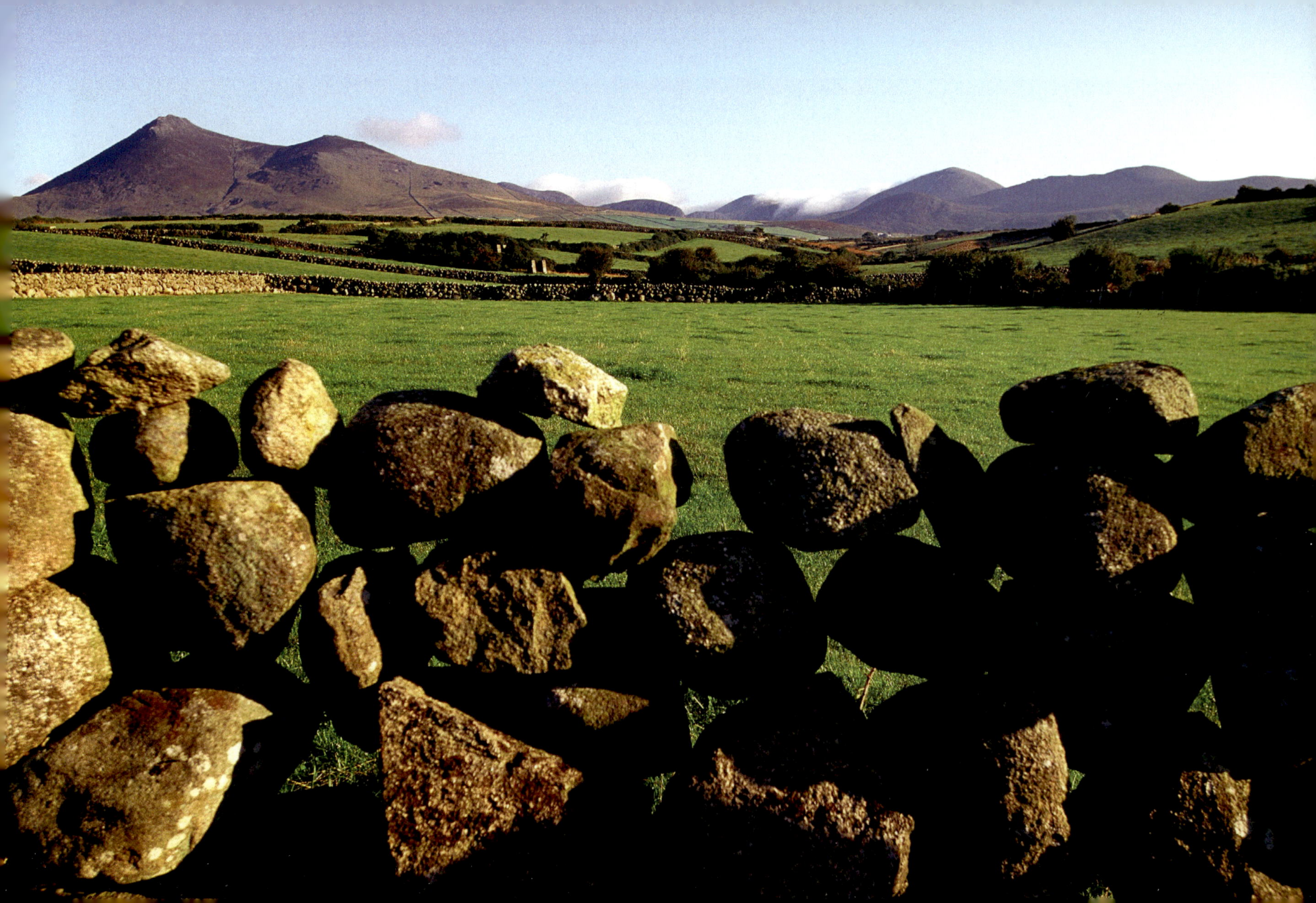

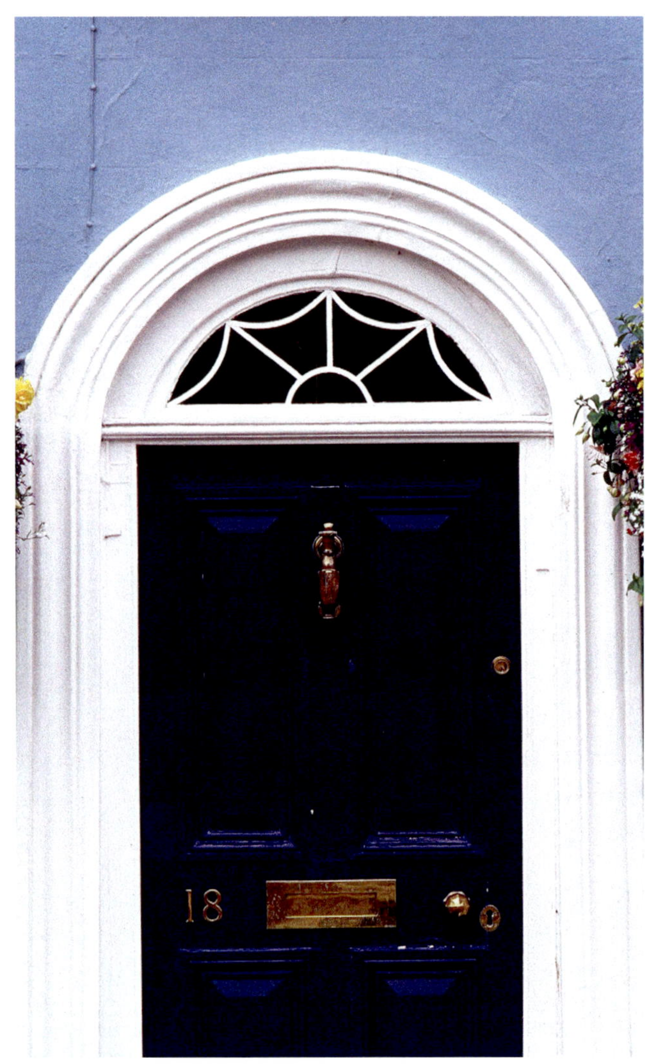

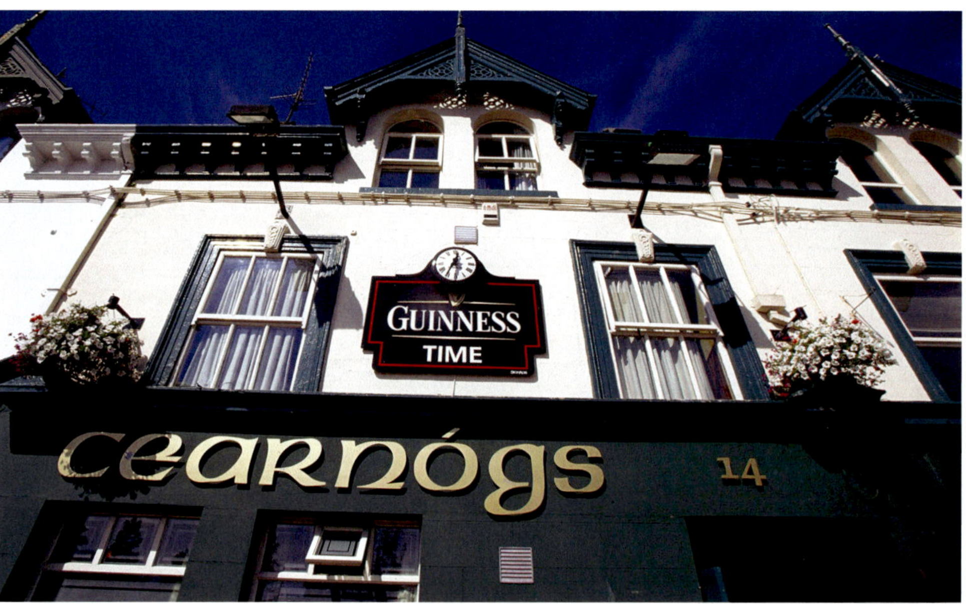

Doorway (left)
Irish doorways are famous from north to south and subject of many photographs and posters.

Warrenpoint (above)
The town is compact and attractive with neat Victorian terraces and wide streets. Visitors are surprised to learn that this is still one of the busiest ports in Northern Ireland, commercial berthing being out of sight further up the Lough.

Mountains of Mourne (right)
The ridge of mountains gently slope towards the sea into Dundrum Bay. This well forested area is wonderful for walking.

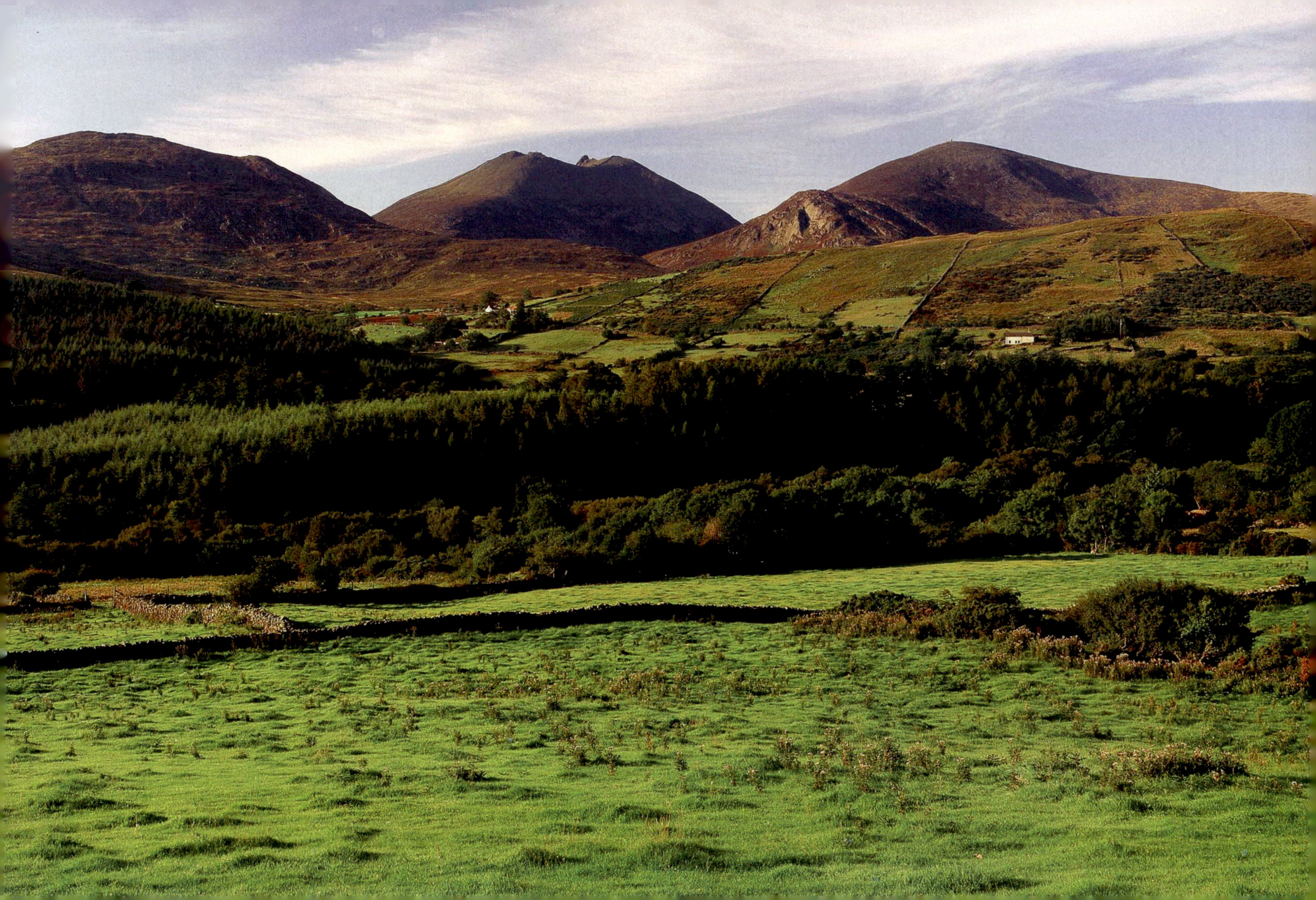

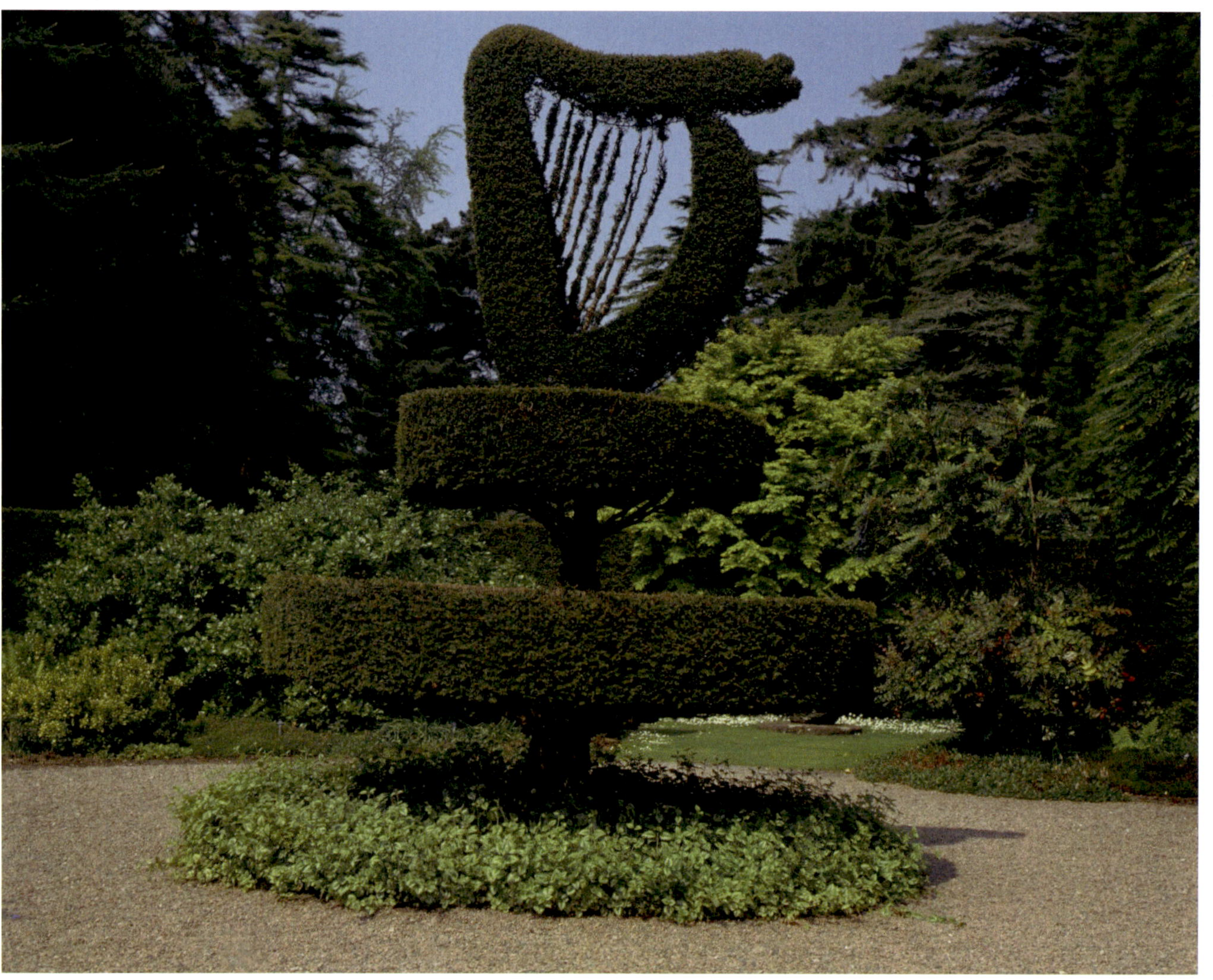

Mount Stuart House and Gardens (left)

The boyhood home of Robert Stewart, Lord Castlereagh, the gardens are among the finest in Europe, with an unrivalled collection of plants, colourful parterres, and vistas.

Silent Valley (right)

The Silent Valley and Ben Crom reservoirs supply thirty million gallons of water a day to Belfast and County Down. All around the dam lie beautiful parkland and wonderful countryside.

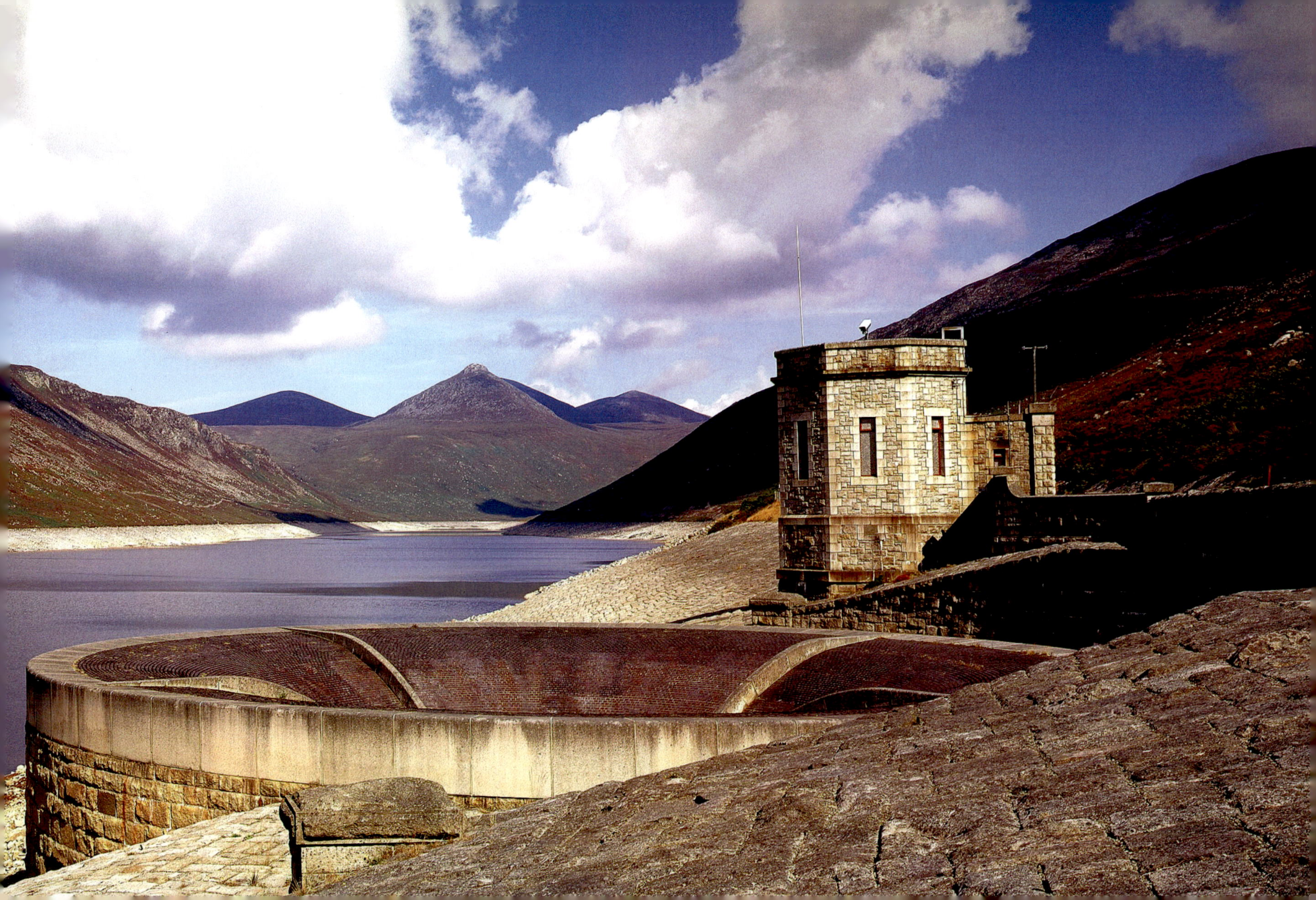

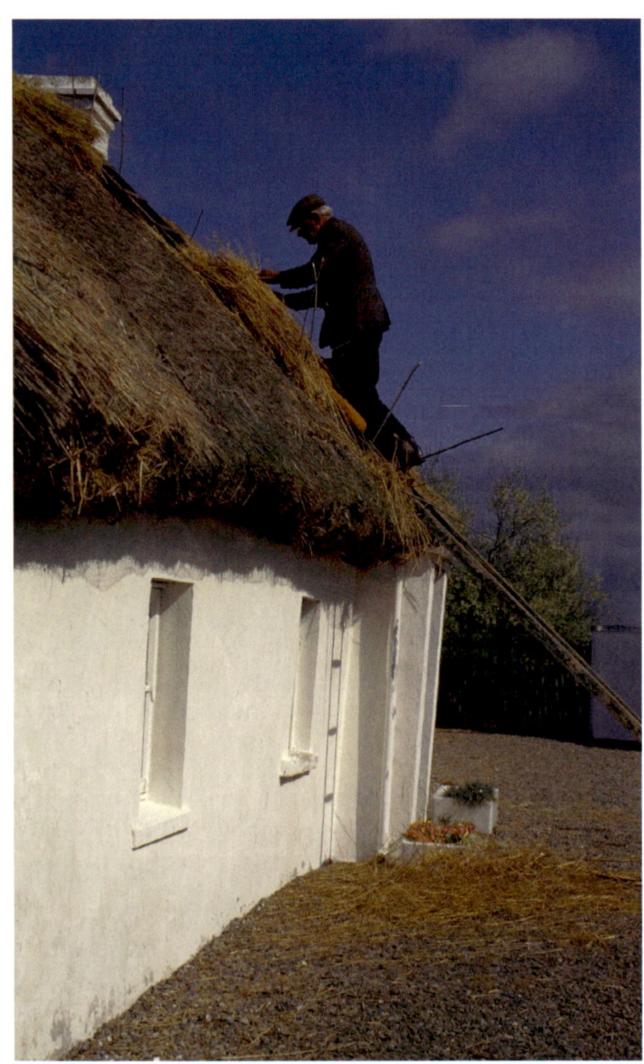

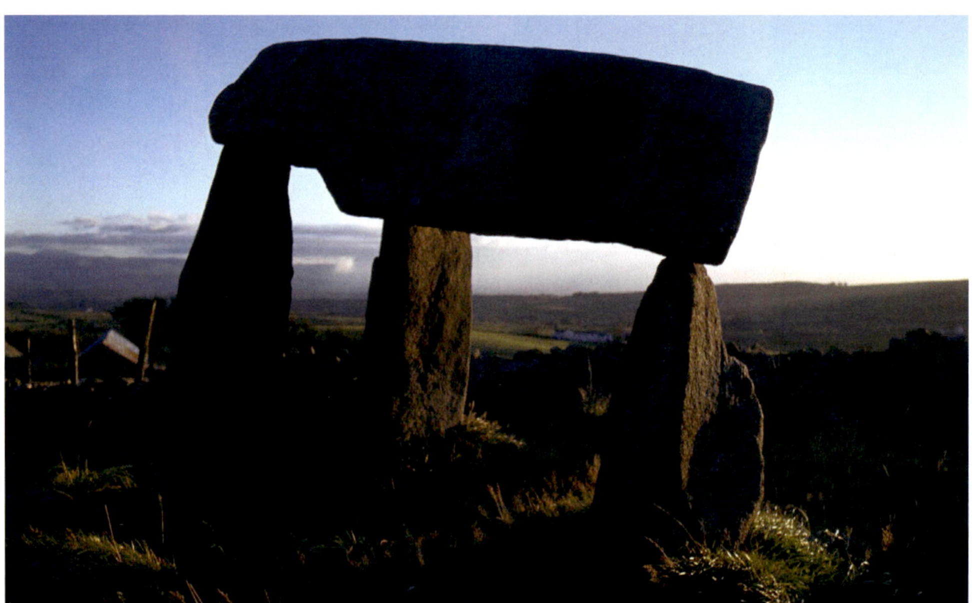

Thatched Cottage, Maghery (left)
The typical Irish house has changed little over the centuries. Traditionally it is a single-storey rectangle with a thatched roof of high quality straw or reeds. In the wild and windy westerly regions the thatch is tied to the roof with ropes.

Legananny Dolman (above)
South of Ballynahinch on the slopes of Slieve Croob mountain stands the Legananny Dolmen, one of Ireland's finest Neolithic tombs.

Gosford Park (right)
Gosford Forest Park at Markethill was formerly part of Gosford Castle, a mock-Norman battlemented extravaganza.

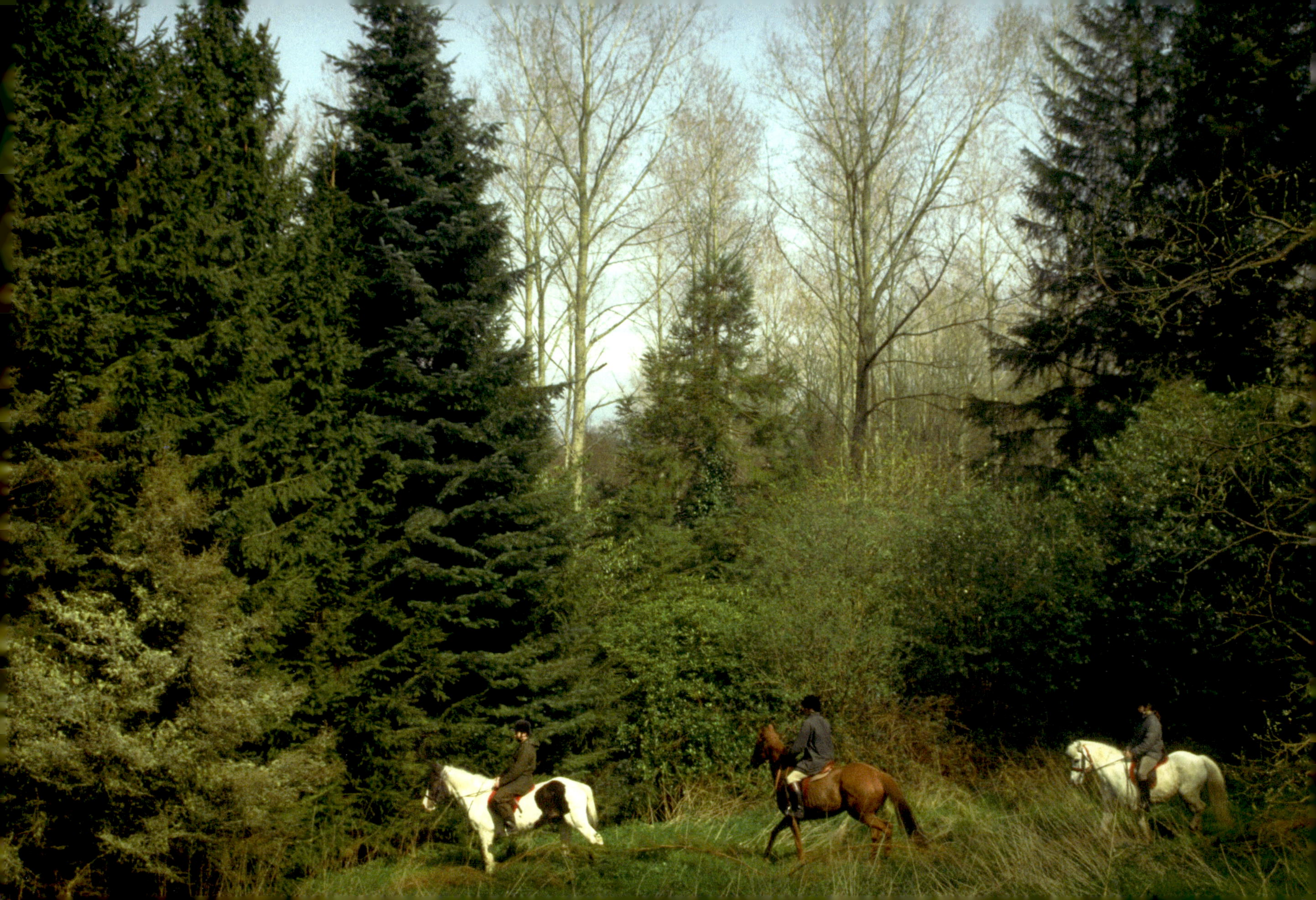

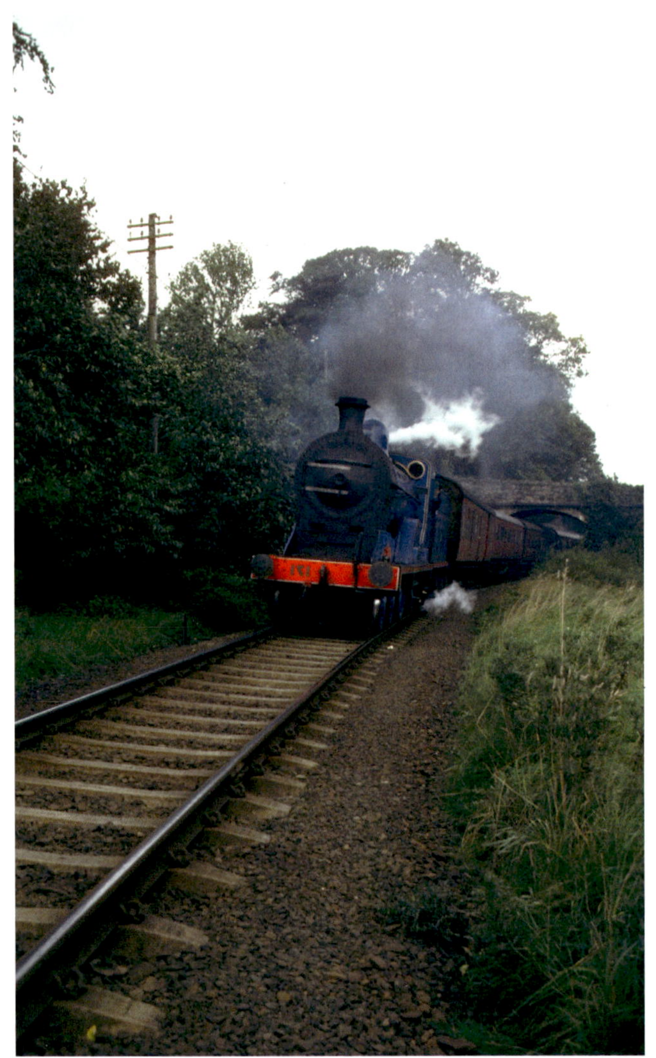

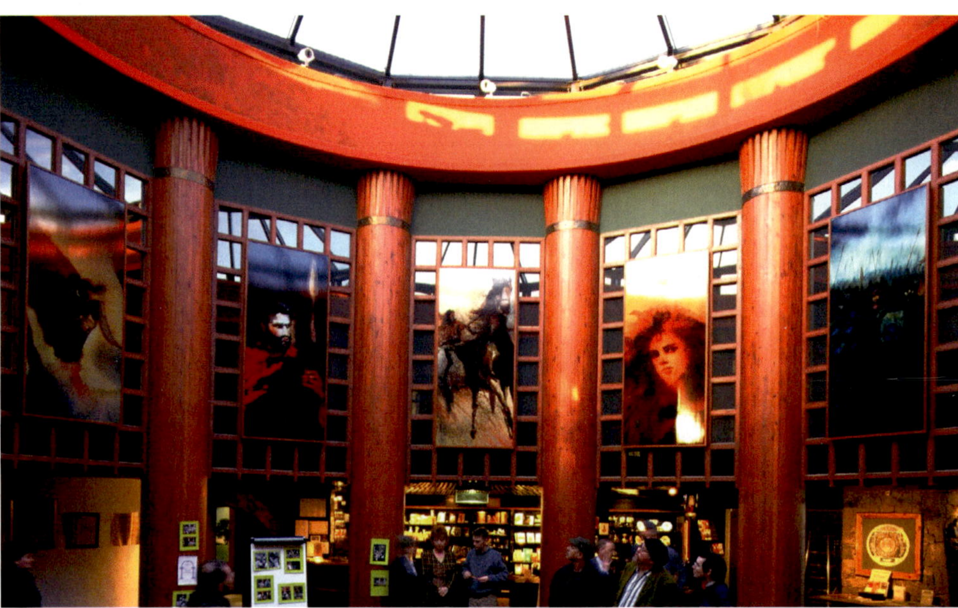

Slieve Gullion (left)
No 171 is an "S" class 4-4-0 locomotive built by Beyer-Peacock of Manchester in 1913 for the Great Northern Railway of Ireland. Named Slieve Gullion, it was preserved after it finished working in the 1960s.

Navan Centre (above)
Opened in July 1993 as a visitor and interpretative centre at Navan Fort, which is situated just outside Armagh, the site is the premier archaeological earthwork in Northern Ireland.

Armagh (right)
View from the Catholic Cathedral over Armagh. The name Armagh comes from the Irish Ard Macha which means "hill of Macha".

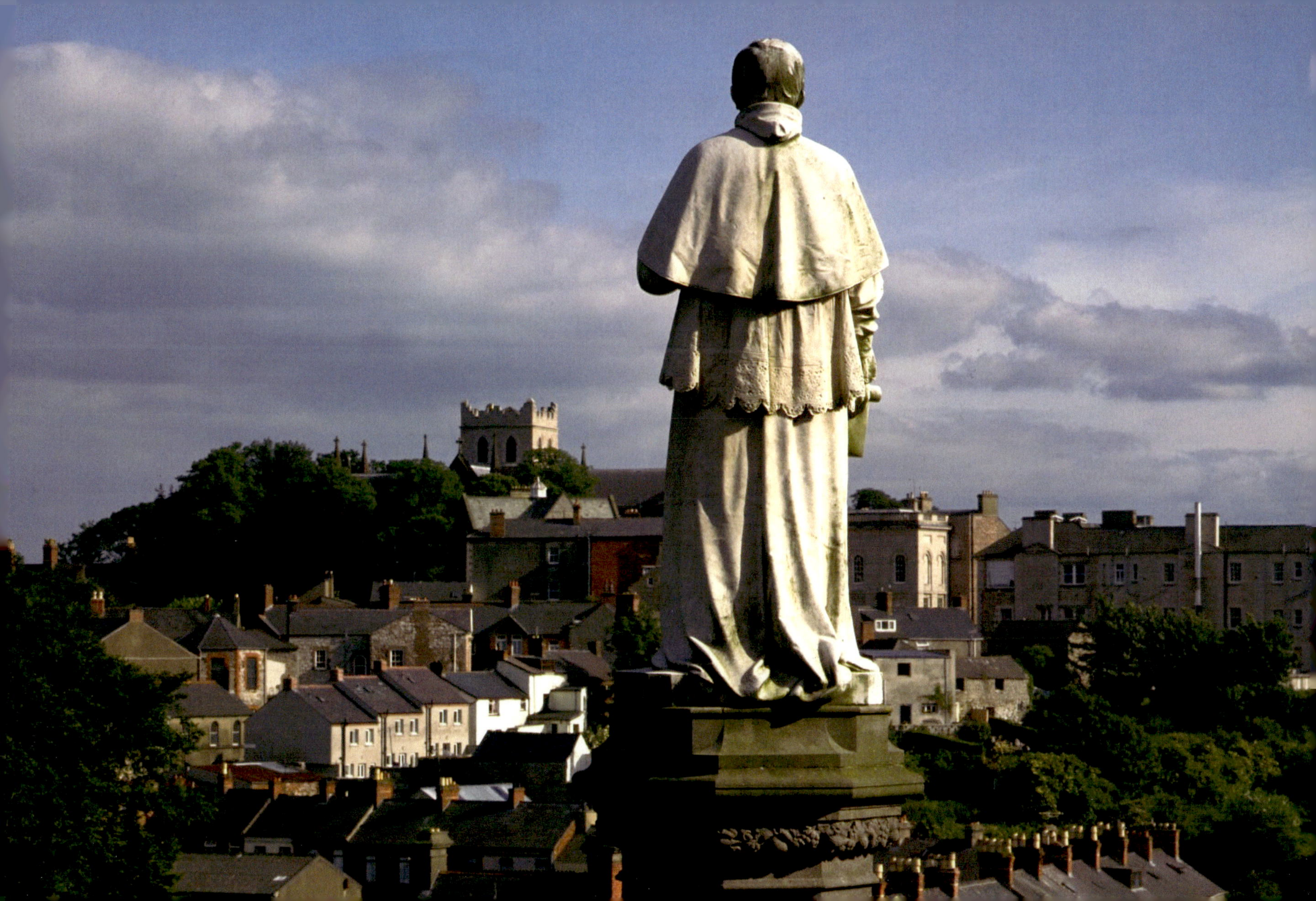

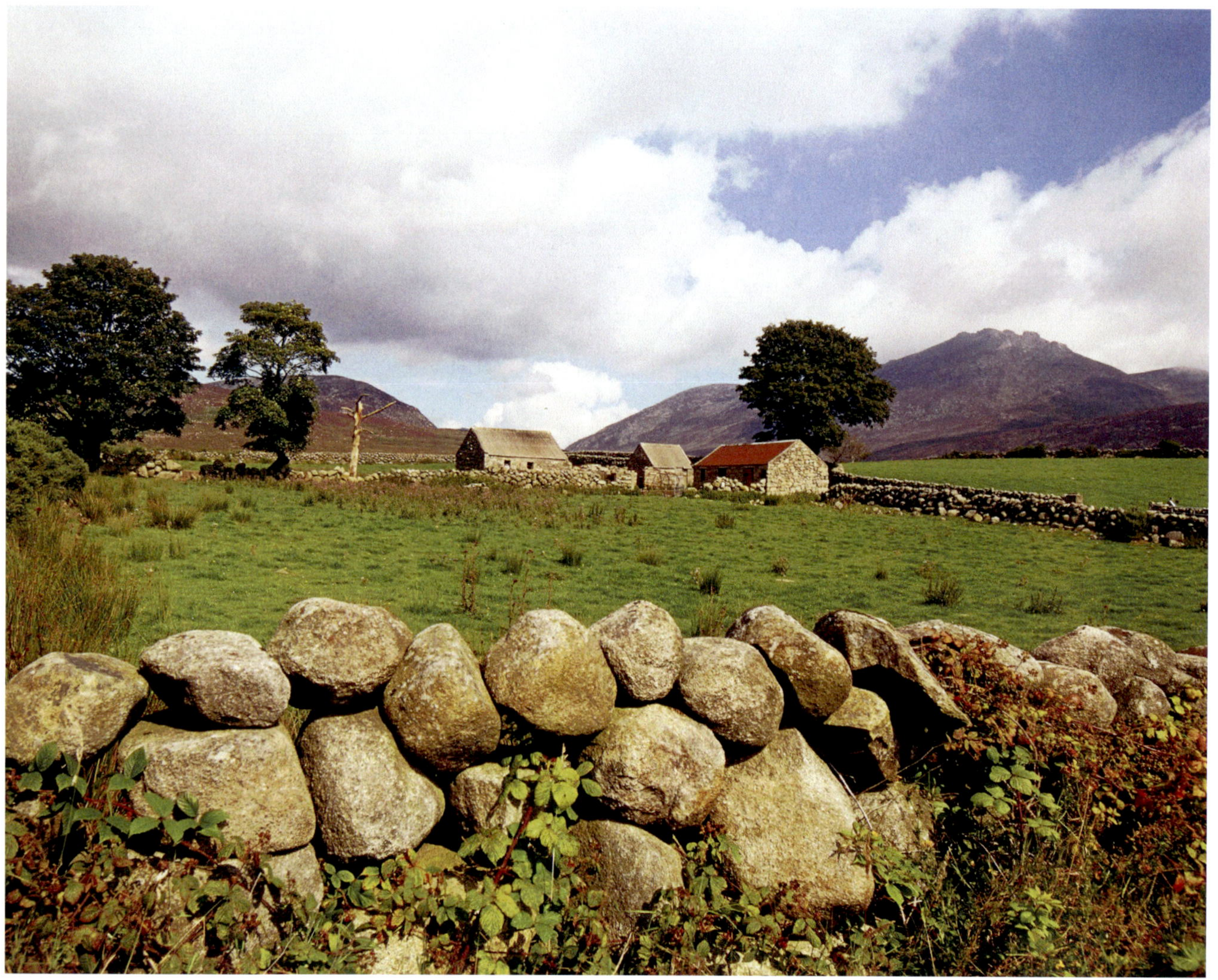

The Mournes (left)
The Mourne Mountains are home to the Silent Valley reservoir.The Silent Valley is surrounded by the Mourne Wall a 22 mile stone boundary wall.

Royal County Down Golf Course (right)
One of the oldest Golf Clubs in Ireland with traditions dating back for more than one hundred years. Situated in Newcastle, where in the immortal words of Percy French, "The Mountains of Mourne sweep down to the sea", Royal County Down is not only a fine test of golf but has accompanying scenery that is spellbinding.

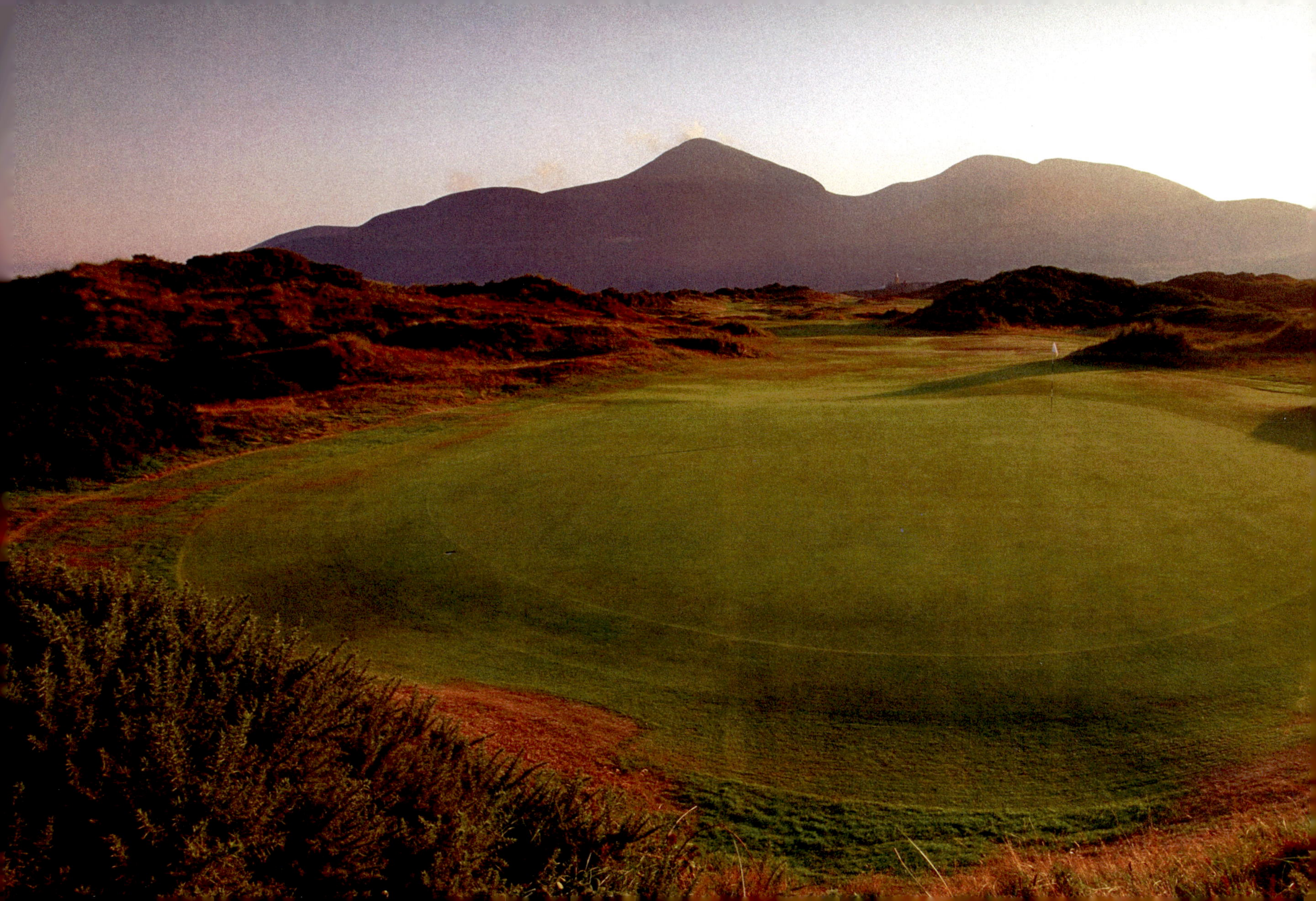

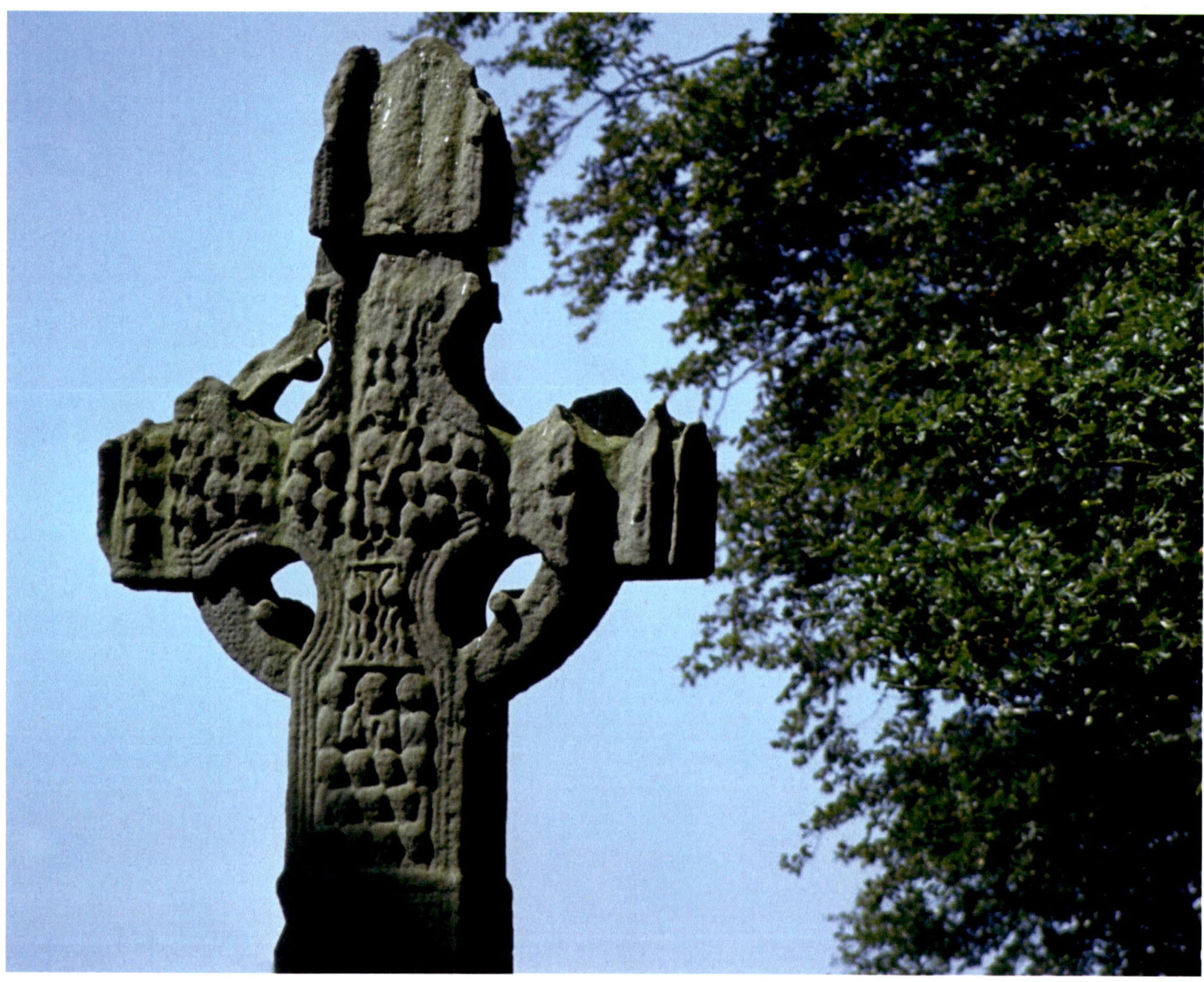

Ardboe Cross (left)

A national monument, which dates from the 10th century, Ardboe Cross is believed to be the first high cross in Ulster. It stands 18.5 feet tall and its 22 panels depict biblical scenes.

Beaghmore Stone Circles (right)

This is a mysterious complex of seven Bronze Age stone circles and alignments built over six thousand years ago.

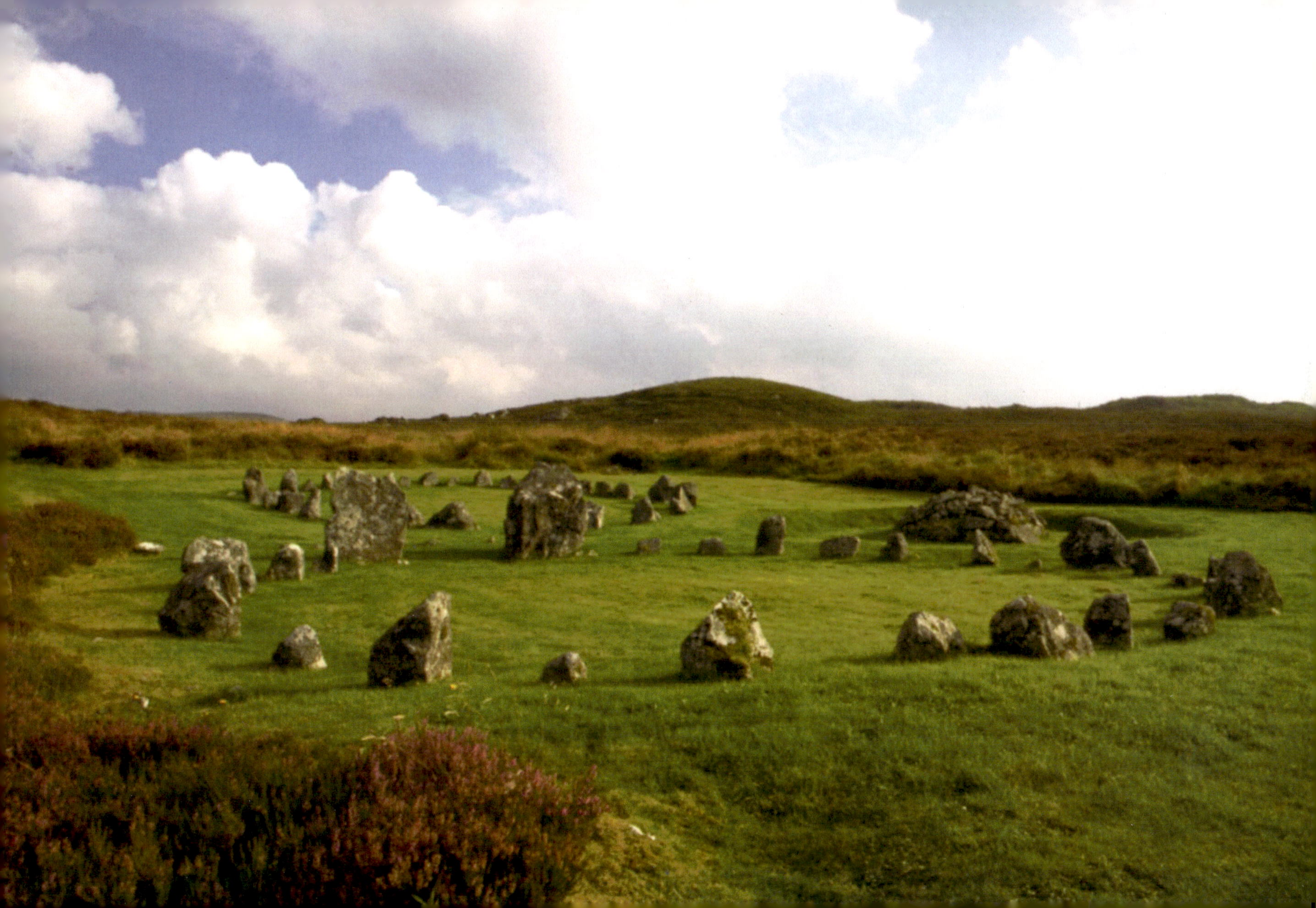

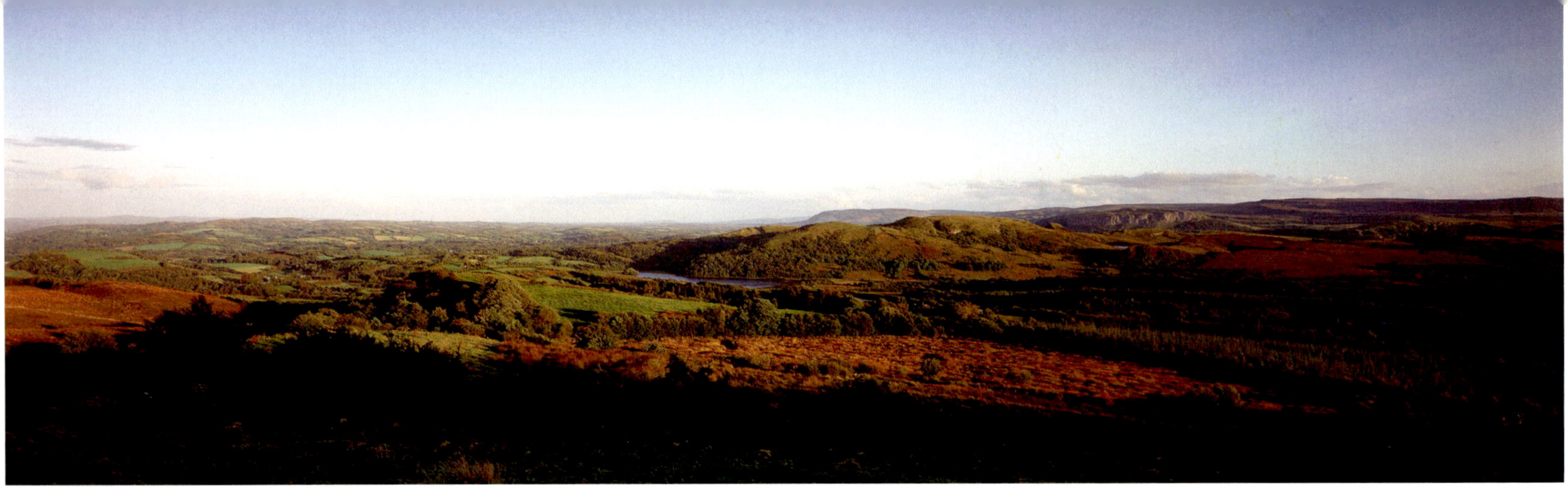

Fermanagh (above and below)

Ireland is known for its fine fishing and Lough Erne is renowned for its trout. Fishermen arrive in spring to go "dapping"—when they sit in a small boat casting locally caught mayflies to attract trout. Lower Lough Erne contains a number of holy islands on which there are the remains of ancient religious settlement and numerous interesting and enigmatic stone carvings and remains.

Enniskillen Castle (right)

On the banks of the Erne, the castle was built in 1612. The Keep houses the Museum of the Royal Inniskilling Fusiliers.

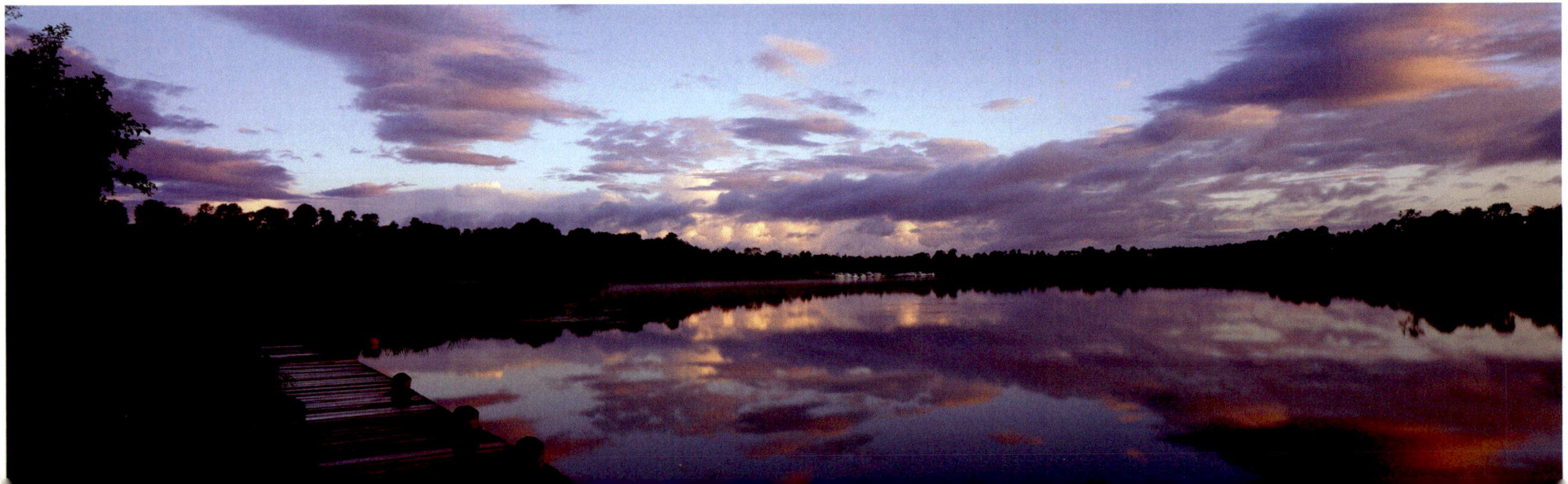

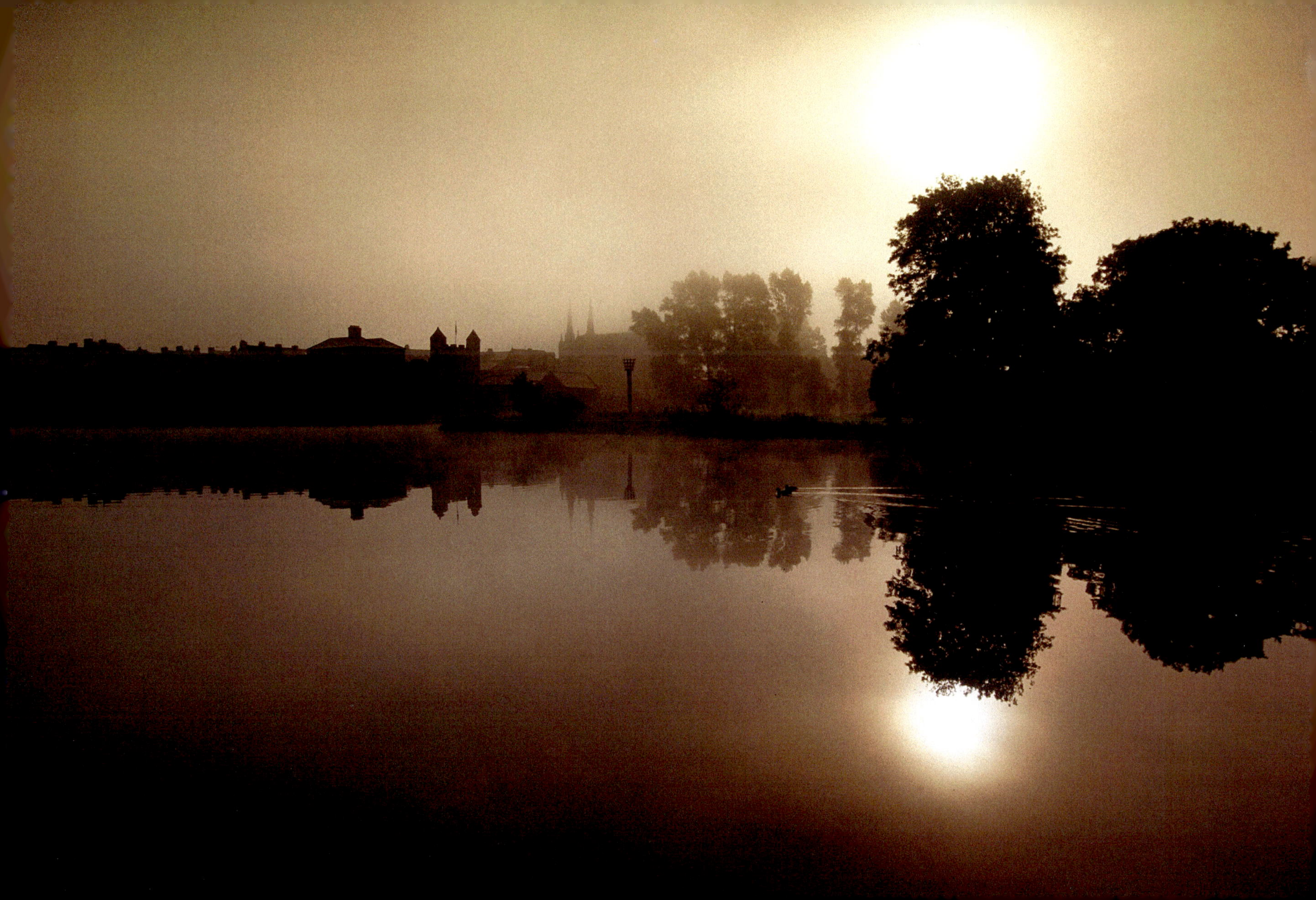

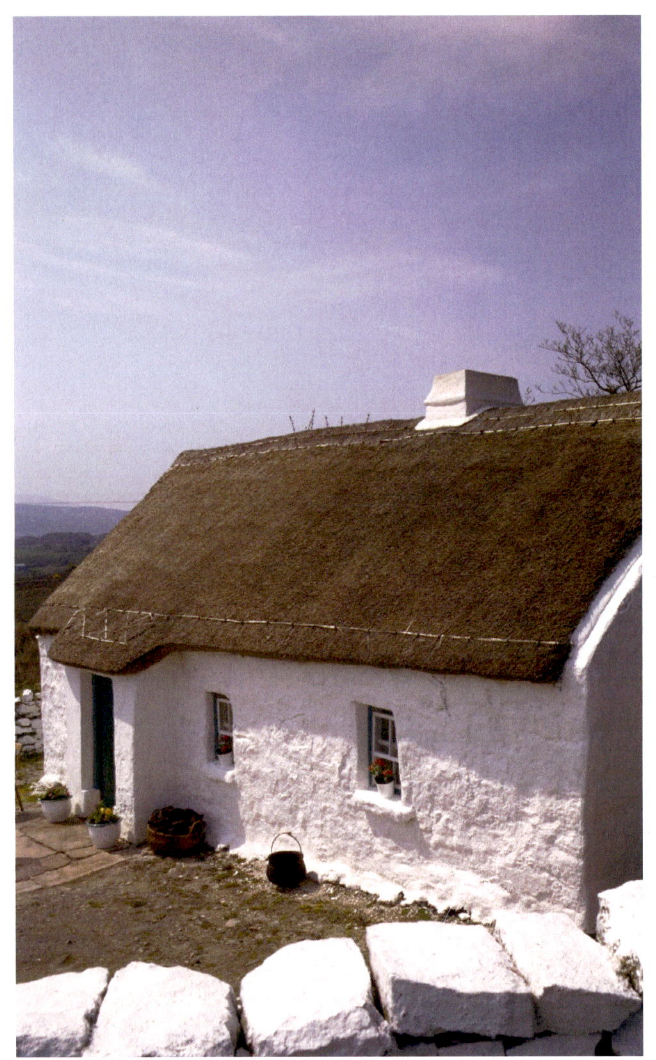

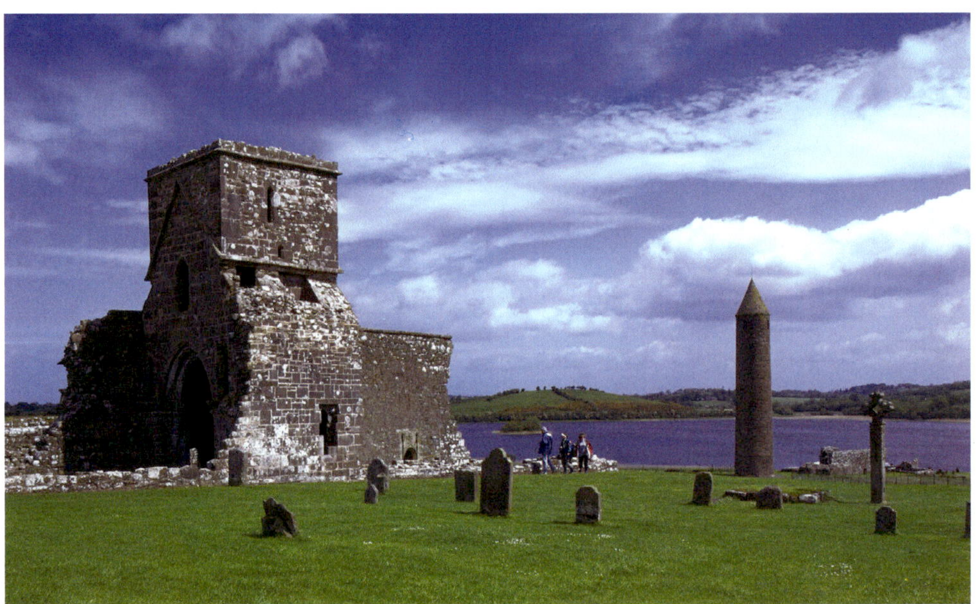

Margaret Gallagher's Cottage (left)
If you want to see how Northern Irelanders lived a hundred years ago, Margaret Gallagher still lives the same way as her ancestors did in this thatched cottage at Belcoo.

Devenish Island (above)
In the Middle Ages there was a chain of island monasteries in Lough Erne. Devenish, pictured, has a wonderfully preserved 12th-century round tower.

Upper Lough Erne (right)
Upstream from Enniskillen the lough gets shallower and numerous small islands dot the waters. Here too are remnants from former times with ancient tombstones and strange stone carvings.

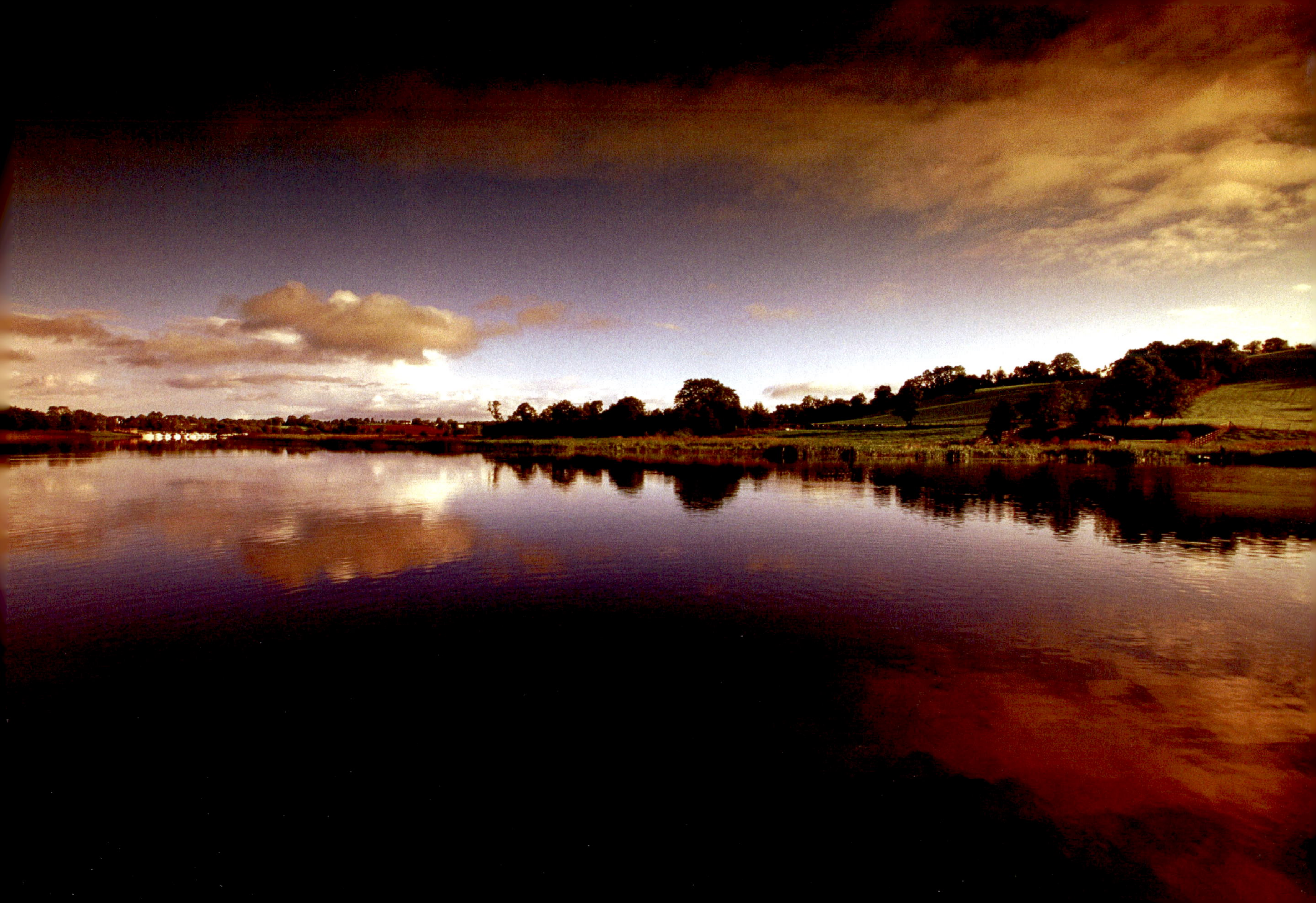

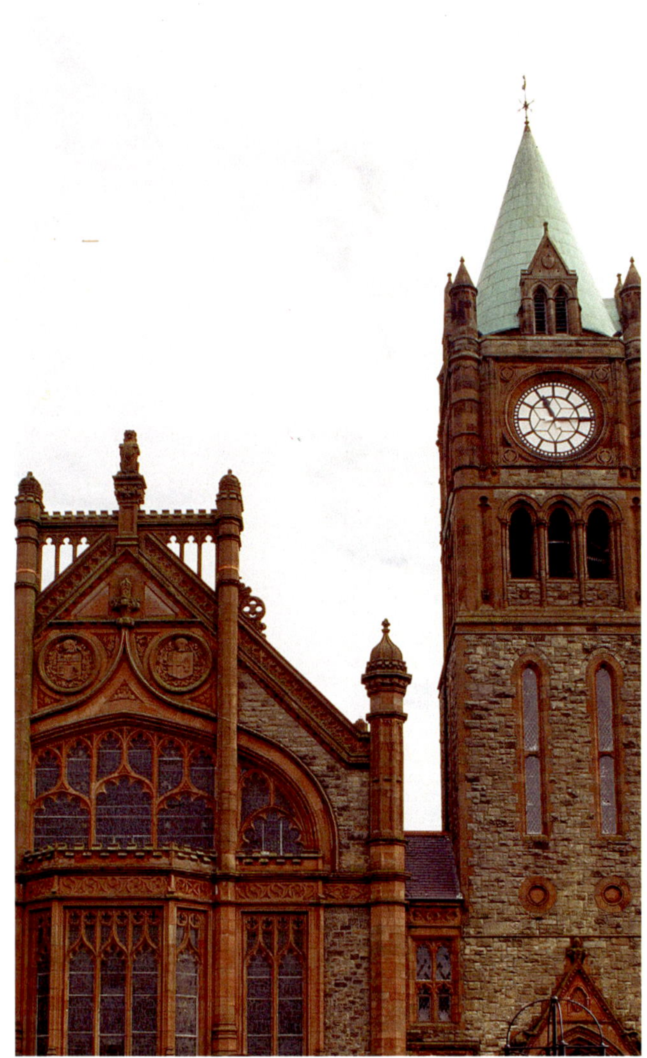

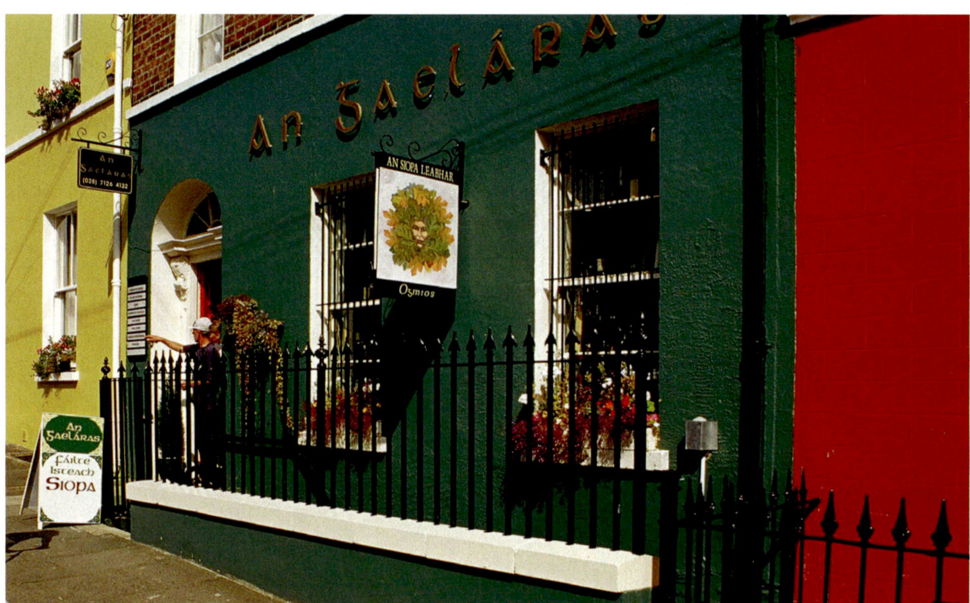

Guildhall, Derry (left)
The Neo-Gothic Guildhall was built in 1912. Its delightful interior is the main civic and cultural centre and the stained glass windows tell the history of Derry.

Derry Shop (above)
Irish shops and, especially, pubs are often painted in bright cheerful colours, perhaps the better to be seen through the winds and rains of winter.

St. Eugene's Cathedral (right)
Designed in the Gothic Revival style, this is Derry's Catholic cathedral, nestled in the heart of the Bogside district just beyond the city walls. The foundation stone was laid in 1851, but work continued until 1873. The spire was added in 1902.

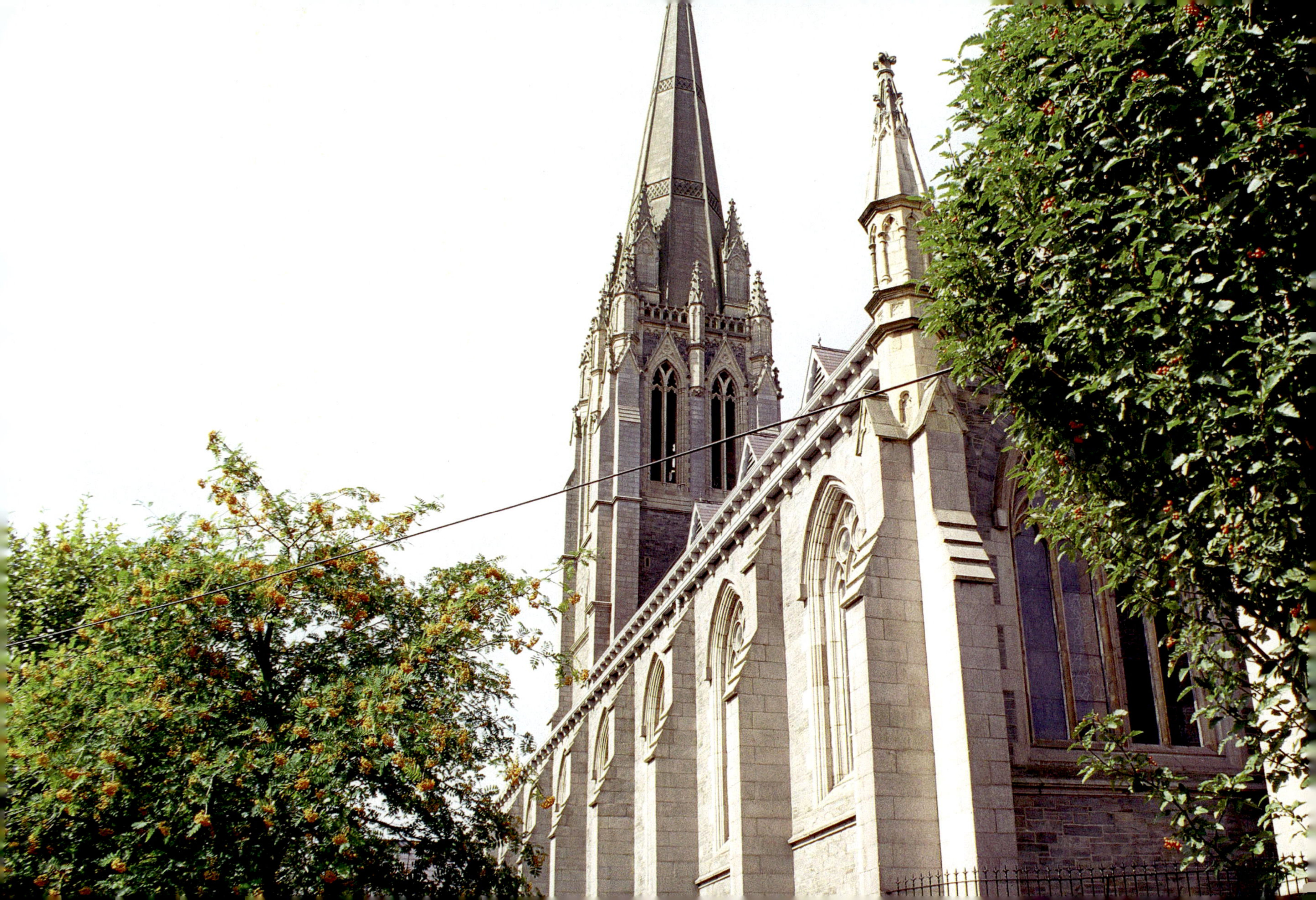

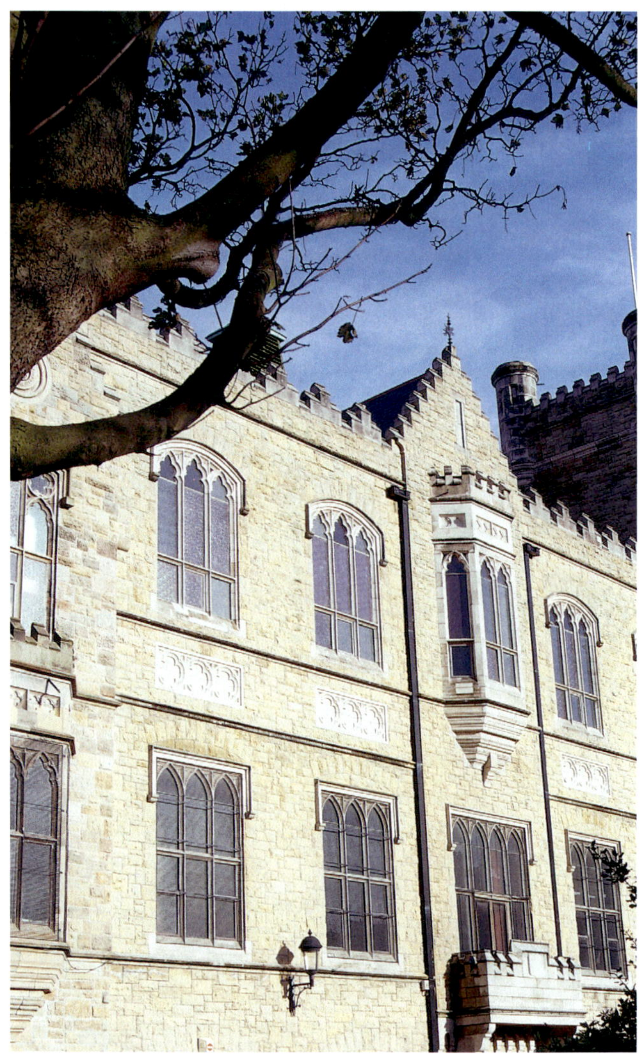

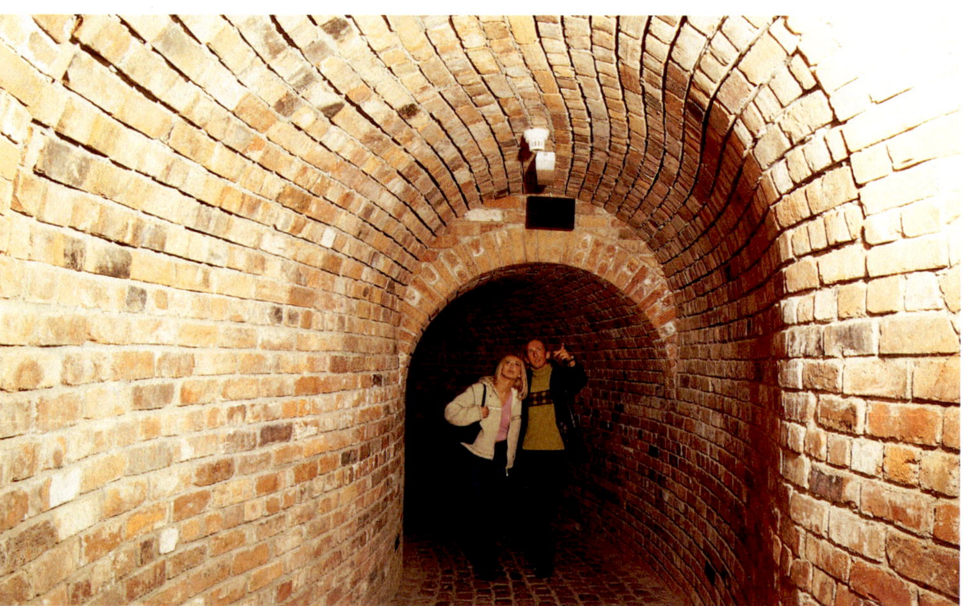

Apprentice Boys Hall (left)
The hall, built in 1873, is the centre of events held each year to commemorate the Great Siege of 1689—events that include the Apprentice Boys parade each August.

Derry Tower Museum (above)
Opened in 1992, the museum tells the story of Derry from its origins in the 6th century right up to the present day. Just inside the city walls, the 16th-century tower house was built originally for the O'Donnells.

Carlisle Square Sculpture (right)
The statue is situated at the city end of Craigavon Bridge and was unveiled in July 1992. It represents friendship and reconciliation and is the artistic embodiment of the "hands across the divide" aspiration.

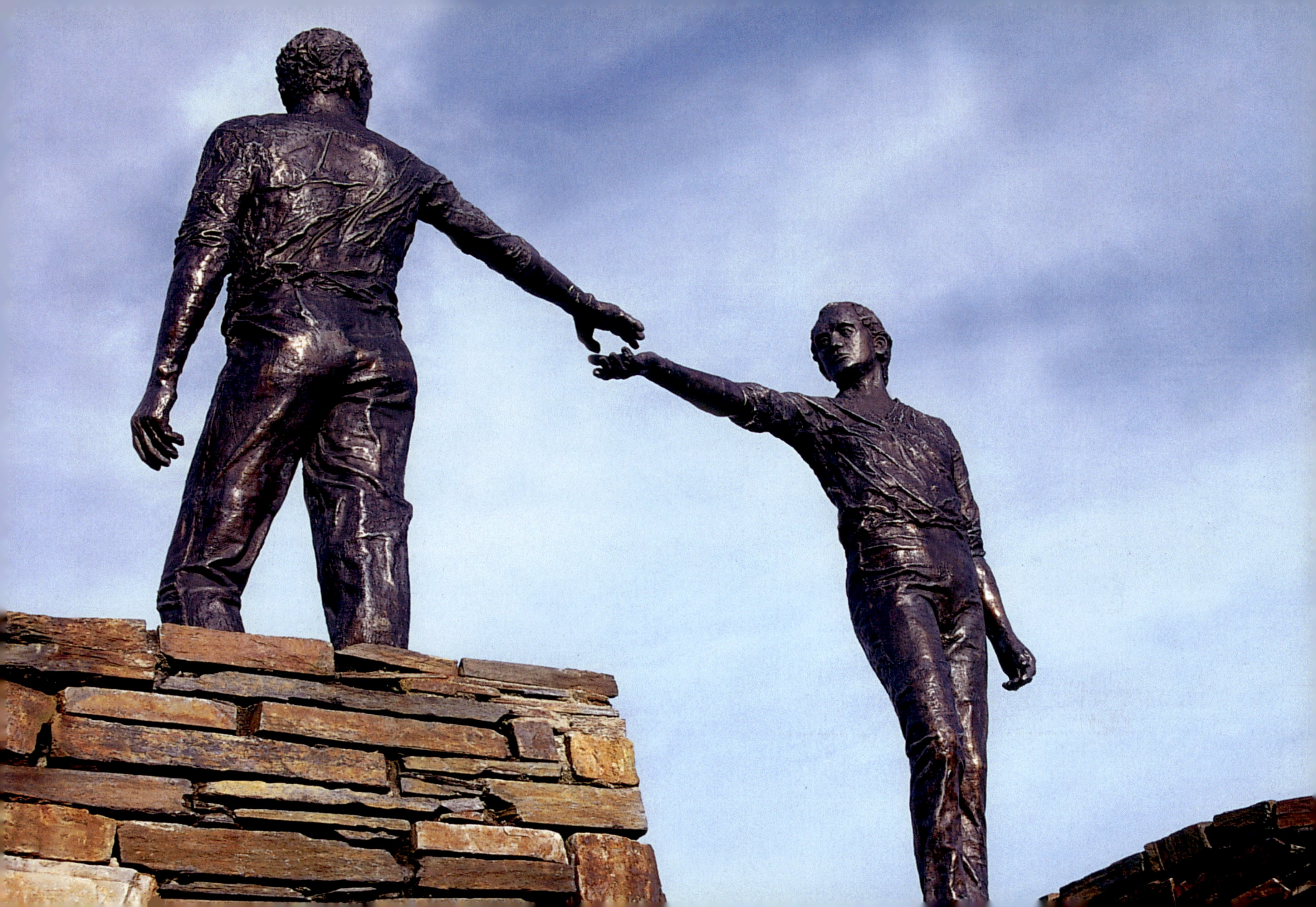

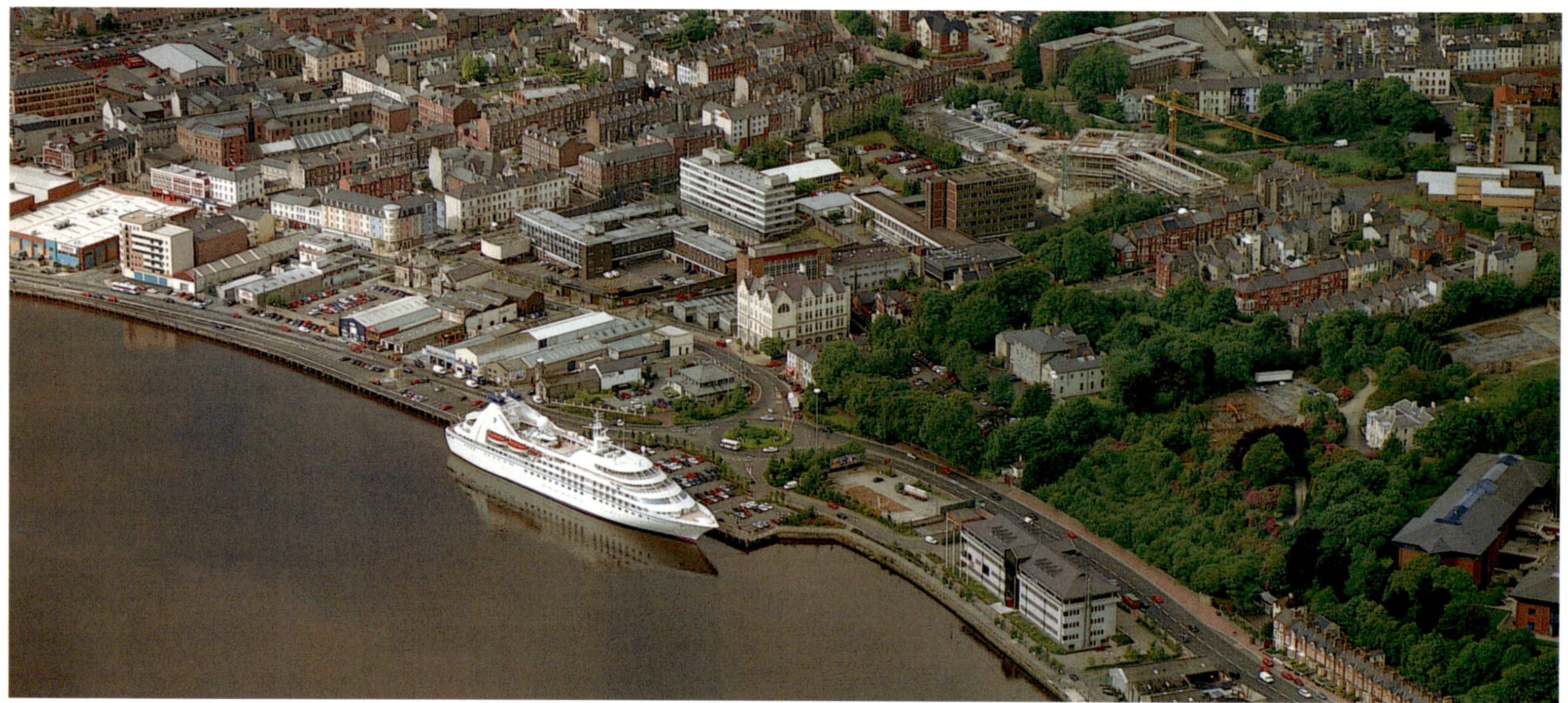

Derry aerial (above)

A bird's eye view of the sprawl of Derry. It gets its name from St Columba who founded a monastery at Doire (oak grove) later anglicised as Derry in 1613.

St Columb's Cathedral (right)

The cathedral has stood on its prominent site inside the walls of Derry since 1633—the first cathedral built in the British Isles after the Reformation. The interior was restored in the 19th century.

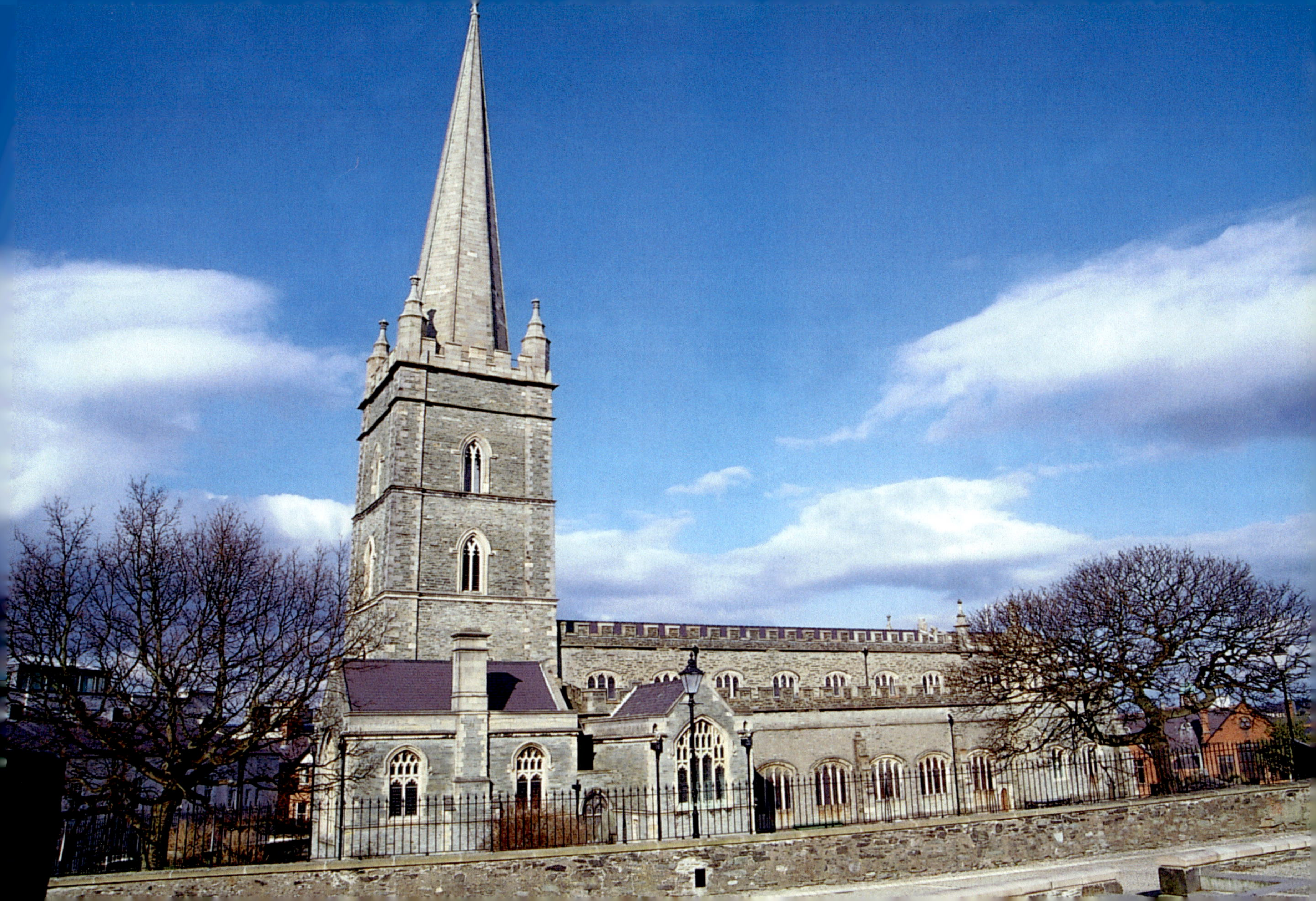

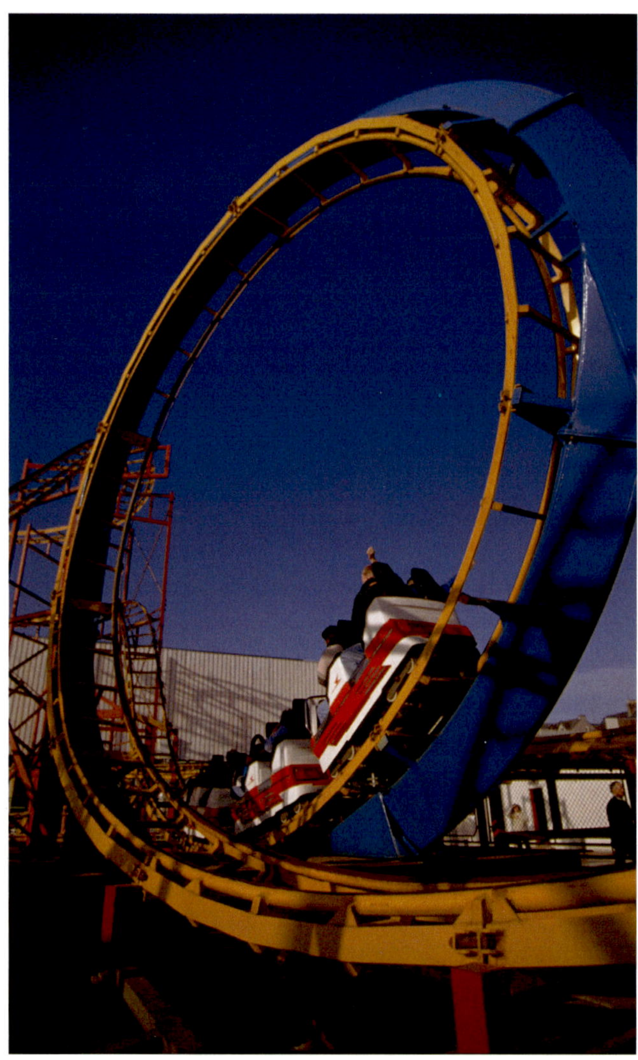

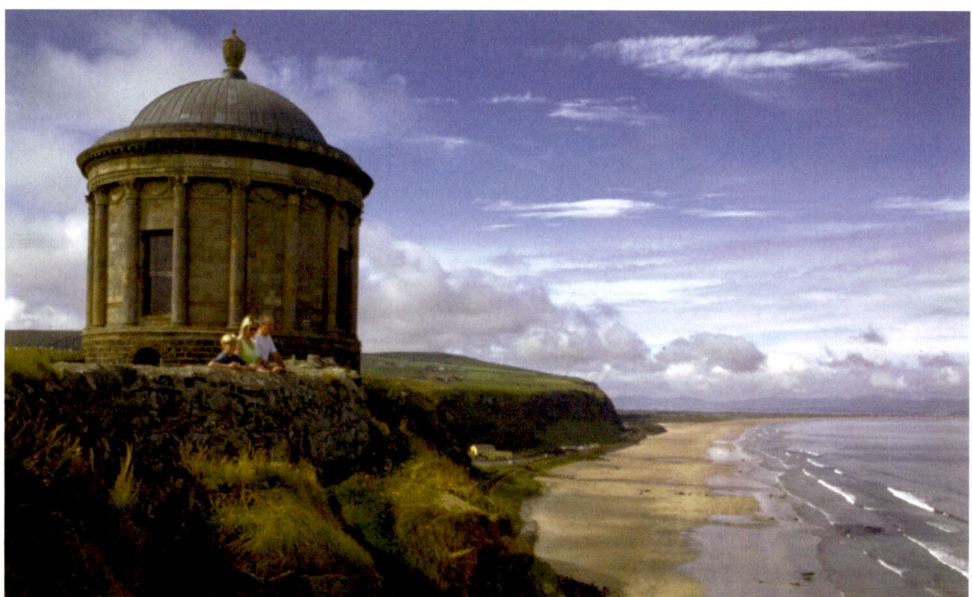

Roller Coaster (left)
Given a strong stomach, a roller-coaster brings out the child in everyone.

Downhill and Mussenden Temple (above)
Set on a stunning wild headland with fabulous views over Ireland's north coast is the 18th century estate of Downhill. It includes the renowned Mussenden Temple, Mausoleum, and palace ruins.

Dunluce Castle (right)
Another view of the castle (see also pages 16/17) which is situated on a dark basalt outcrop on the causeway coast. On a clear day you can look from here to Donegal and round to Islay

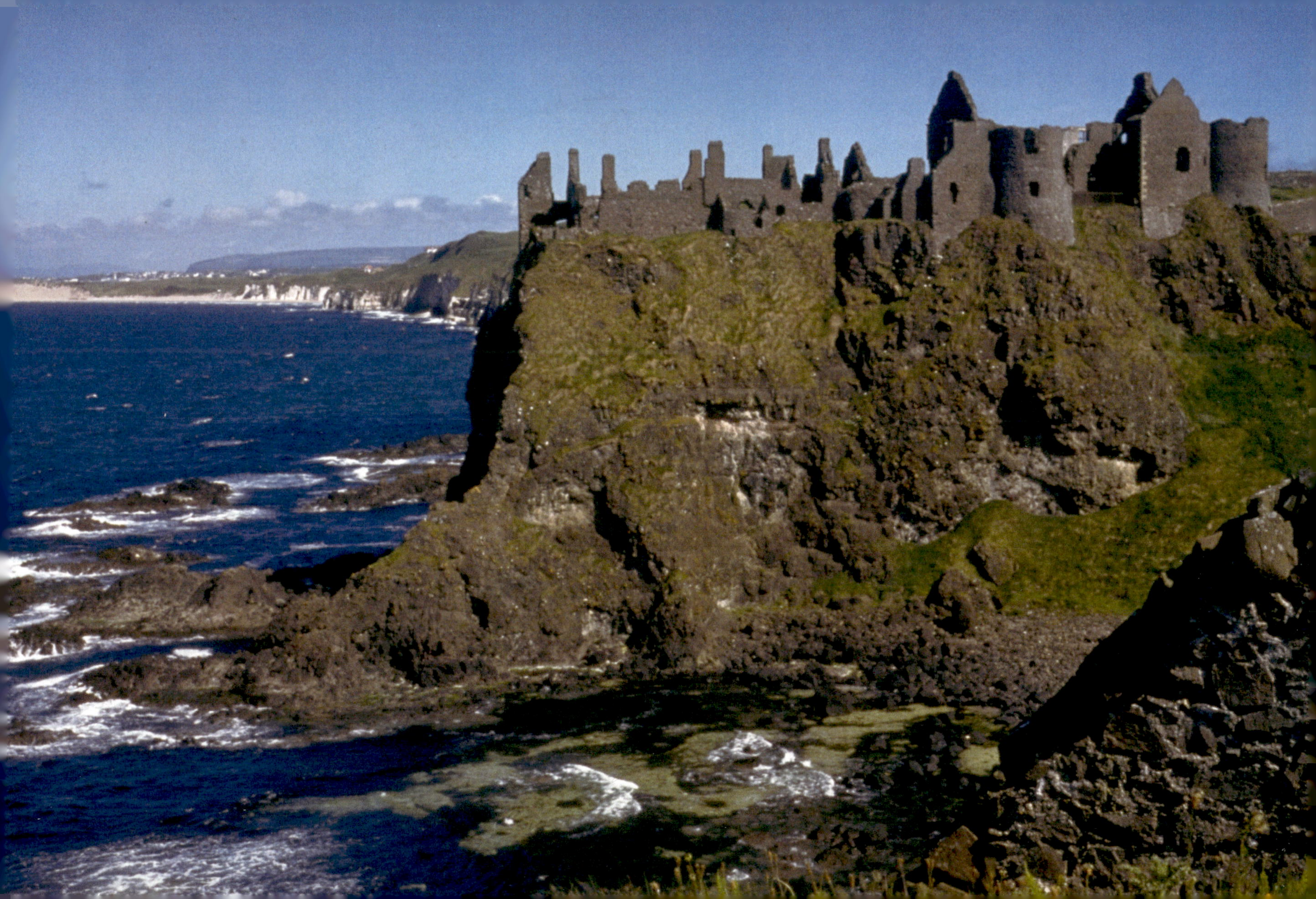

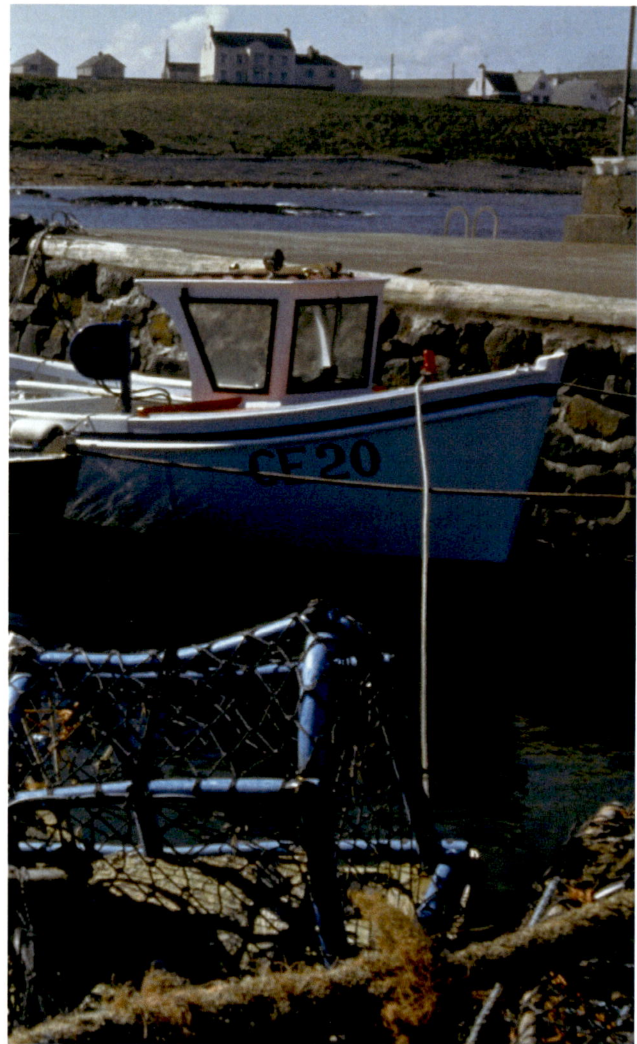

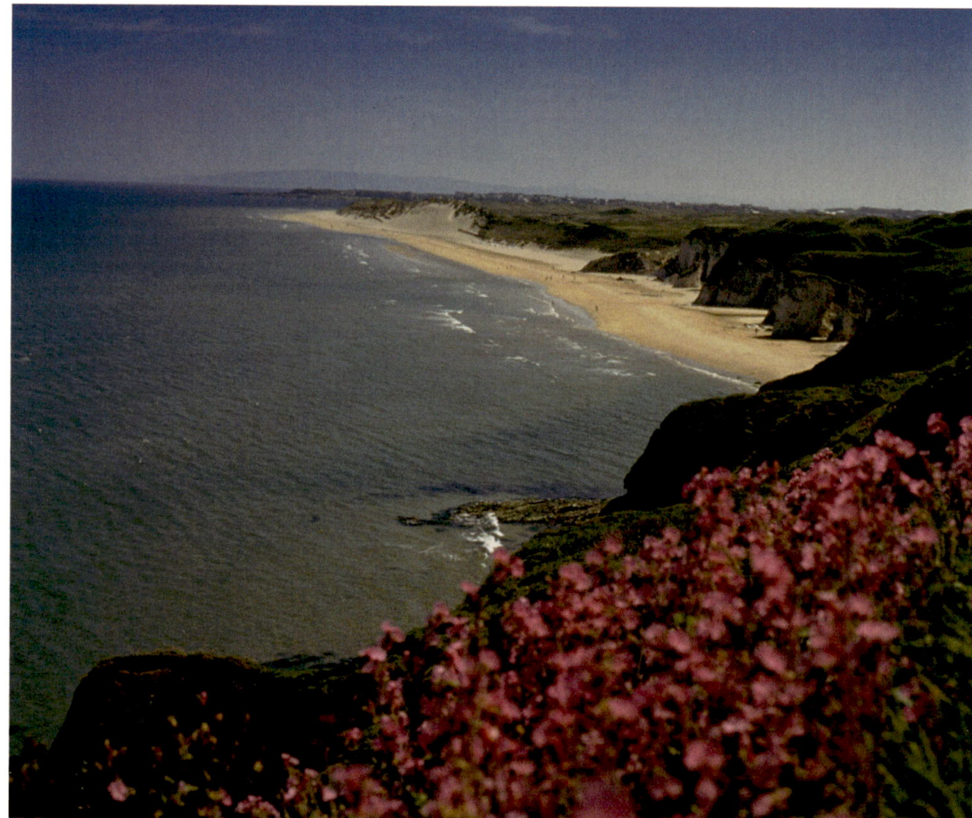

Ireland has a wonderful coastline which is there for everyone to enjoy—whether for cliff walking, lazing on the beach, spotting the amazingly varied fauna and flora, or simply admiring the stunning views.

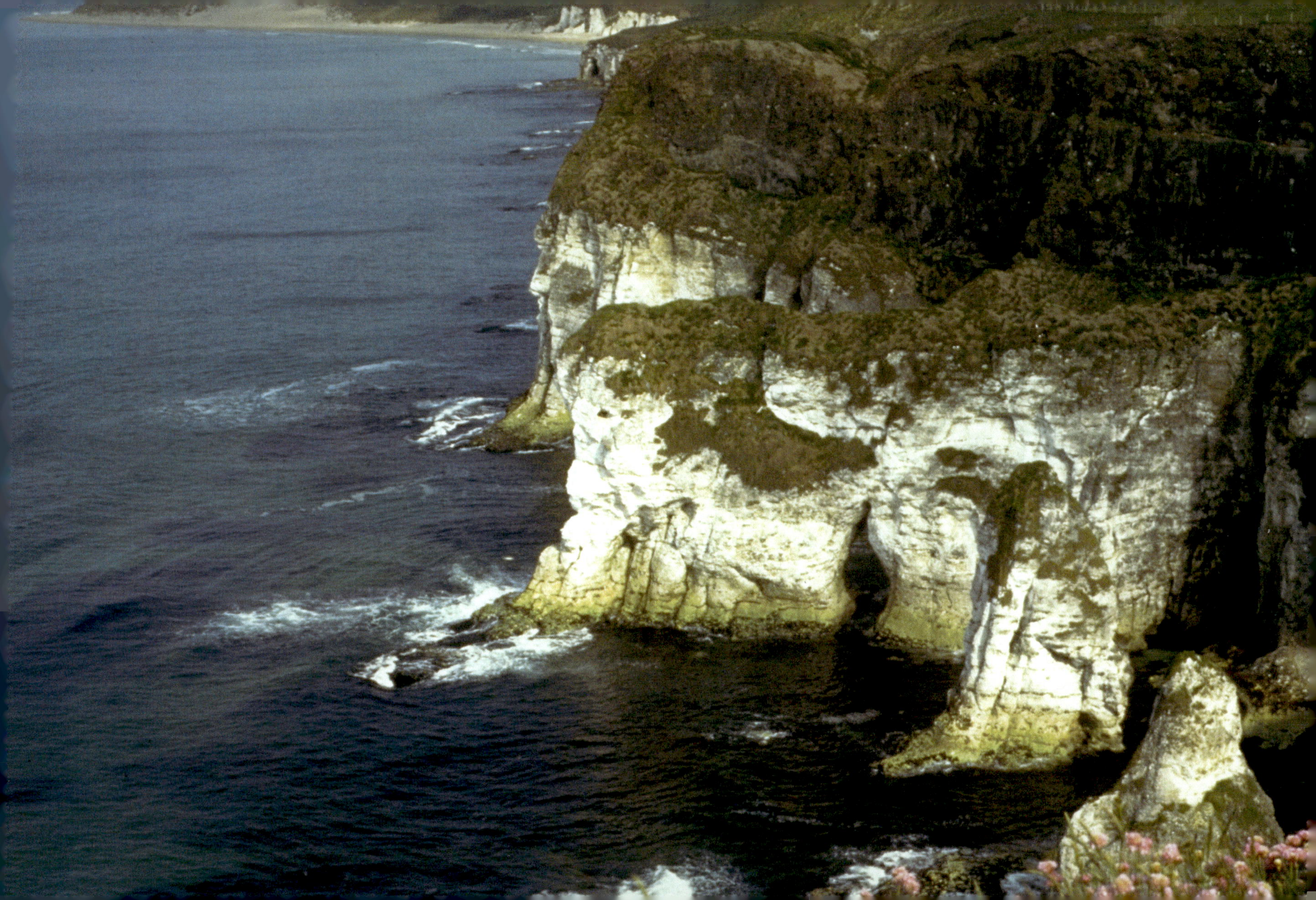

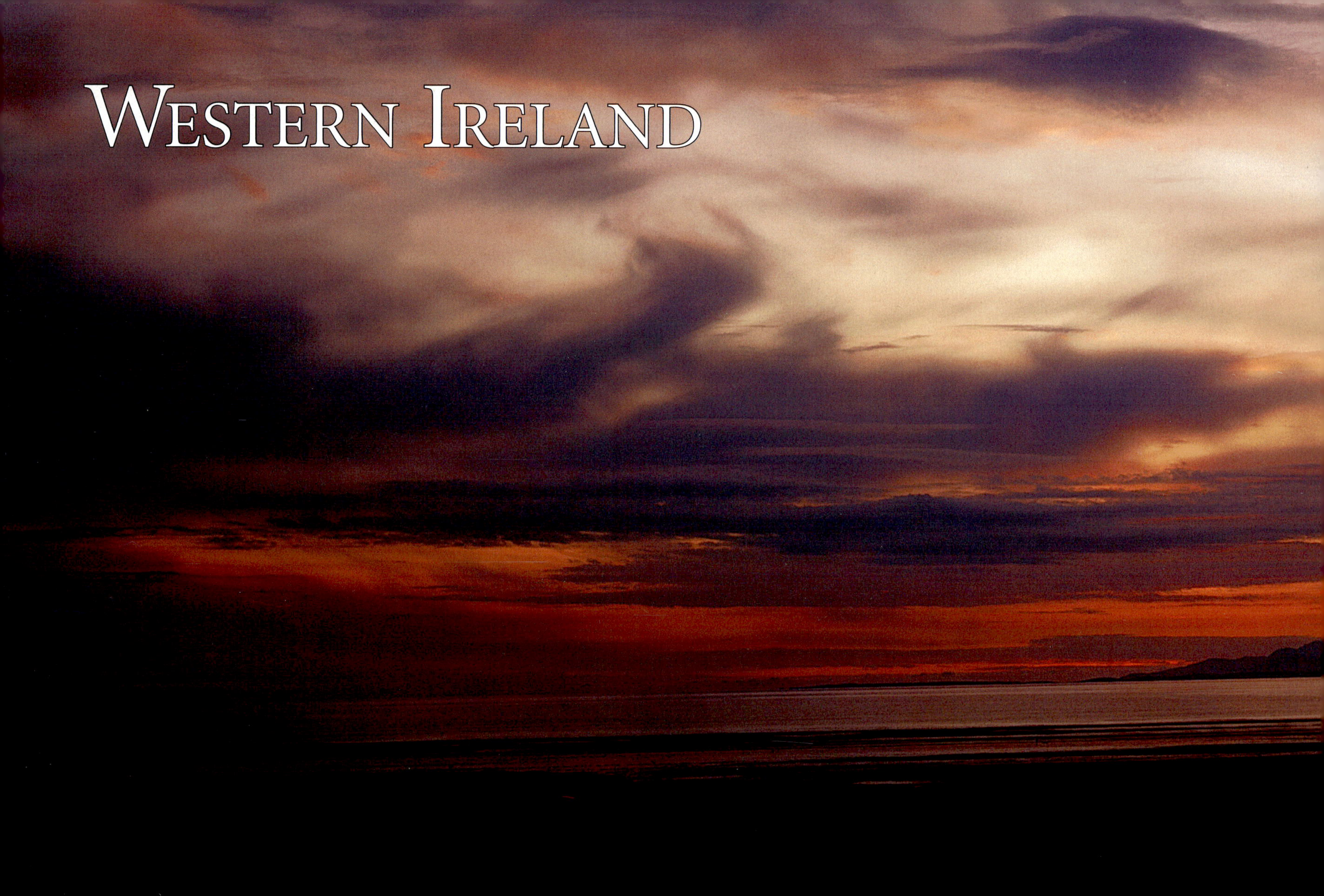
Western Ireland

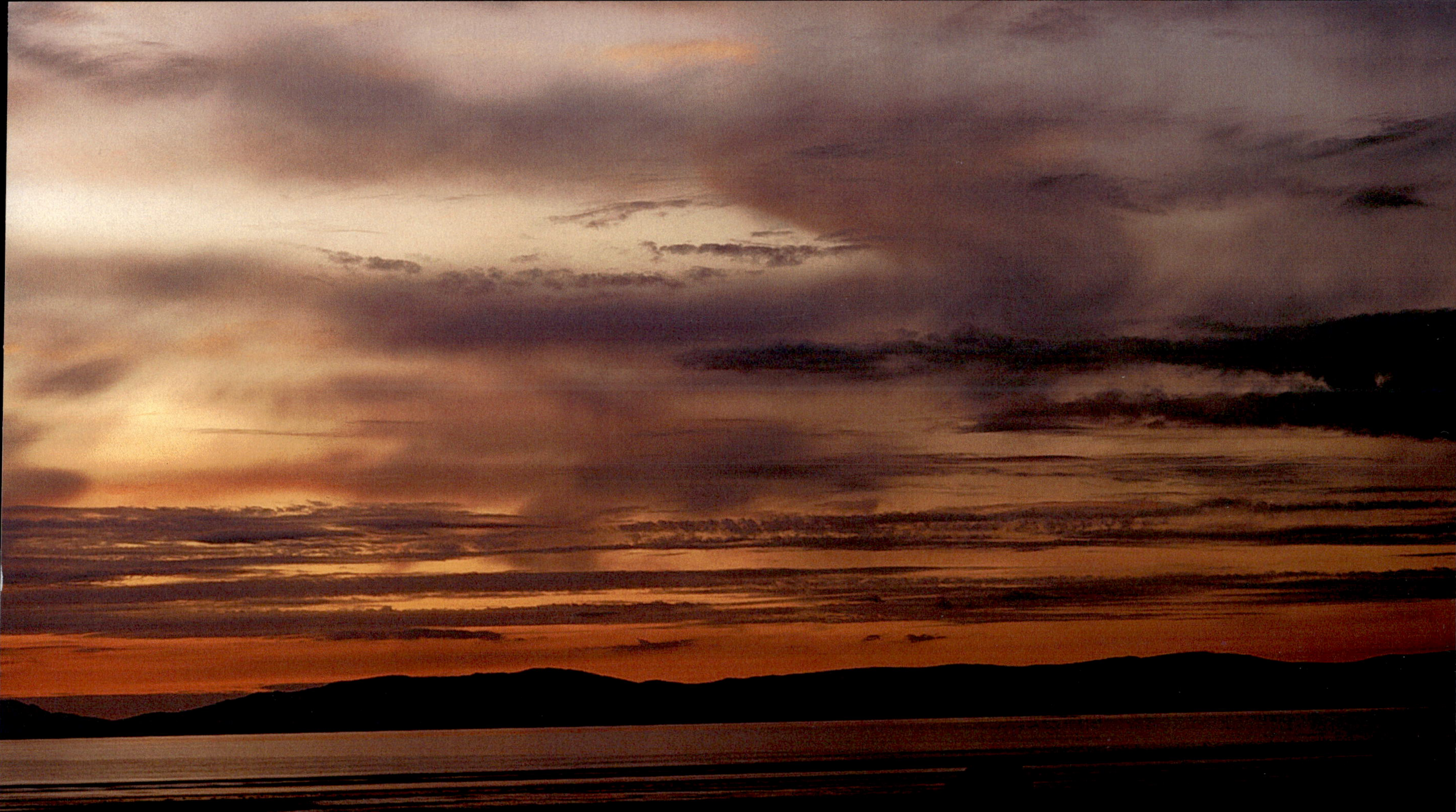

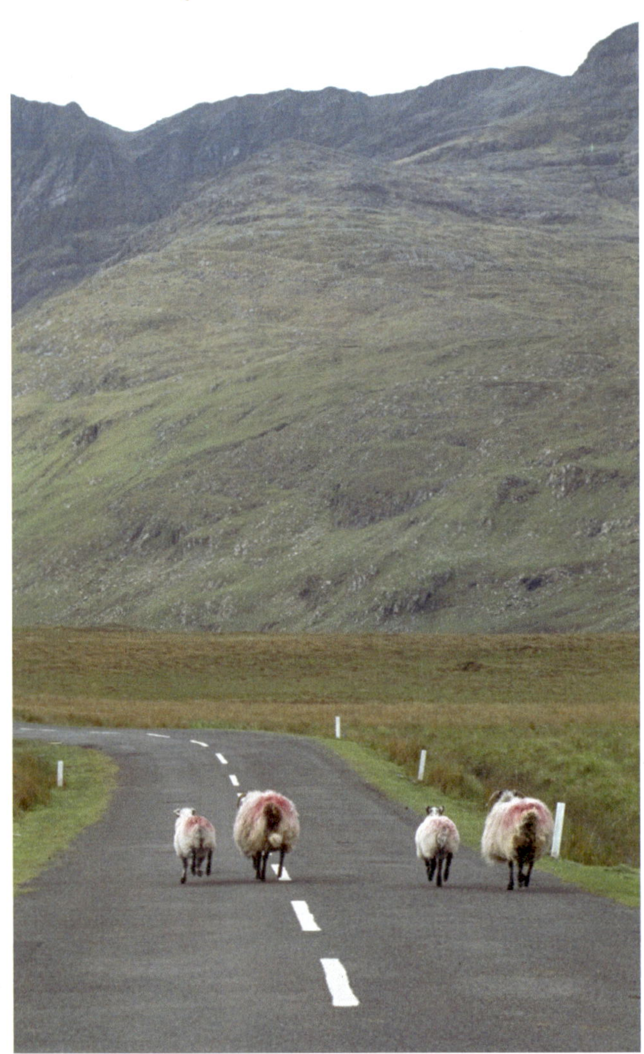

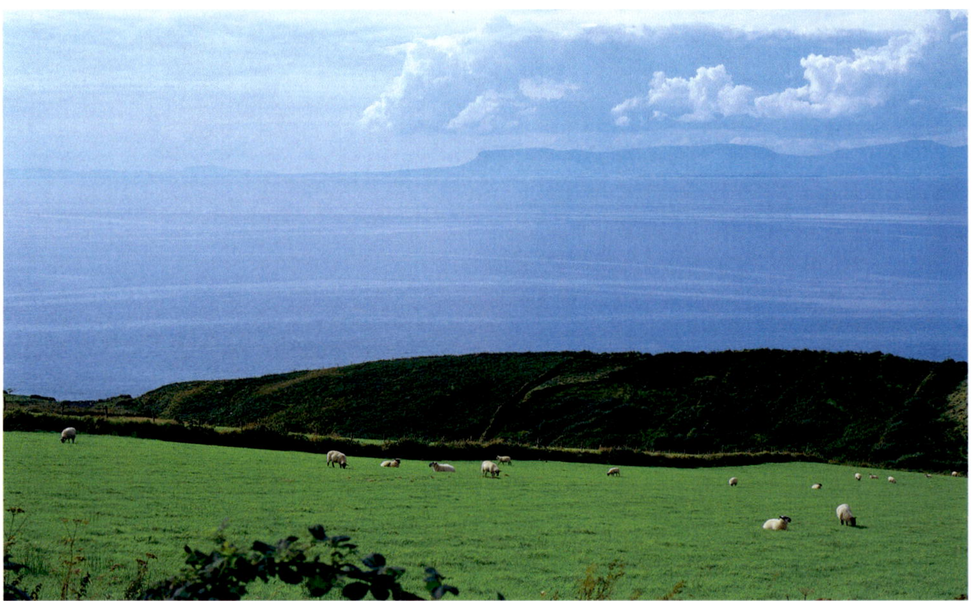

Mweelrea Mountains, County Mayo (left)
Mweelrea (2,670ft) is the highest mountain in Connaught and is guarded on all sides by craggy slopes. There are no easy ascents of this mighty peak and it needs to be approached with caution.

View of Benbulbin (above)
Sligo is a maritime county in the province of Connaught. Benbulbin (1,792ft) is part of the Ox Mountain and is very precipitous on the side facing Sligo Bay.

Cong (right)
The Gaelic name for Cong means a narrow strip of land and the village of Cong is situated on a narrow isthmus of cavernous limestone between Lough Mask and Lough Corrib.

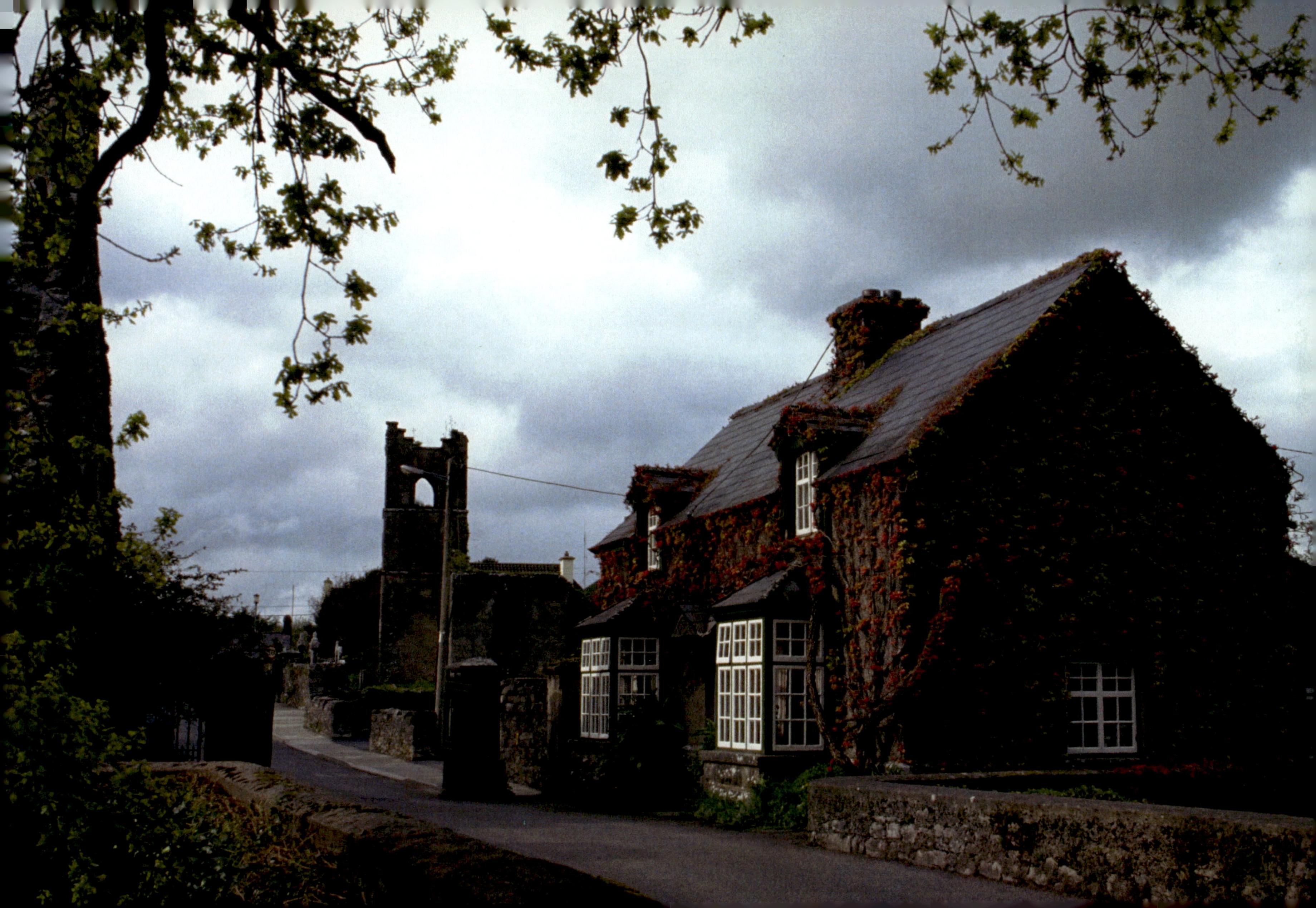

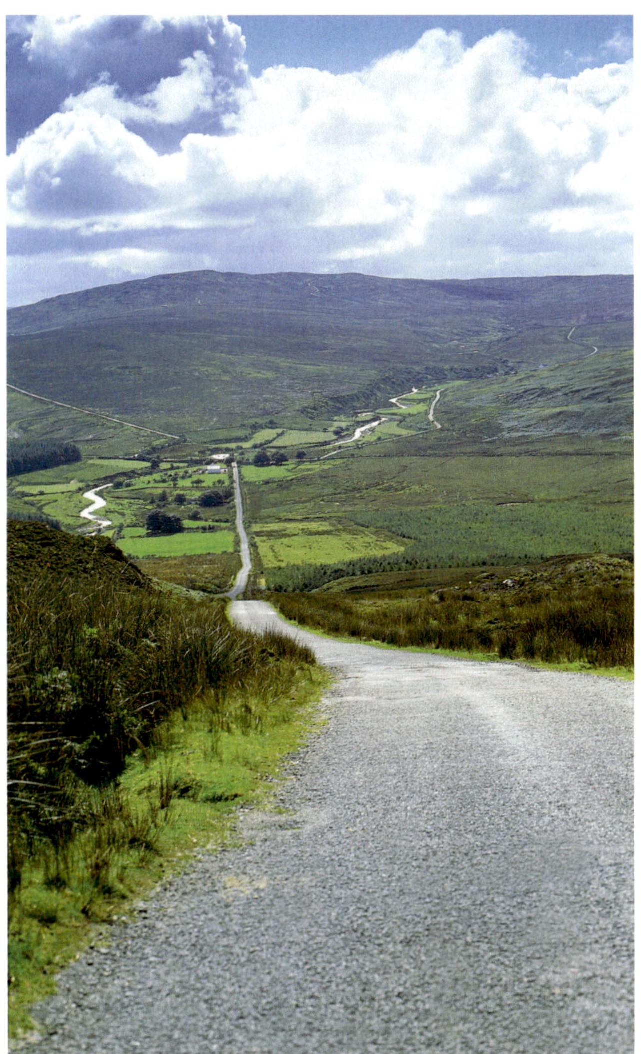

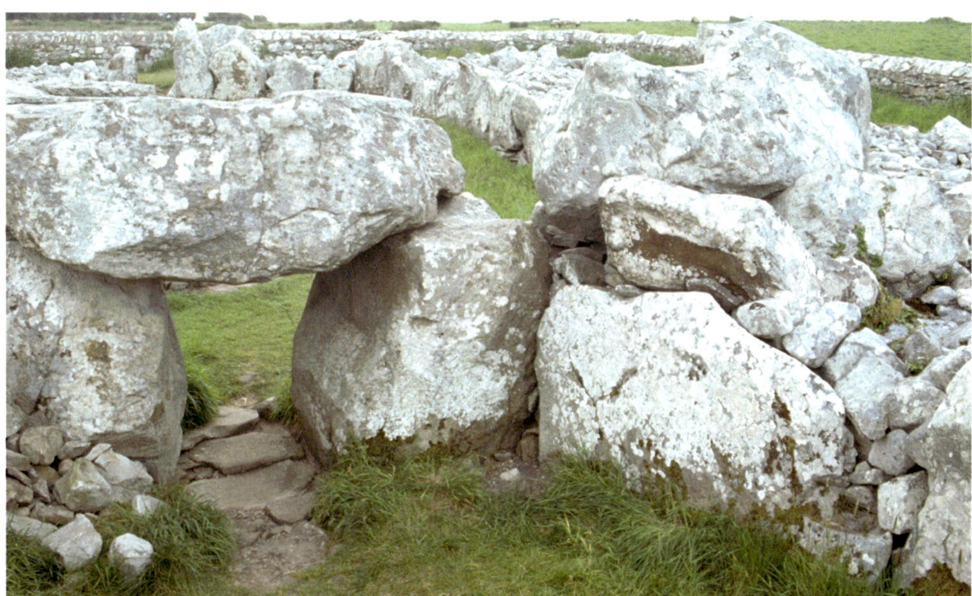

Gap of Mamore (left)
The Gap of Mamore lies between Muff and Buncrana, a very scenic routes through the Urris Mountains, which cover much of the peninsula's interior.

Creevykeel Court Tomb, Bundoran (above)
This classic court tomb has two main burial chambers. It was built by a Stone Age farming community who settled in this area between 3,000 and 3,500 BC.

Kinvara Village (right)
Located in the south-east of Galway Bay, the famous boats of Galway, the Galway Hookers, are often seen in Kinvara harbour. Close to the village is the 16th-century Dun Guaire Castle.

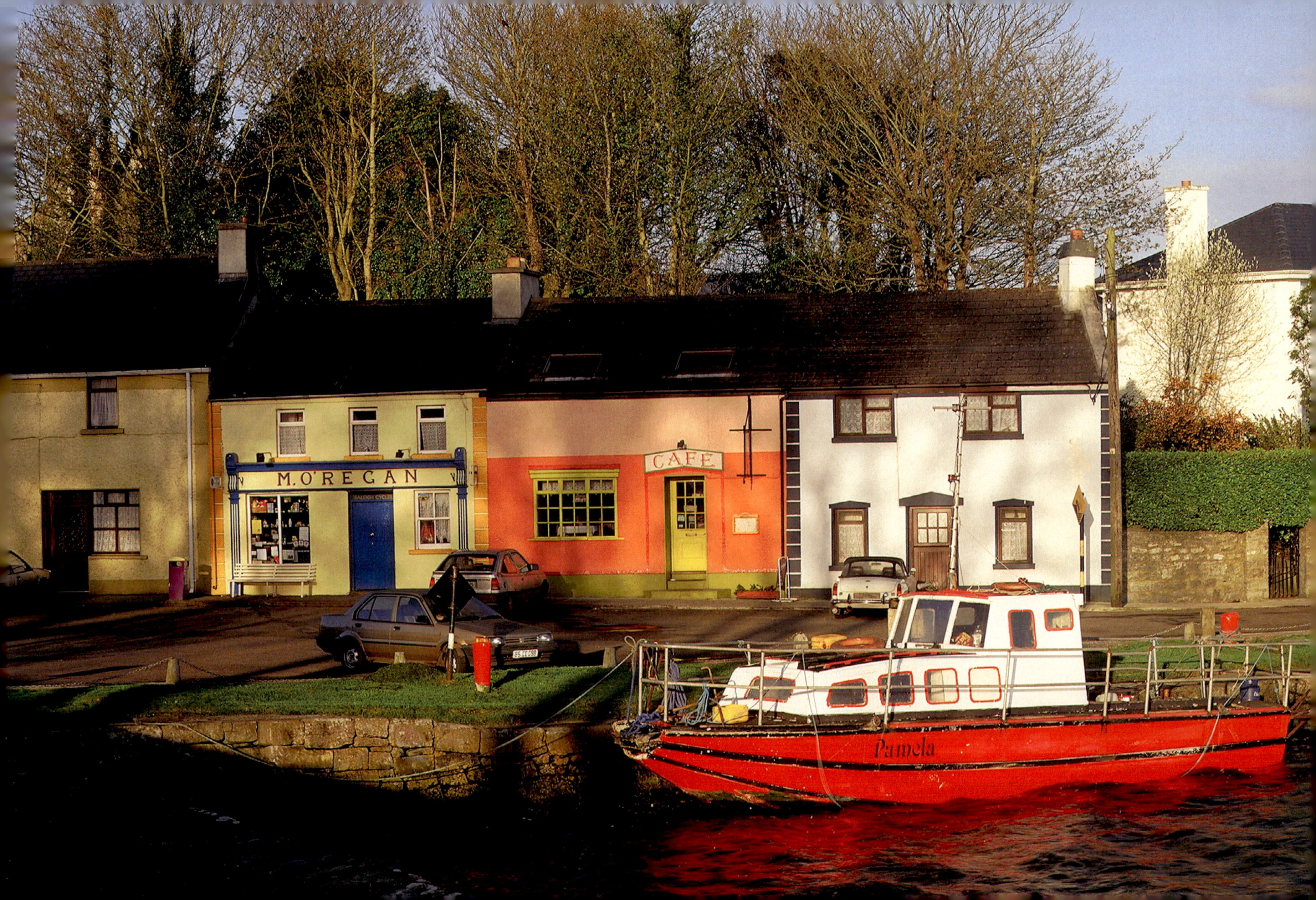
M.O'REGAN
CAFE
Pamela

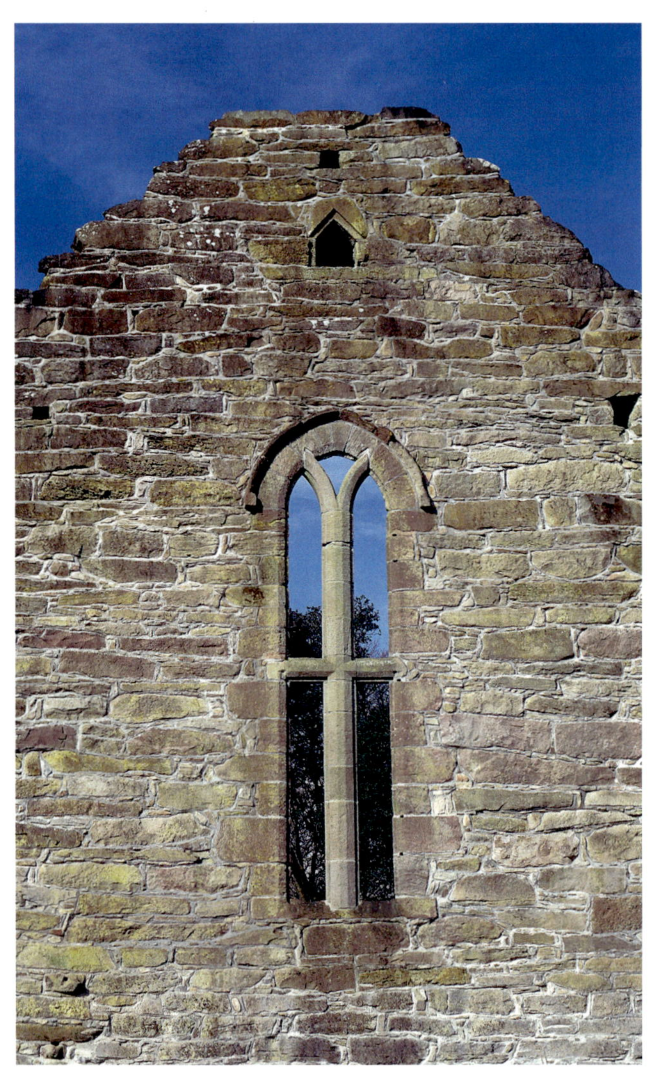

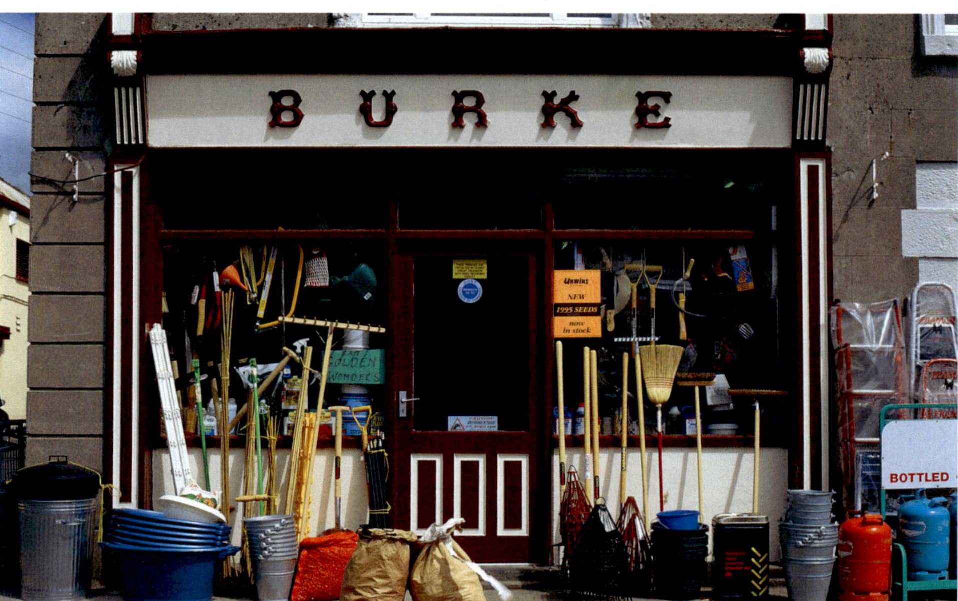

Lough Key Forest Park (left)
Located outside Boyle in the old Rockingham estate, this park includes a temple, stable block, church, disused castle, ice-house, and subterranean passages once used by the servants.

Gort (above)
The quiet town of Gort in County Galway is surrounded by ancient monastic ruins and dramatic countryside. Nearby stands a tree carved with the initials of WBY (William Butler Yeats), GBS (George Bernard Shaw), and many others.

Ashford Castle, County Mayo (right)
The original building dates back to the 13th century Anglo - Norman castle built by the de Burgos family after their defeat of the native O'Connors of Connaught.

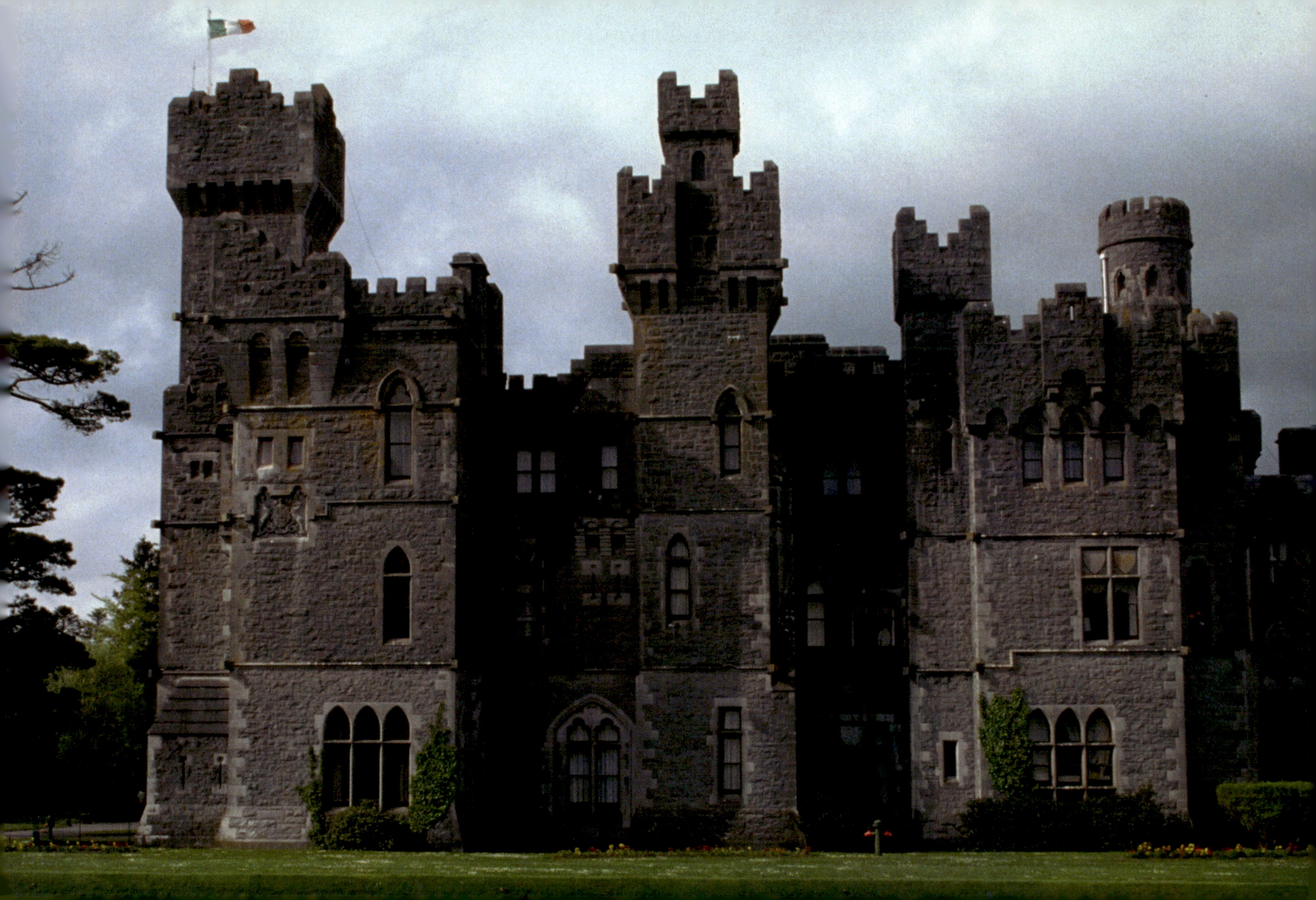

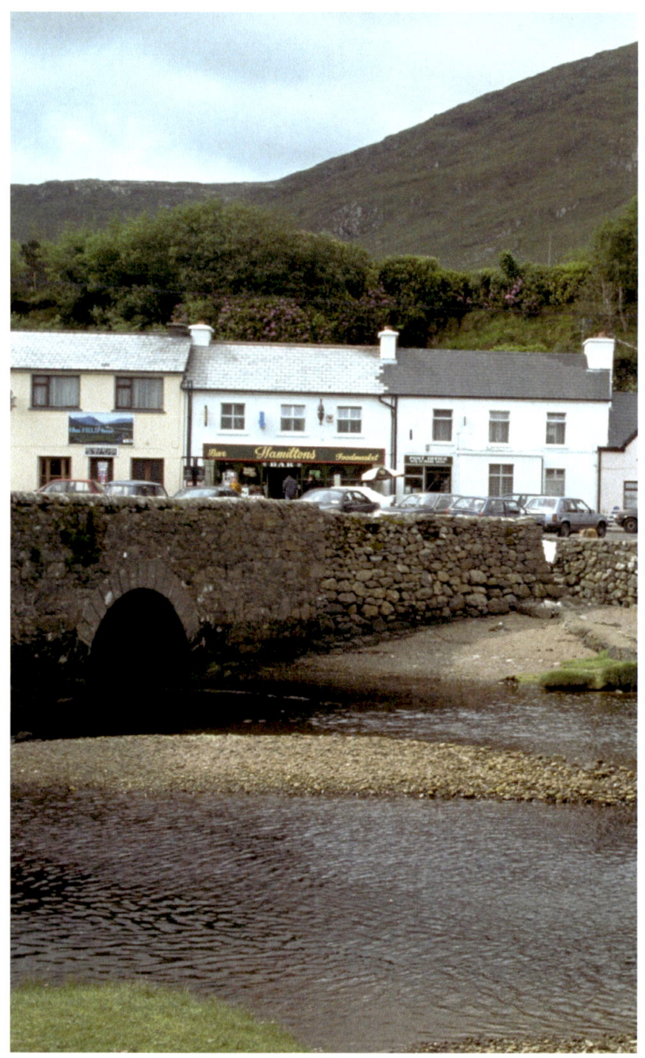

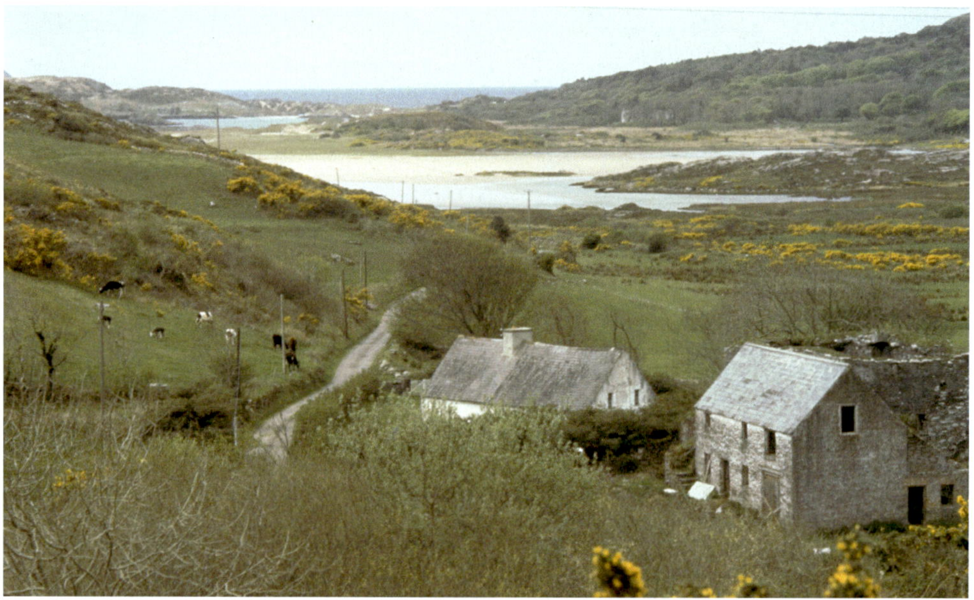

Leenane (left)
Often considered the "Gateway to the Connemara", Leenane, County Galway, is situated at the head of Killary Harbour, Ireland's only fjord.

Galway coast (above)
The second largest of the counties, Galway's coast is broken by deep inlets, bays, and harbours all bordered by rugged cliffs. Offshore are the islands of Inishshark, Inishbofin, Gorumna, Lettermullan, Croagnakeela, and adjoining islets.

Kylemore Abbey (right)
This enchanted fairytale castle in Neo-Gothic style stands dramatically at the foot of a barren mountain in a remote and beautiful part of Connemara.

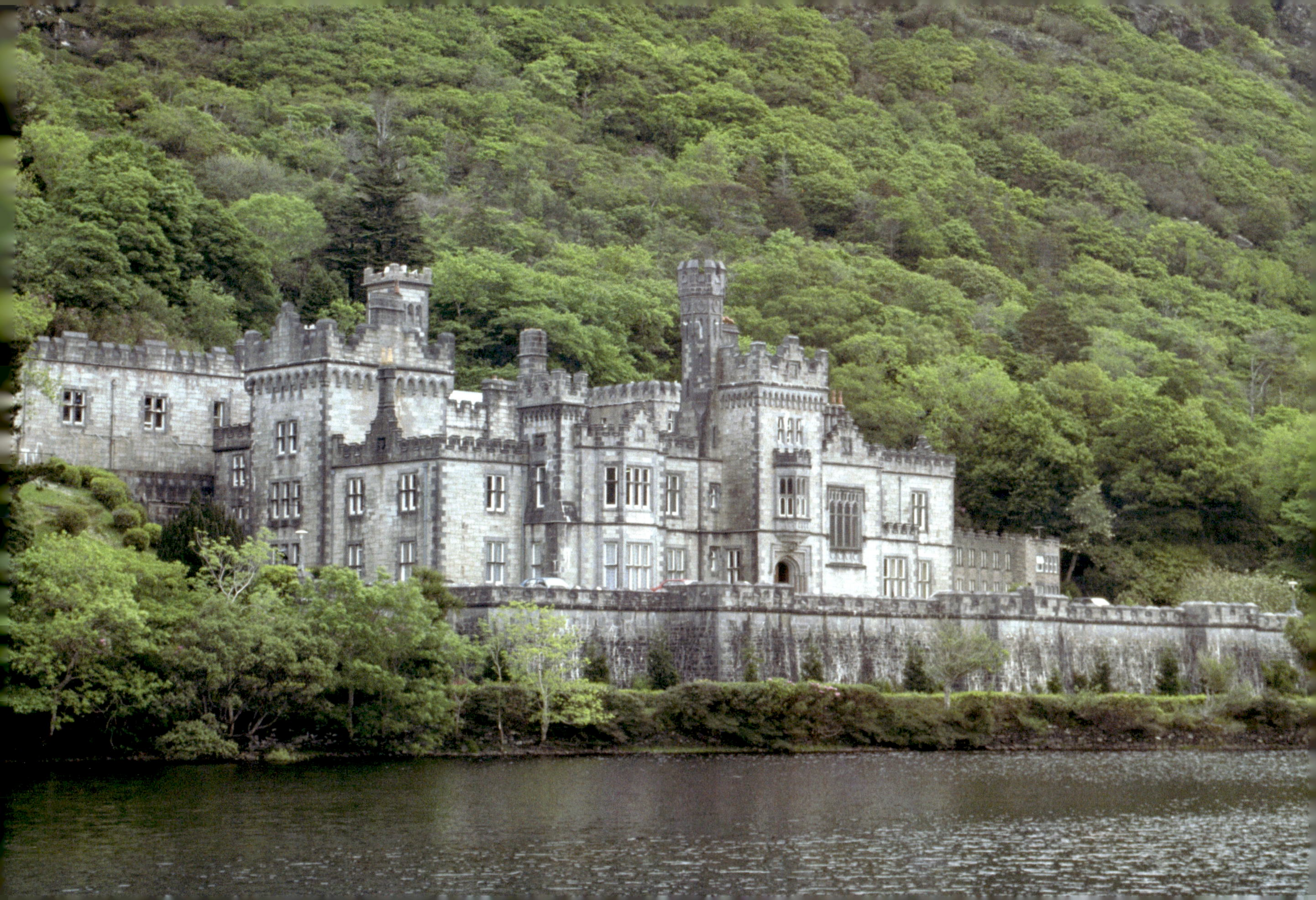

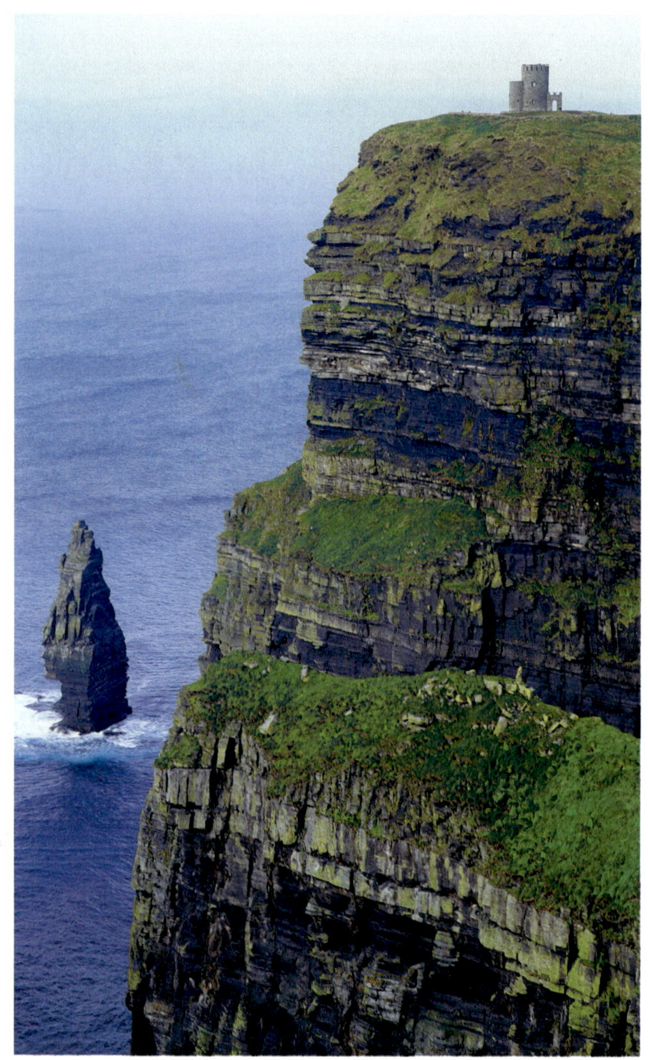

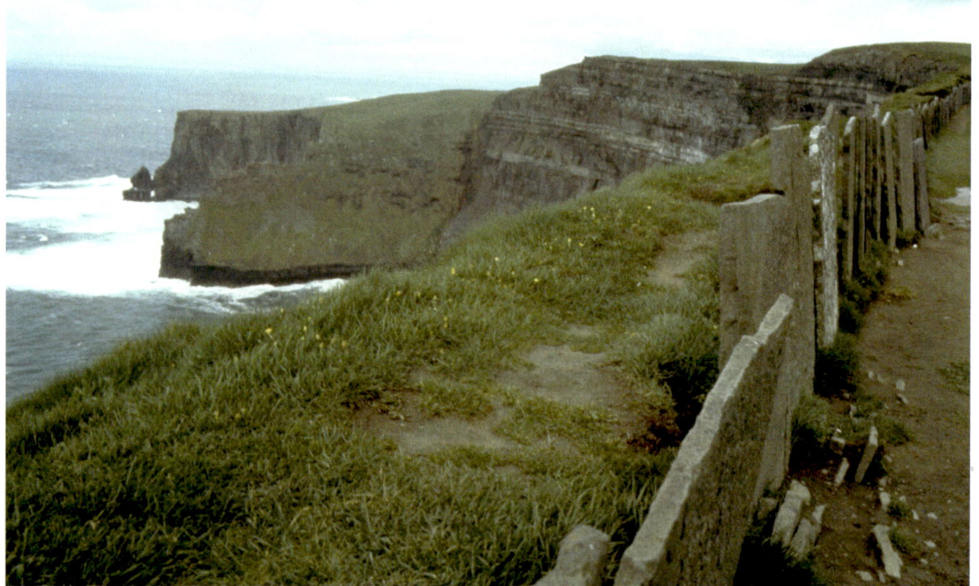

O'Brien's Tower (left)

Standing proudly on a headland of the majestic Cliffs of Moher, O'Brien's Tower was built in 1835 by Cornelius O'Brien a descendant of Brian Boru, and the O'Briens of Bunratty Castle, Kings of Thomond.

Cliffs of Moher (above and right)

The cliffs run along five miles of County Clare's rugged Atlantic coastline and at some points are as high as 600ft above the sea.

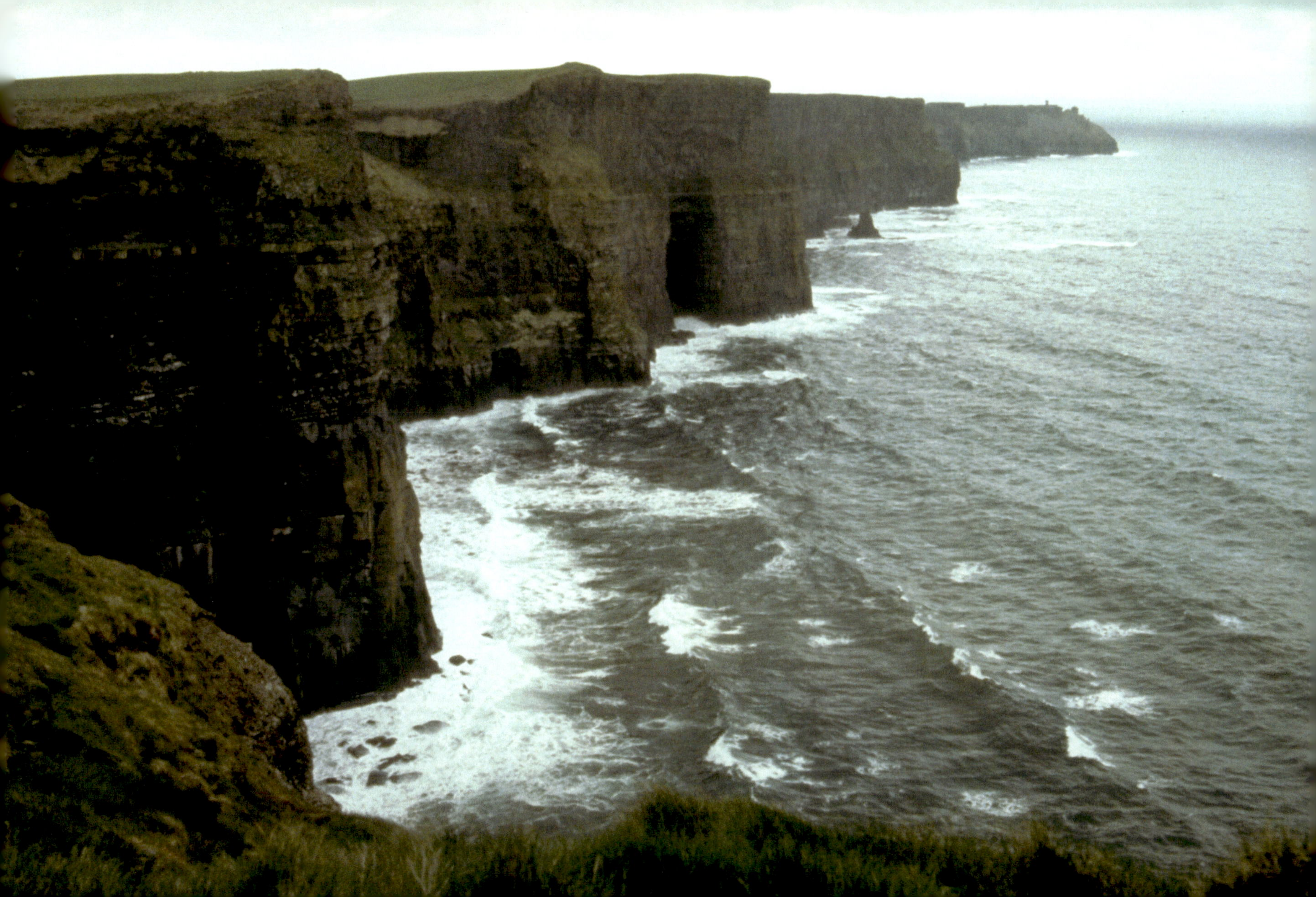

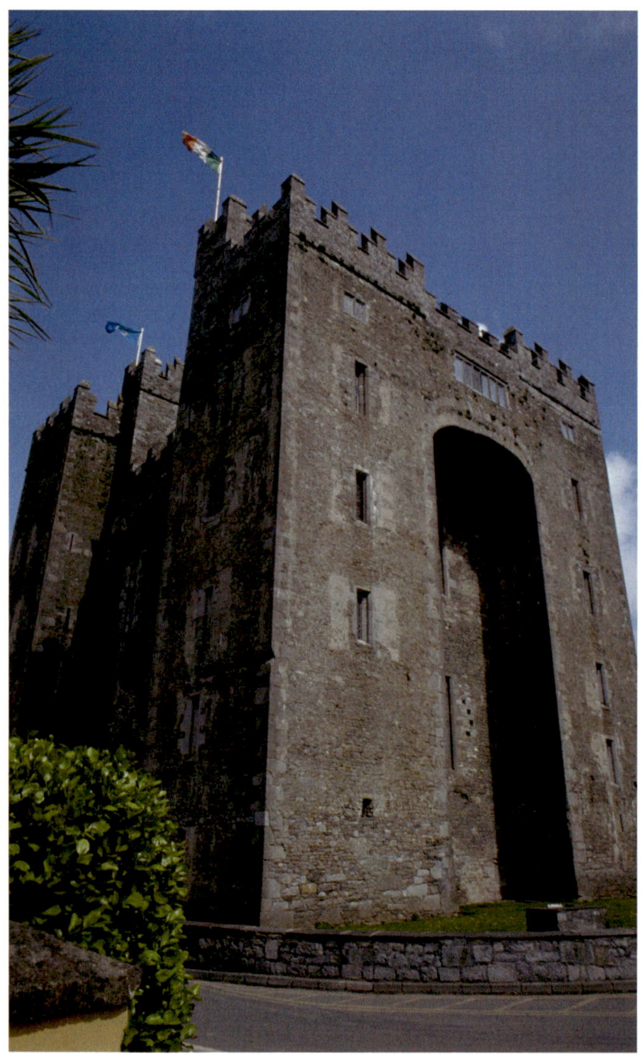

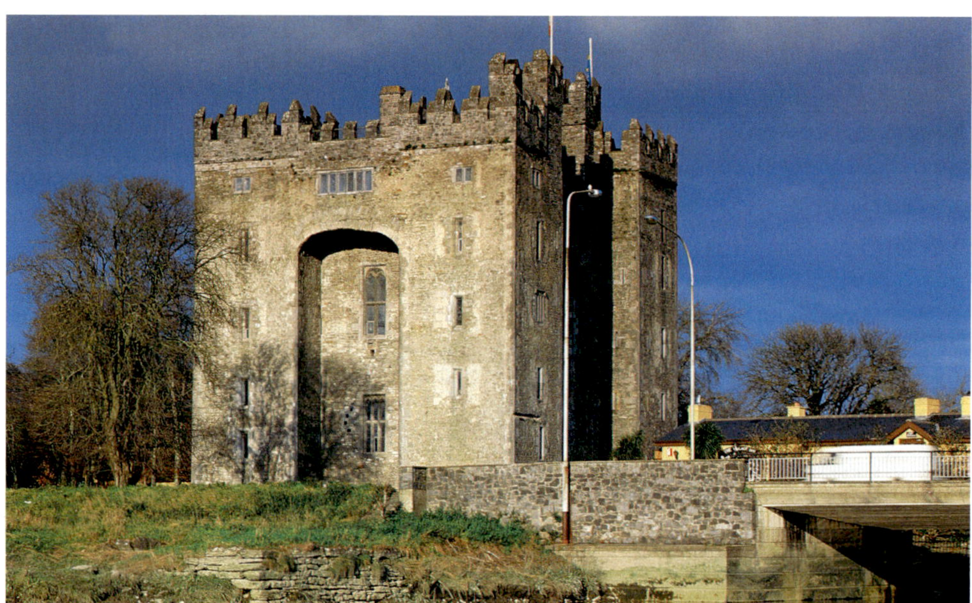

Bunratty Castle (above and left)
Just north of Limerick on the other side of the Shannon, Bunratty lies on the River Ratty. The Vikings built a fortified settlement on what used to be an island and surrounded it with a moat. Thomas de Clare built the first stone structure on the site in the 1270s: the present castle is the fourth or fifth building to occupy the location. One of Ireland's most popular attractions, Bunratty is the most complete and authentic medieval castle in Ireland

Durty Nelly's Pub (right)
In the shadow of the castle, on the main road, is the well-known, popular pub Durty Nelly's.

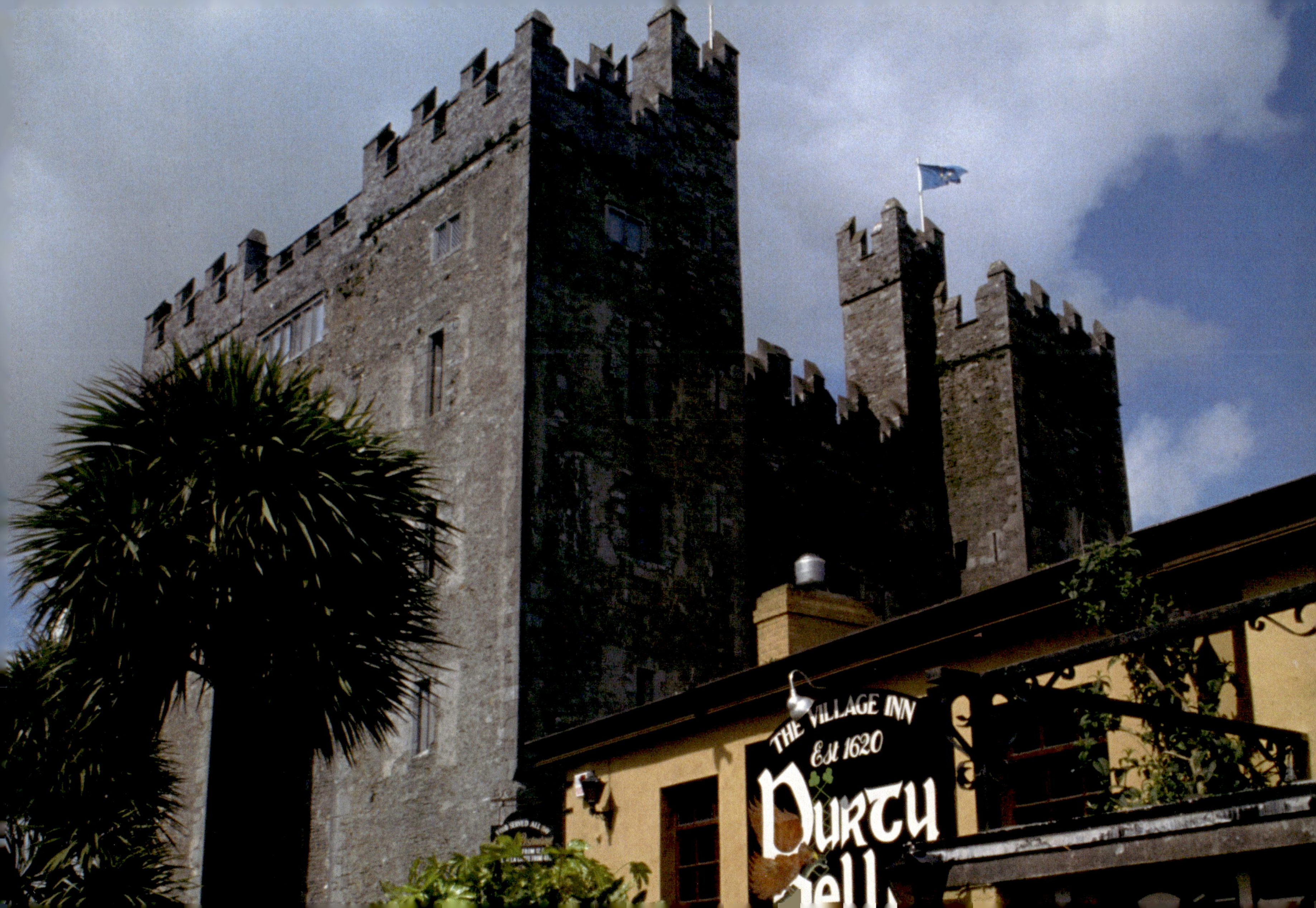
THE VILLAGE INN
Est 1620
Durty

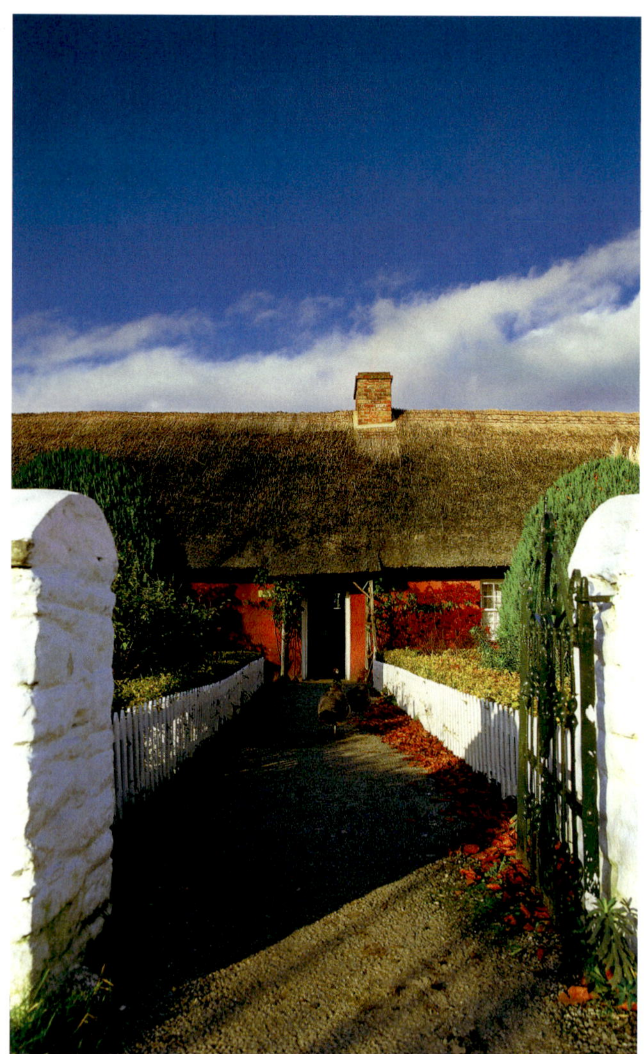

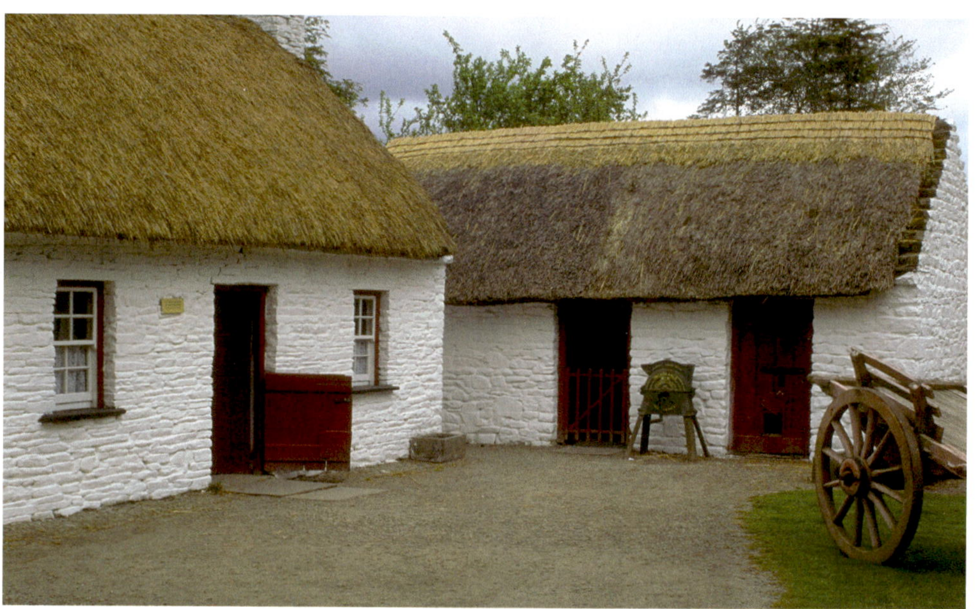

Bunratty Folk Park (left and above)

The Folk Park around Bunratty Castle is a beautifully reconstructed evocation of small town life in Ireland at the turn of the century. It contains typical 19th century rural and urban dwellings, eight farmhouses, a waterfall, a blacksmith's forge, a village street, and a village hotel and pub.

The Burren (right)

Poulnabrone Portal tomb. The name Burren is from the Irish—bhoireann, meaning a stony place. Its formation has lain unspoiled since the ice-age and is composed of karstic limestone, the largest area of such in western Europe.

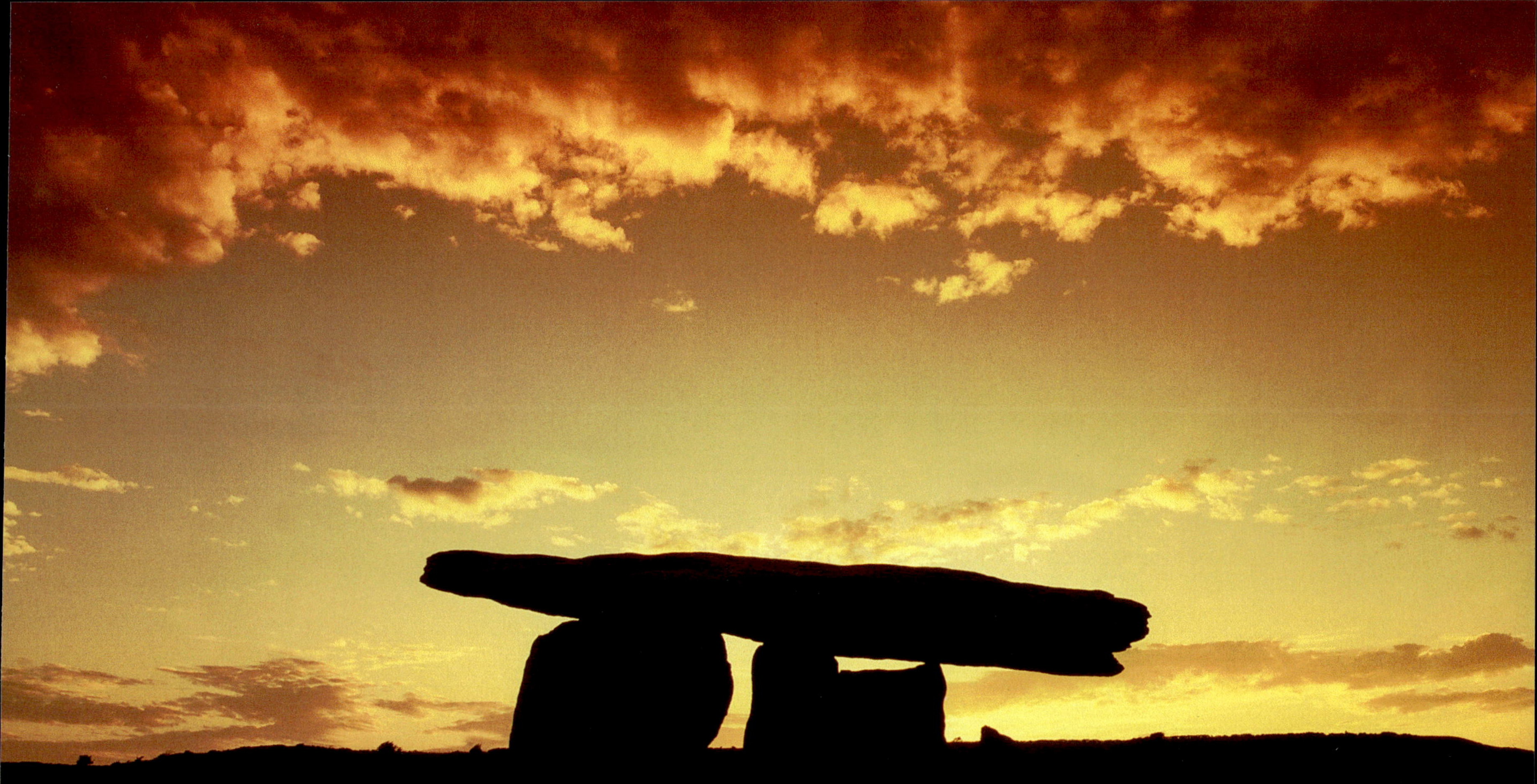

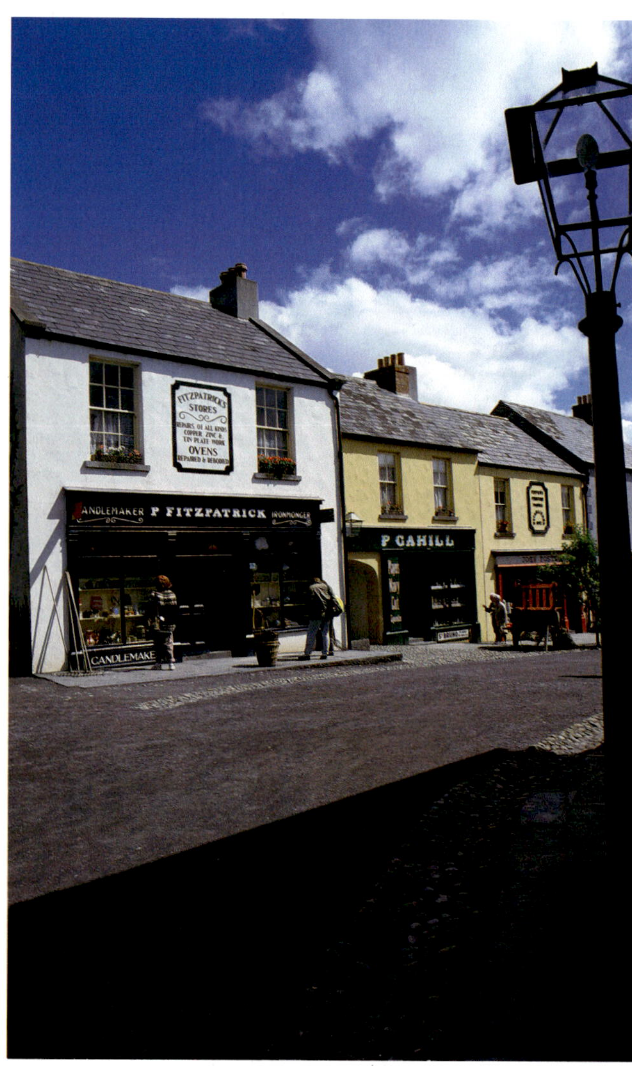

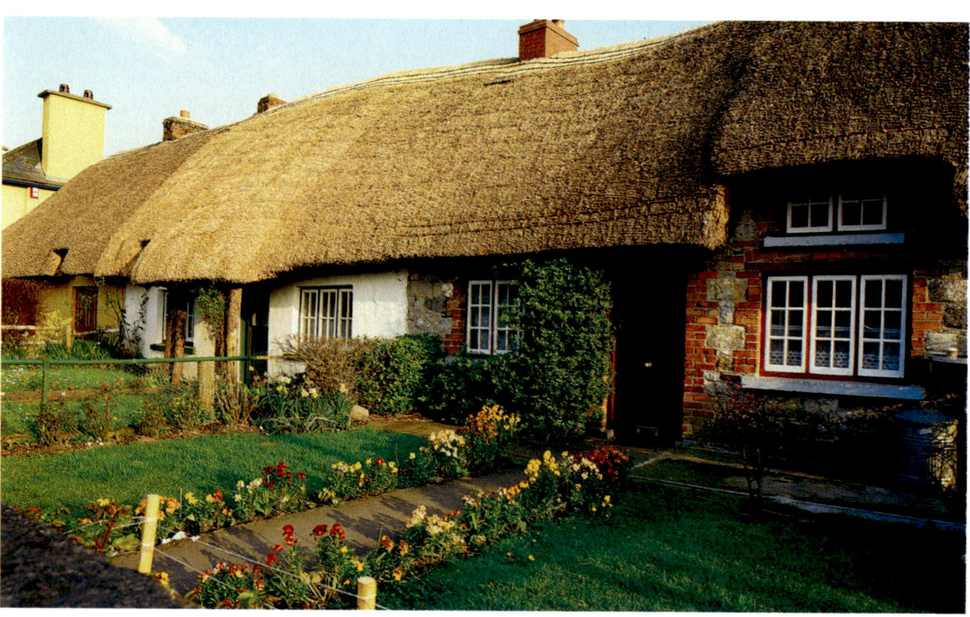

Bunratty Folk Park (left)
The park provides a fascinating insight into the way the Irish lived from the 15th century; the village street is complete with post office, school, doctor's house, hardware shop, printer's, drapery shop, and pawn shop.

Cottage in Adare (above)
Situated on the River Maigue, Adare (Gaelic name: "Ath Dara"— the "ford of the oak"—from the combination of water and woodland) dates back, at least, to the early 13th century.

Dunguaire Castle (right)
The castle bridges thirteen centuries of Irish history, from the skirmishes, battles, and sieges that characterise its colourful past, through to the literary revival of the 20th century.

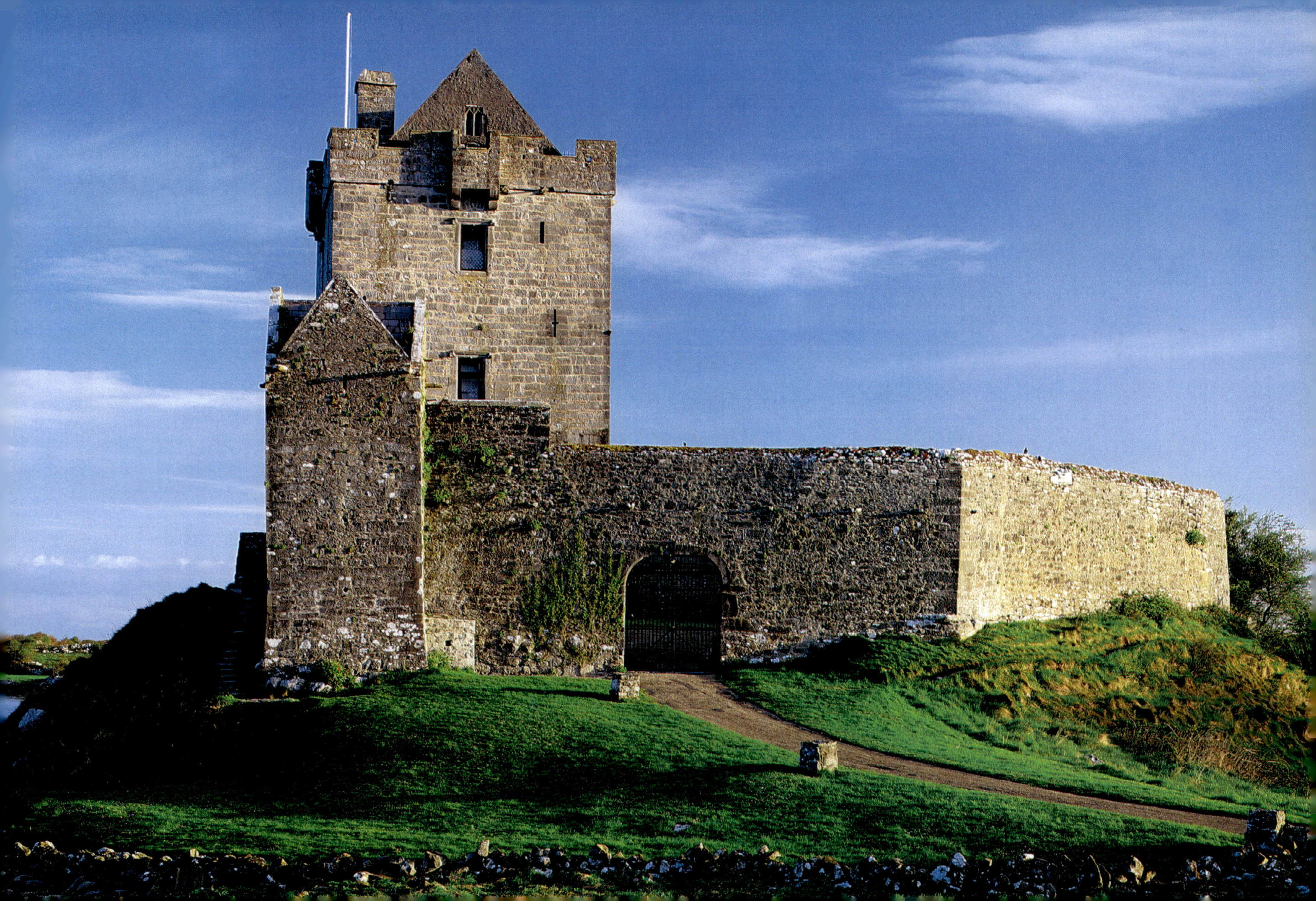

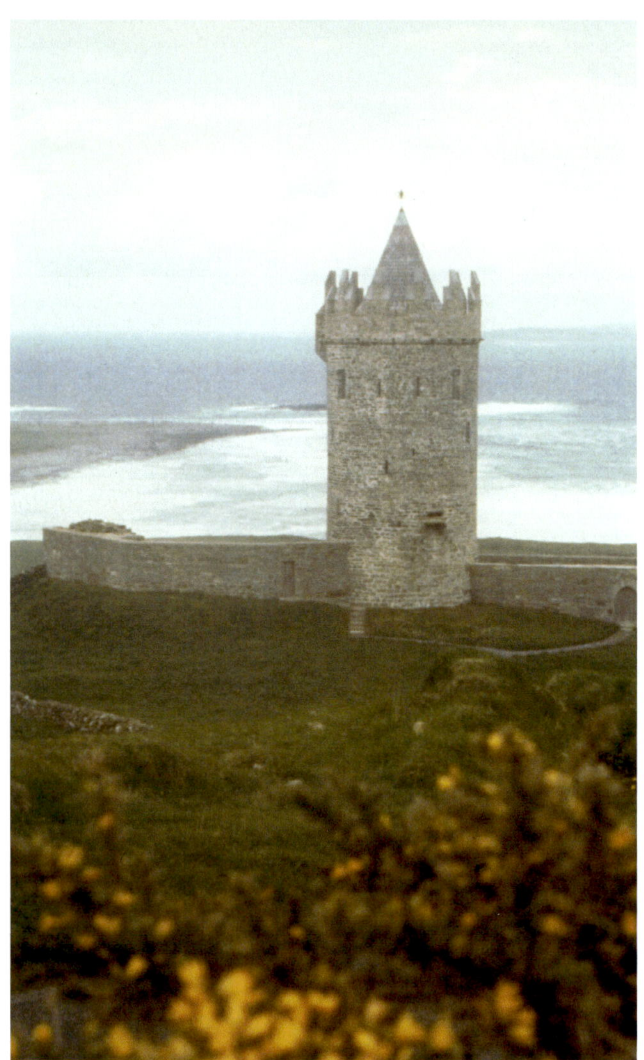

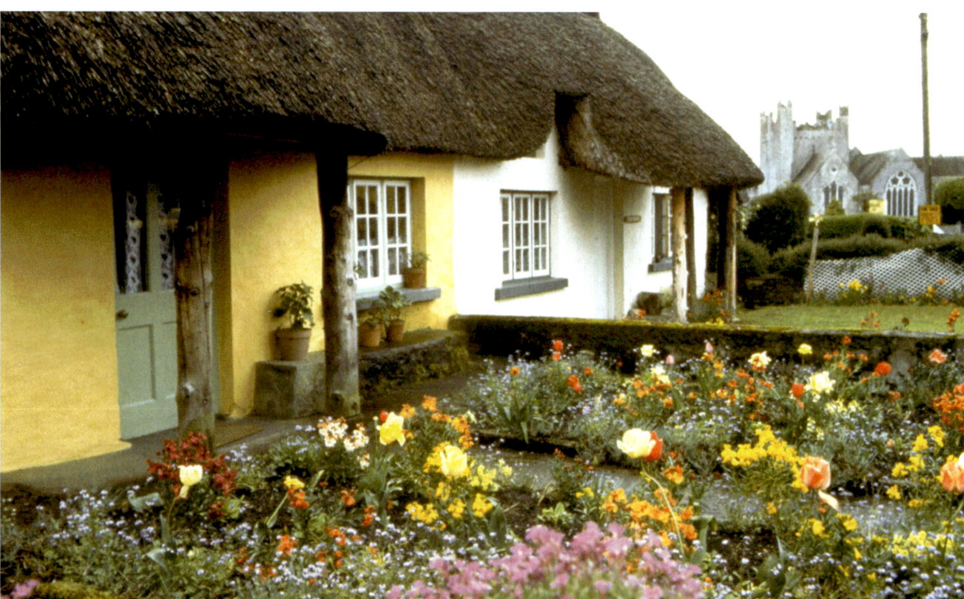

Lisdoonvarna (left)
The spa town of Lisdoonvarna, Country Clare, is perhaps now known less for its sulphur and chalybeate springs than its summer matchmaking festival

Adare (above)
Adare in Limerick is often called Ireland's prettiest village, consisting of one street with a row of beautiful 18th century thatched cottages.

Rosserk Friary (right)
Founded as a Franciscan Friary in 1640, the church is cruciform in shape, with a bell-tower suspended over the chancel arch—an interesting architectural feature.

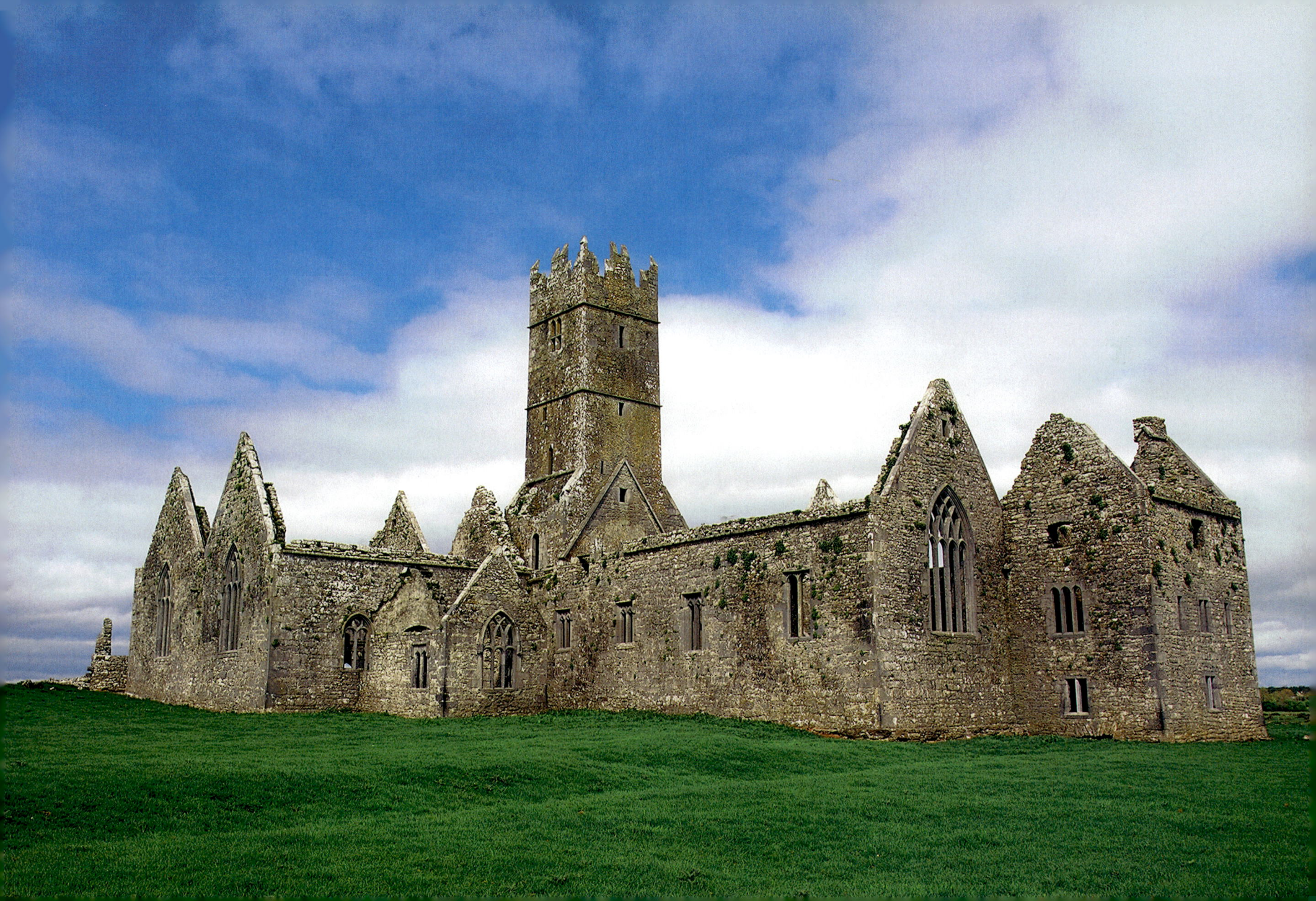

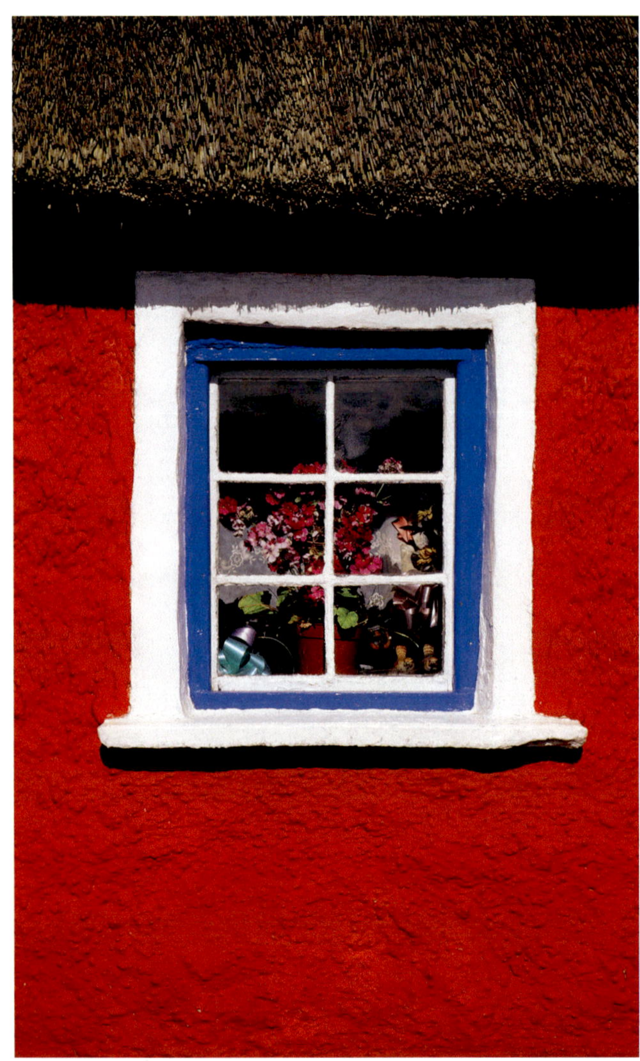

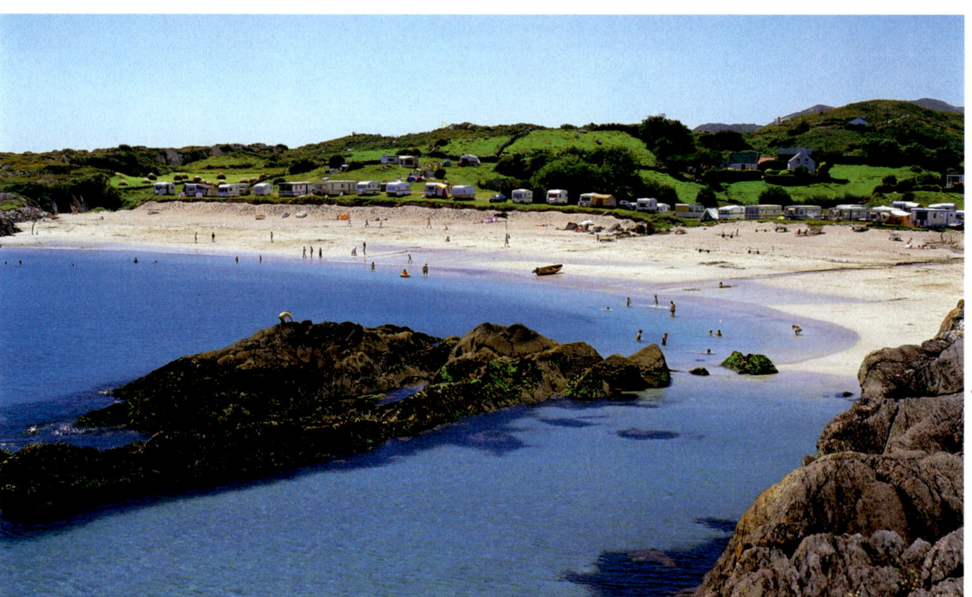

Askeaton (left)
Situated on the banks of the River Deel, Askeaton has an ancient bridge of five arches connecting the opposite sides of the town. This is a typical house exterior.

Dingle Coast (above)
Another beautiful beach on the Dingle peninsula.

Adare Manor (right)
Once the family seat of the Earl of Dunraven, this 18th century manor house is set in 840 acres of formal gardens and parkland set along the River Maigue.

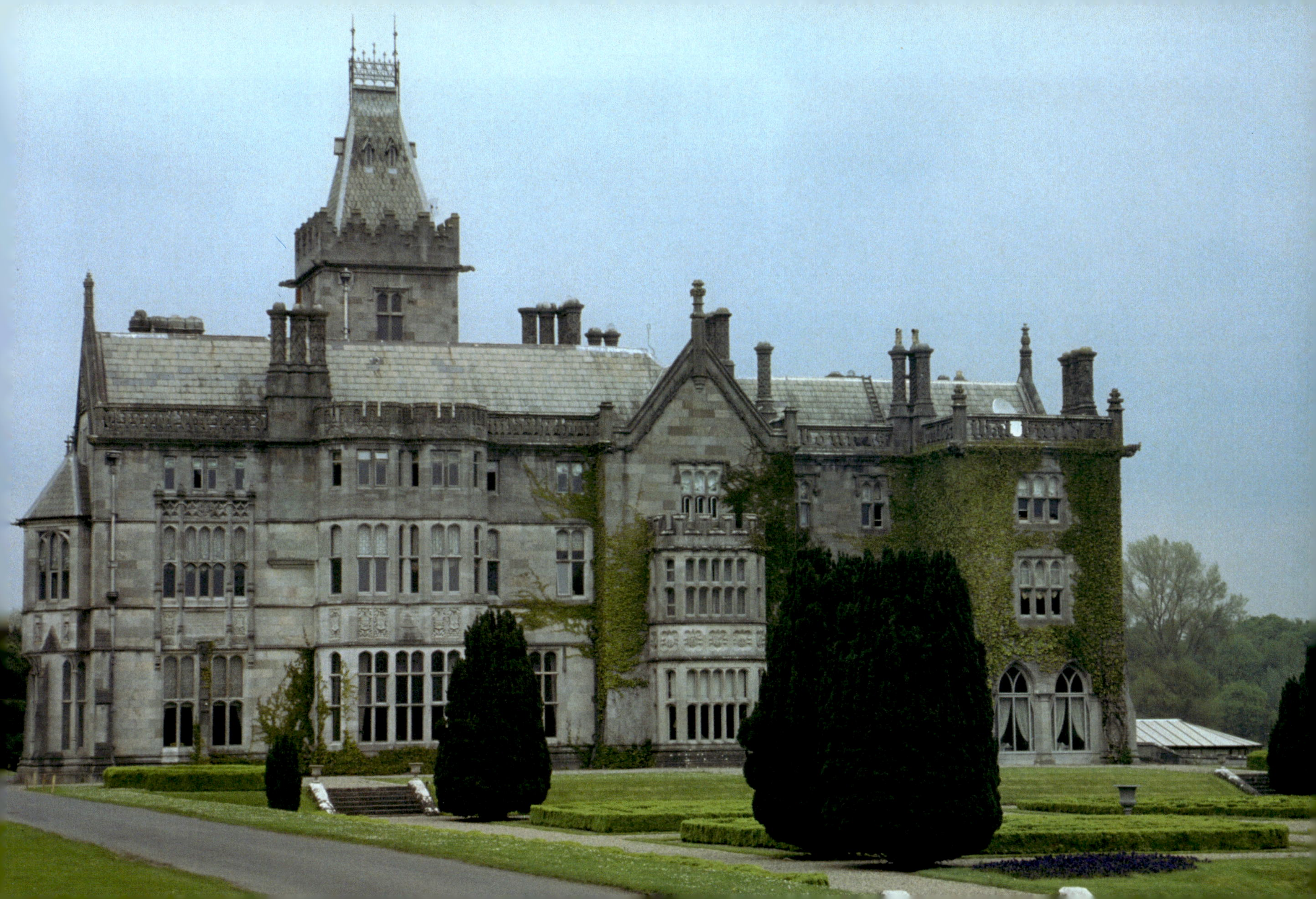

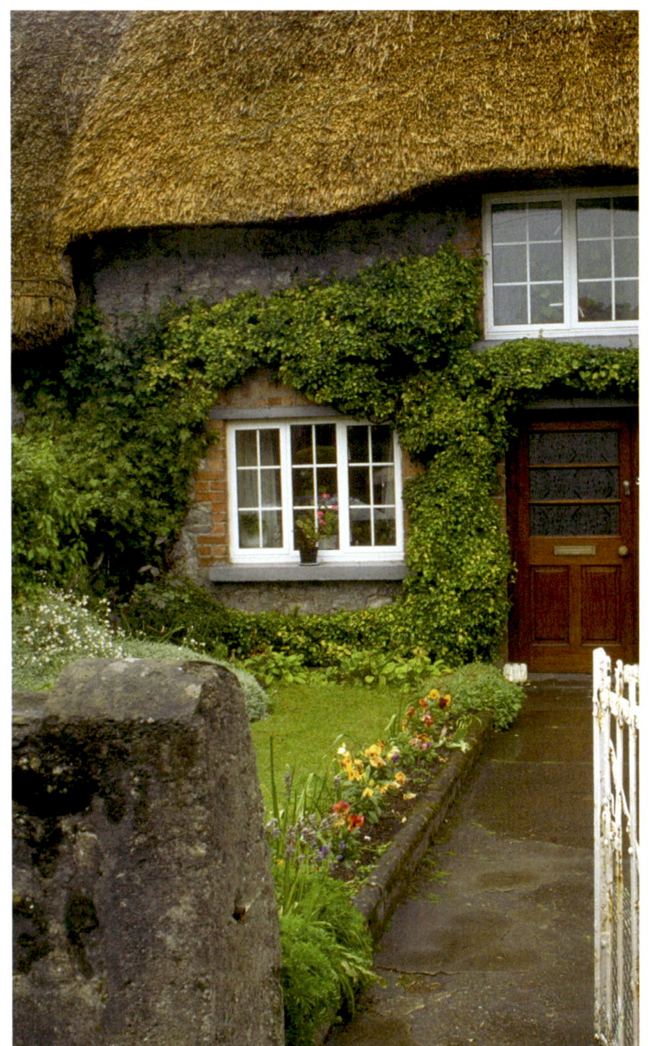

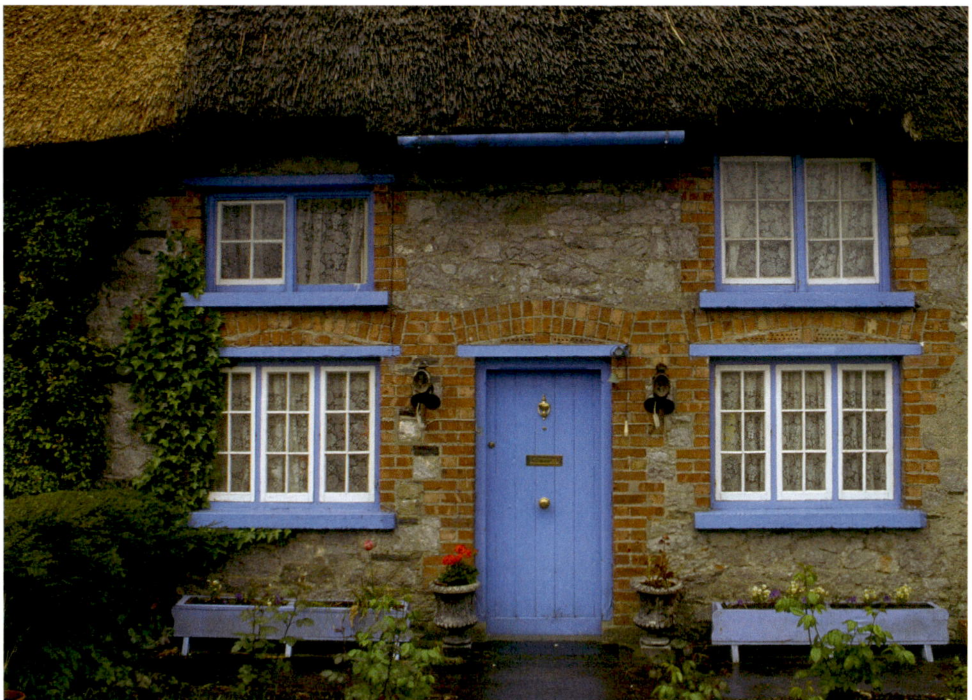

Adare Houses

Three more examples of Adare's pretty cottages. The old town stood on the northern bank of the river, but was destroyed during the 16th century wars. Almost all of the present village was built in the 19th century.

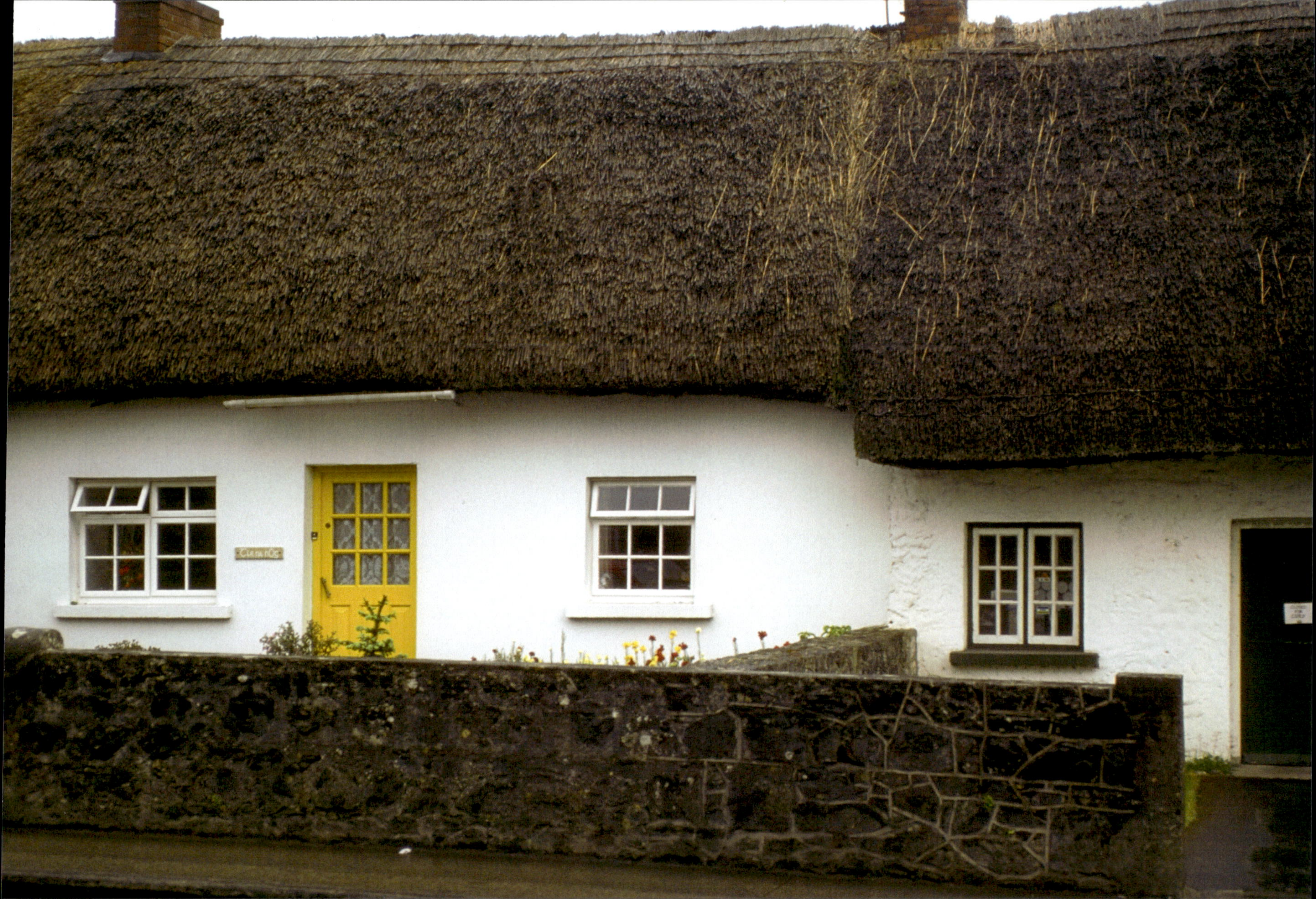

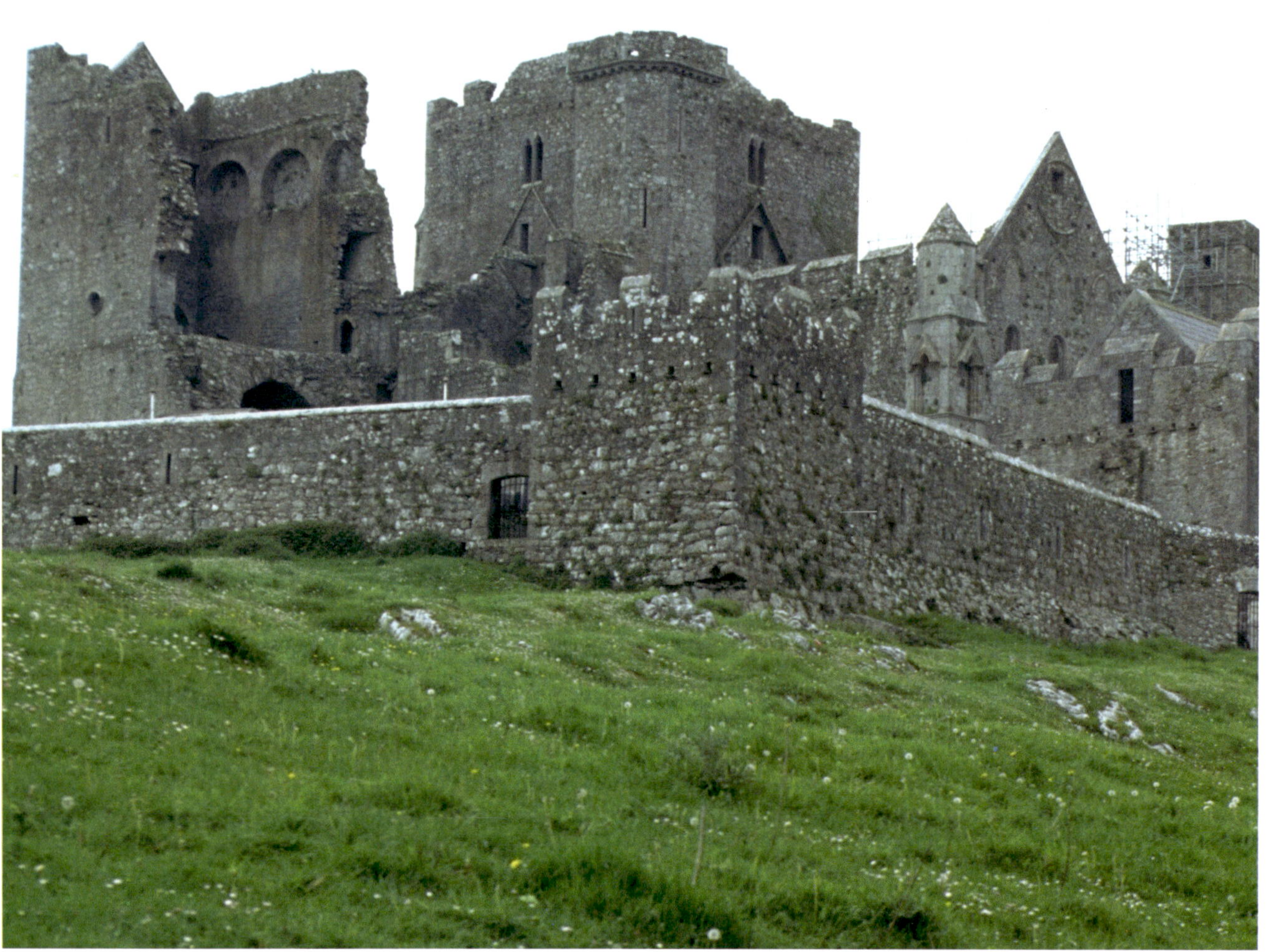

Rock of Cashel (left)

One of the most spectacular archaeological sites in Ireland, the Rock of Cashel, Tipperary, is composed of the Hall of the Vicars Choral, the cathedral, the round tower, and Cormac's Chapel.

Cahir Castle (right)

The Butlers were granted lands here in 1192, but they didn't build their first castle until the 13th century. The castle is still in remarkable condition and one of the largest in Ireland.

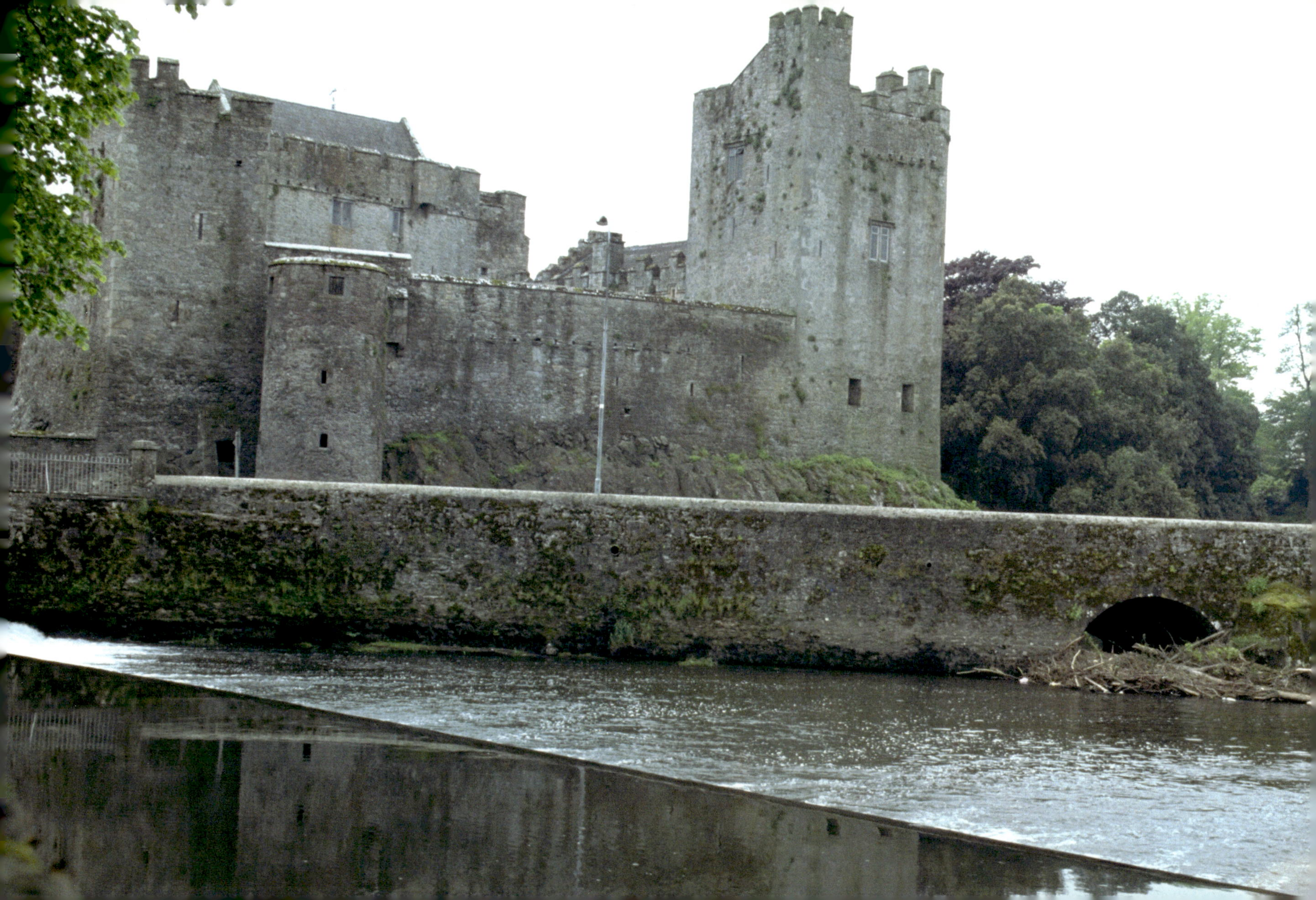

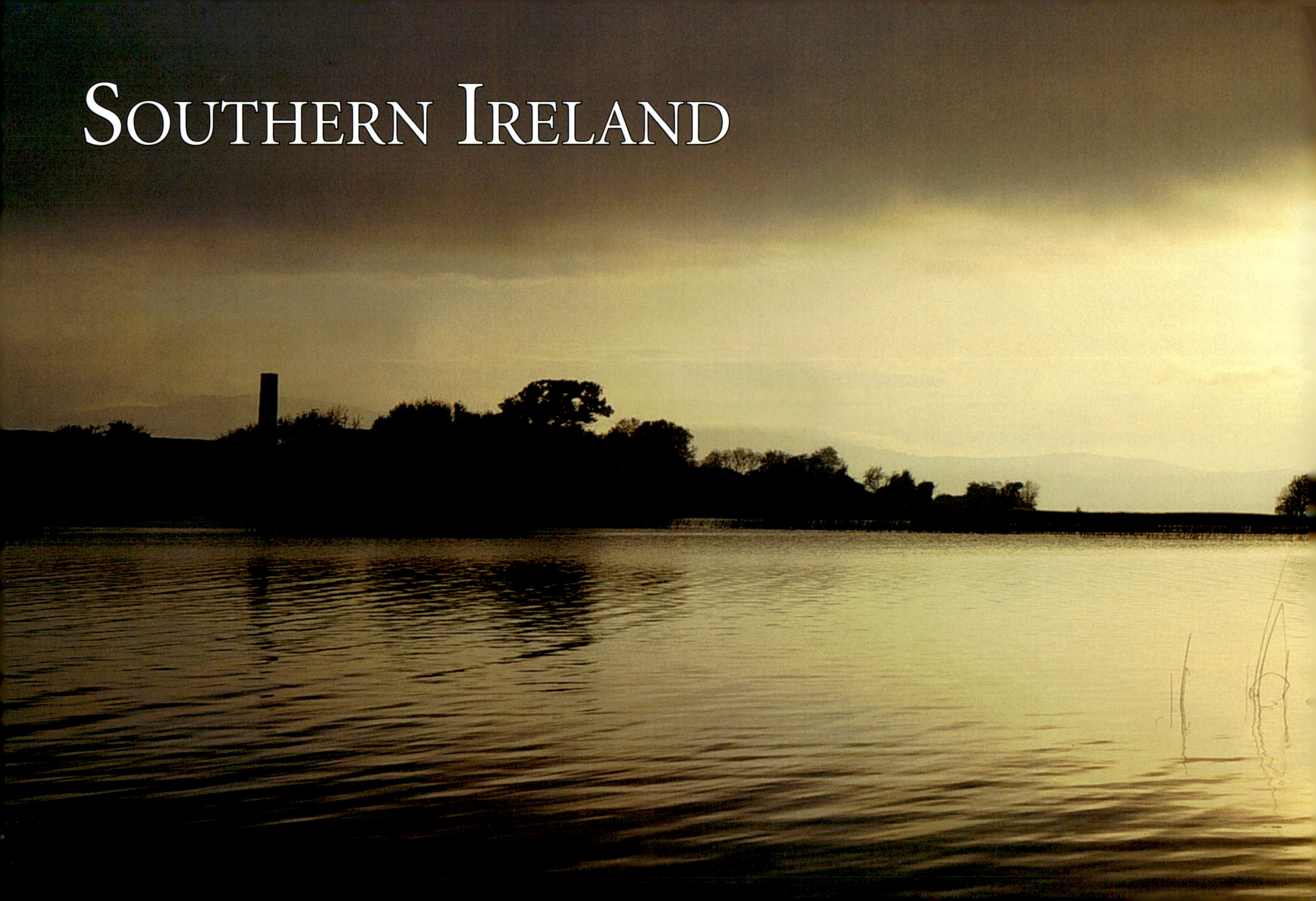

SOUTHERN IRELAND

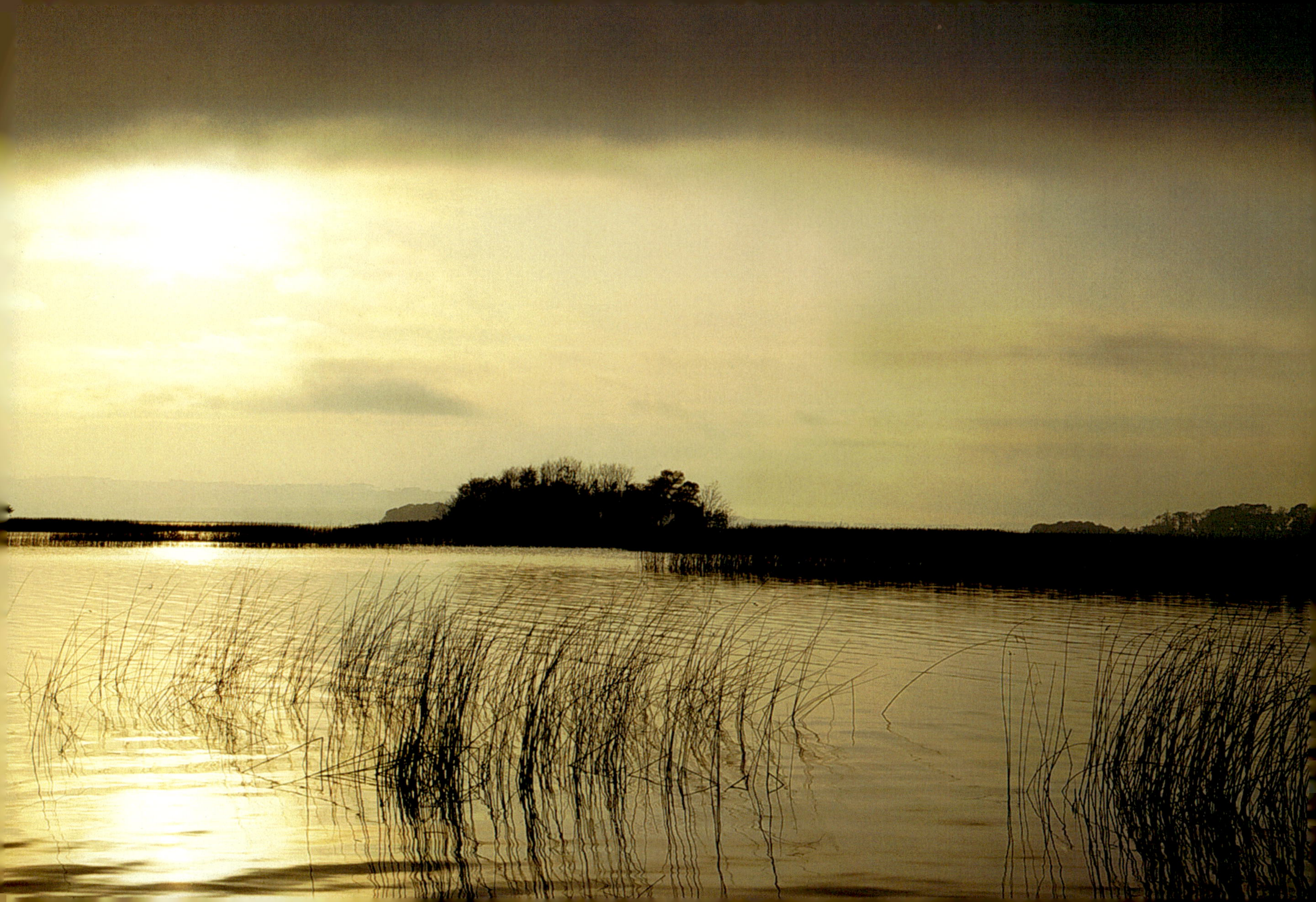

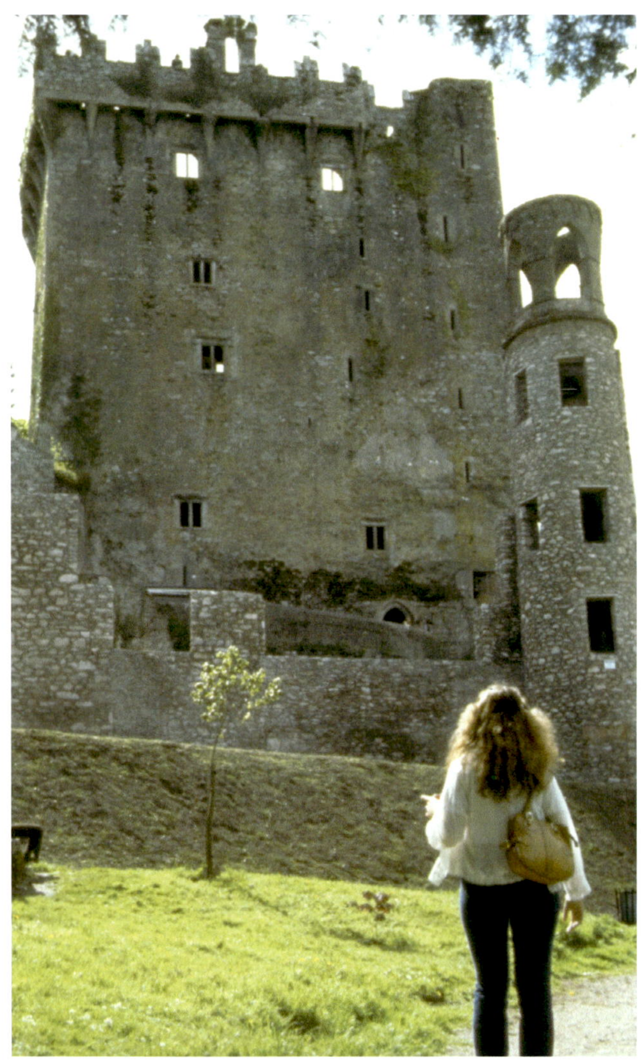

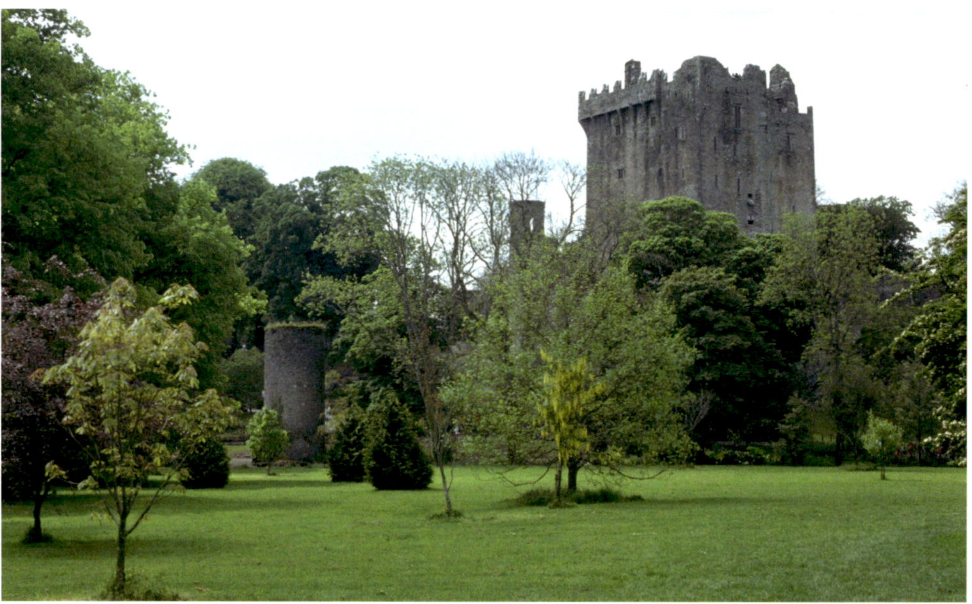

Blarney Castle, Cork (above and left)

A timber hunting lodge built in the 10th century was replaced by a stone castle in 1210 to become Blarney Castle. The present building was completed by the King of Munster in 1446. On the top storey of the castle, just below the battlements, is the Blarney Stone. If you can reach it, kissing s said to give the kisser the gift of persuasive eloquence—blarney.

Baltimore (right)

The seaside village in County Cork was famously attacked by Algerian pirates in June 1631. Two inhabitants were killed and over a hundred were captured and taken away as slaves.

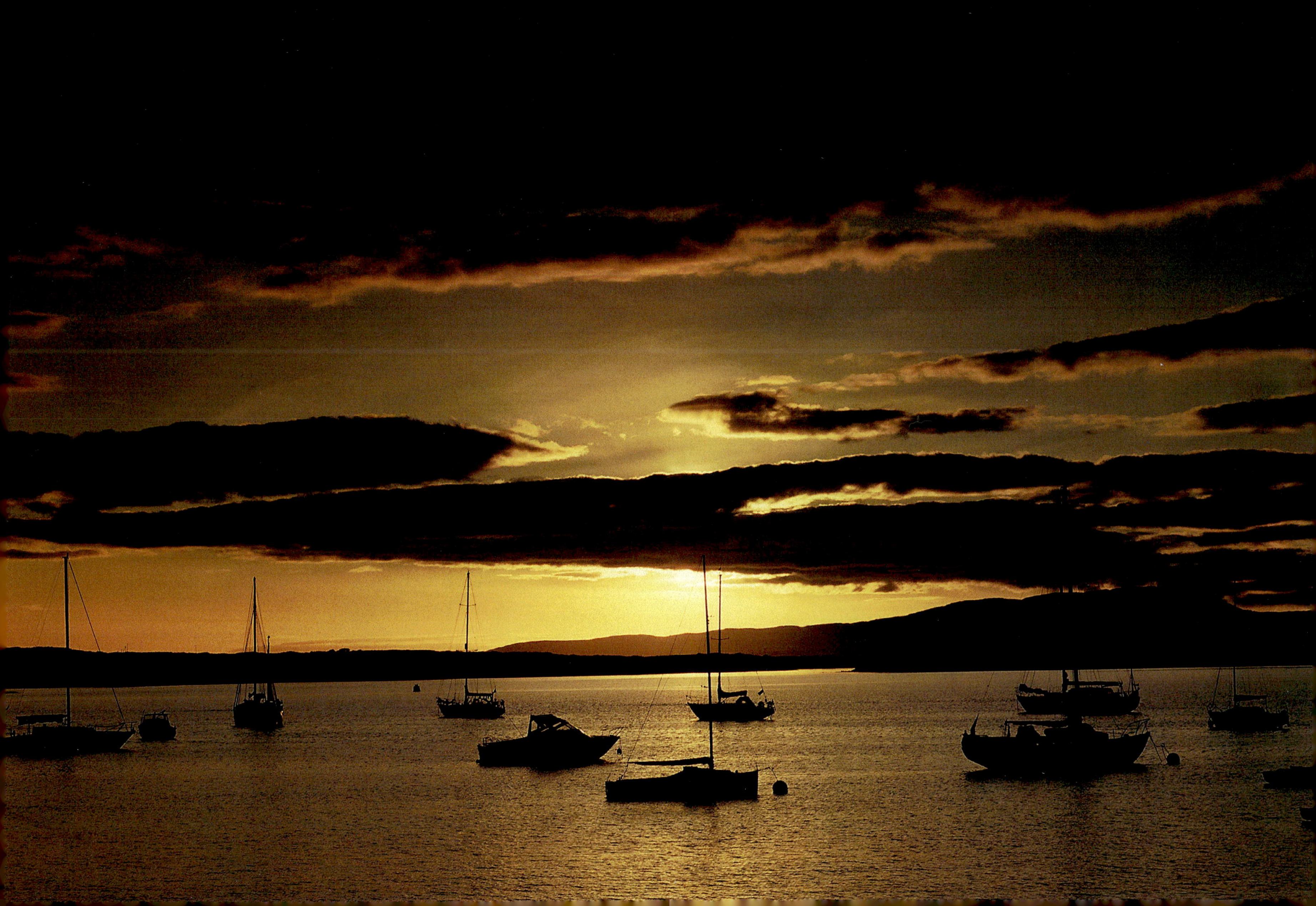

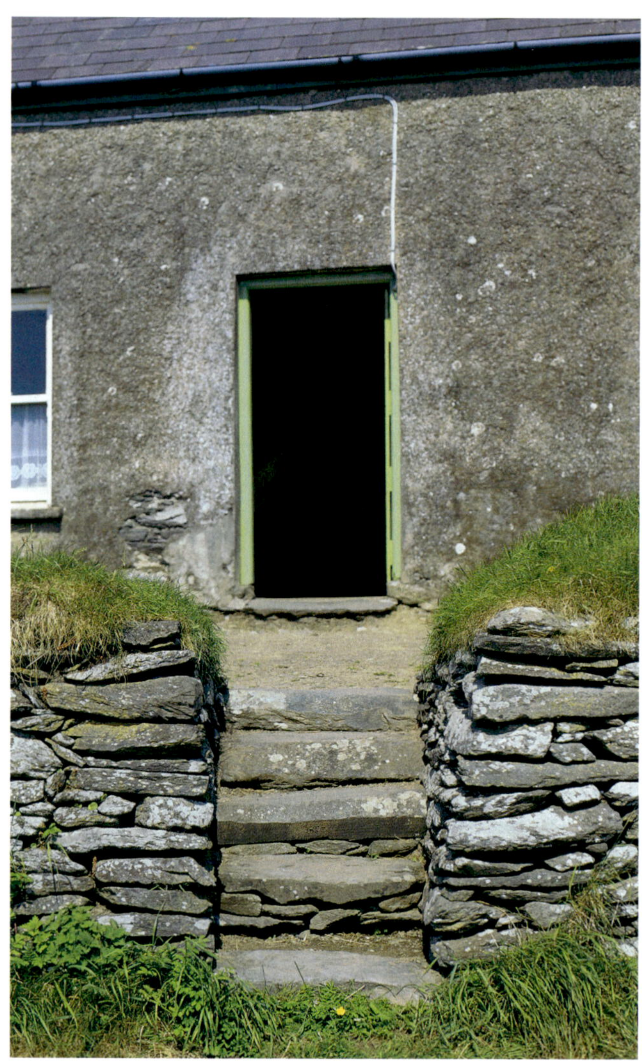

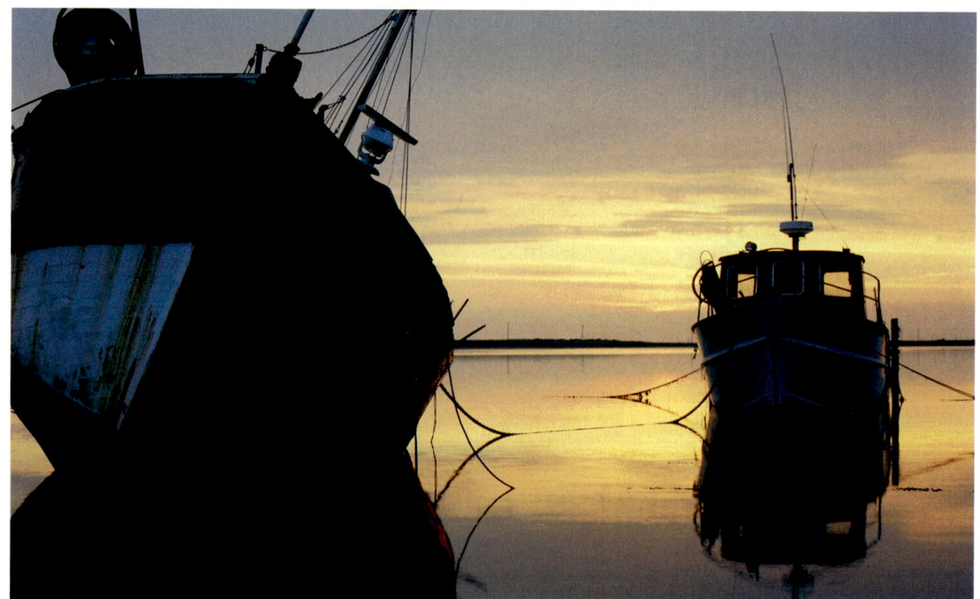

Old House, Dingle (left)
This peninsula has supported various tribes and populations for almost 6,000 years. Because of its remote location, and lack of specialised agriculture, there are over 2,000 existing prehistoric monuments.

Fenit Back Strand (above)
St Brendan, patron saint of Kerry and famous as Brendan the Navigator (484-577), who, it is suggested, may have discovered America, was born near this small port.

Conor Pass (right)
The highest mountain pass in Ireland has breathtaking views over the top of Brandon Bay all the way to County Clare in the far distance.

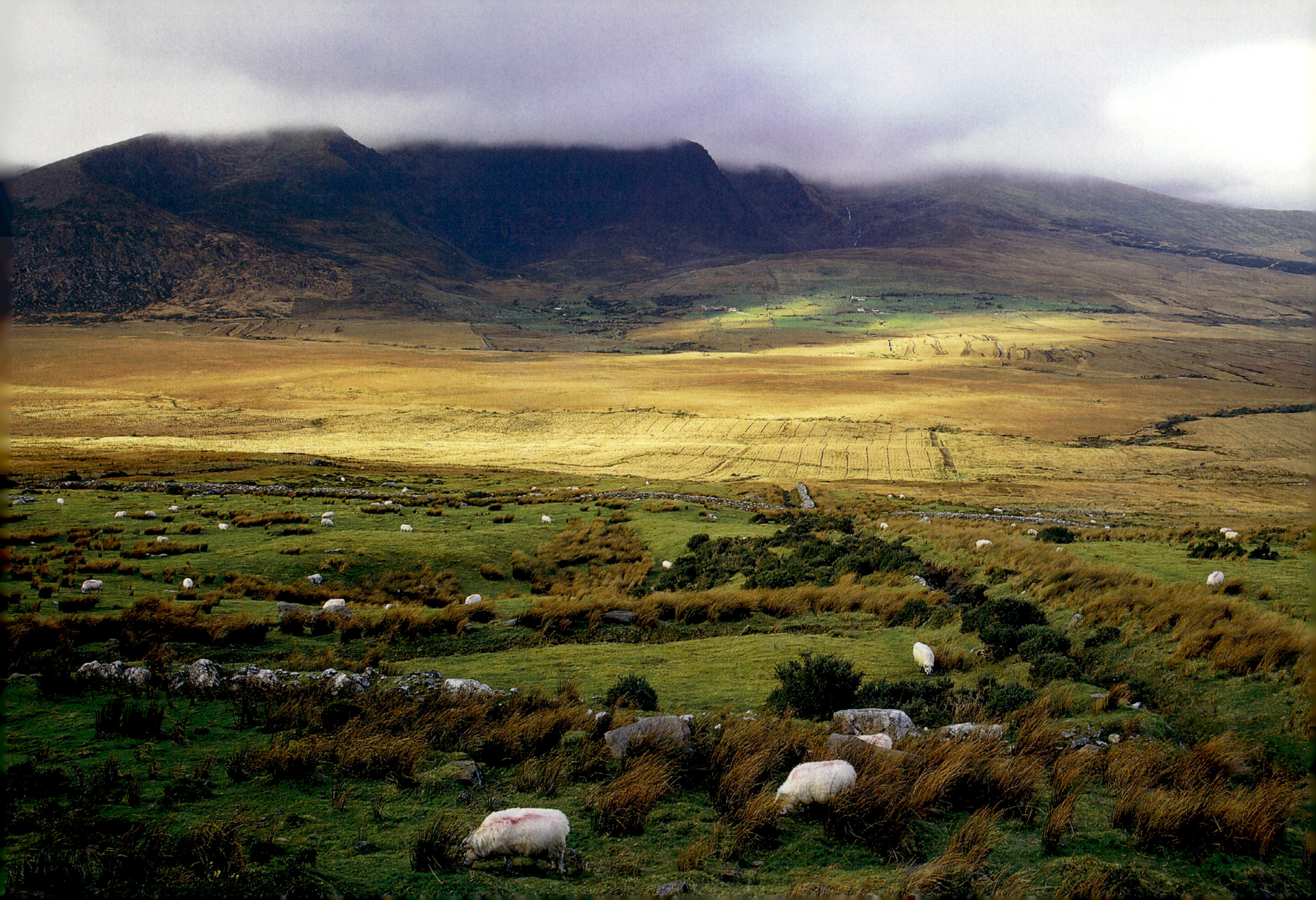

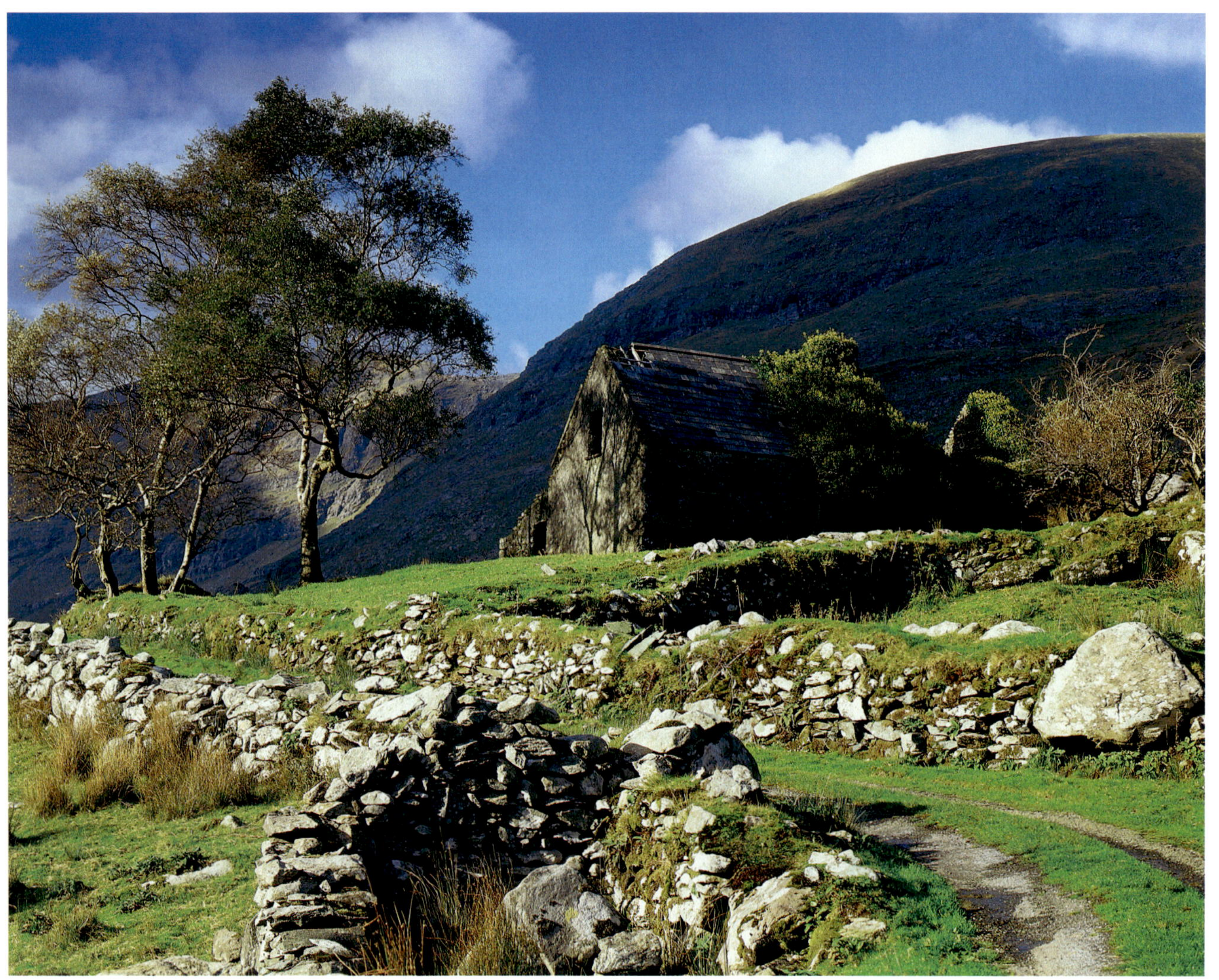

Black Valley, Killarney (left)
In the heart of rugged mountain scenery lies the Black Valley, part of Killarney National Park. This came into being in 1932 when the Muckross estate was presented to the nation

Coumeenole Beach (right)
The rugged beauty of the area was immortalised in the movie Ryan's Daughter which features the beach.

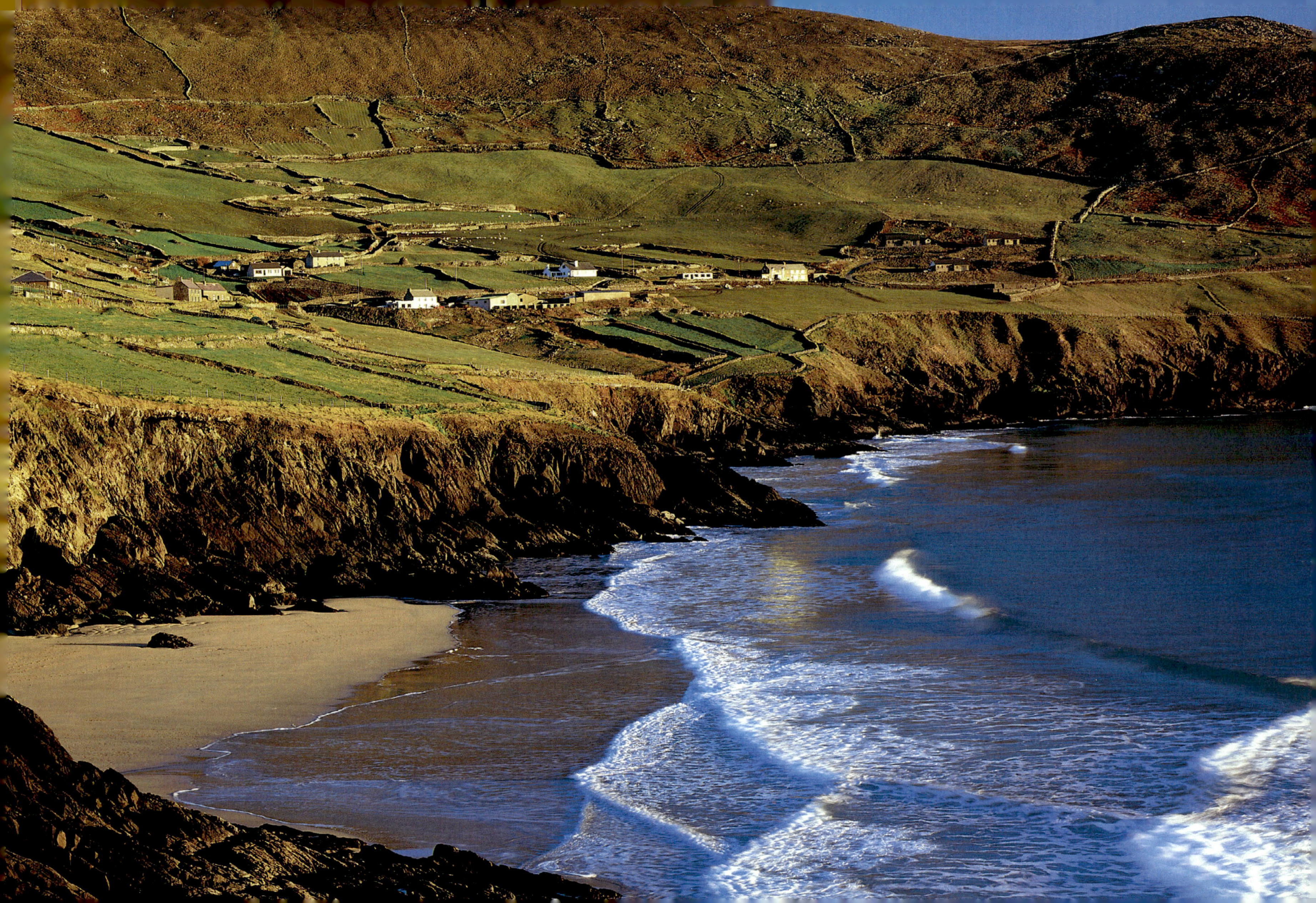

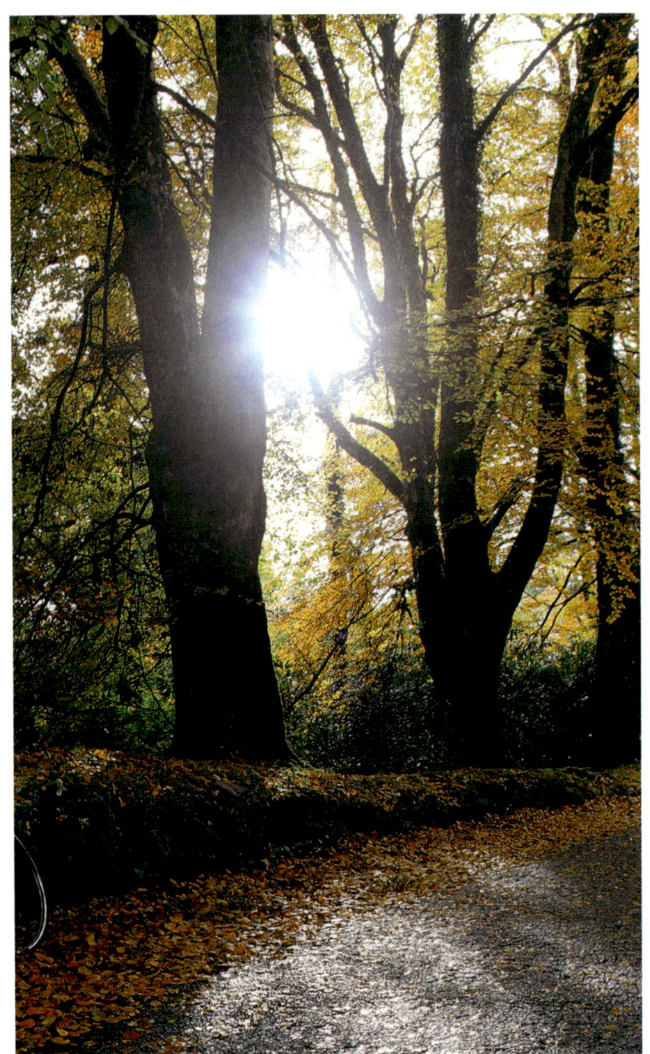

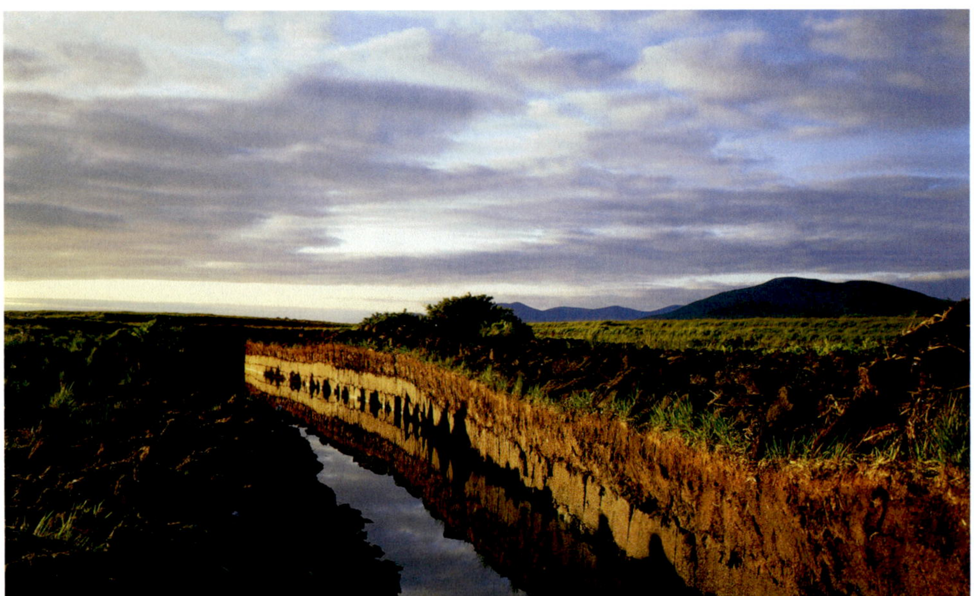

Derreen Gardens (left)
Planted 100 years ago by the fifth Lord Landsdowne, Derreen Gardens lie beside Kilmackillogue Harbour in Lauragh. The famous woodland gardens contain many stunning azaleas and rhododendrons.

Glenbeigh (above)
A popular holiday base situated where the Behy River flows into Dingle Bay, Glenbeigh nestles at the foot of Seefin Mountains (1,621ft).

Ballyheigue Bay (right)
County Kerry lies in the extreme south-west of Ireland. It is characterised by rocky headlands which jut out into the Atlantic.

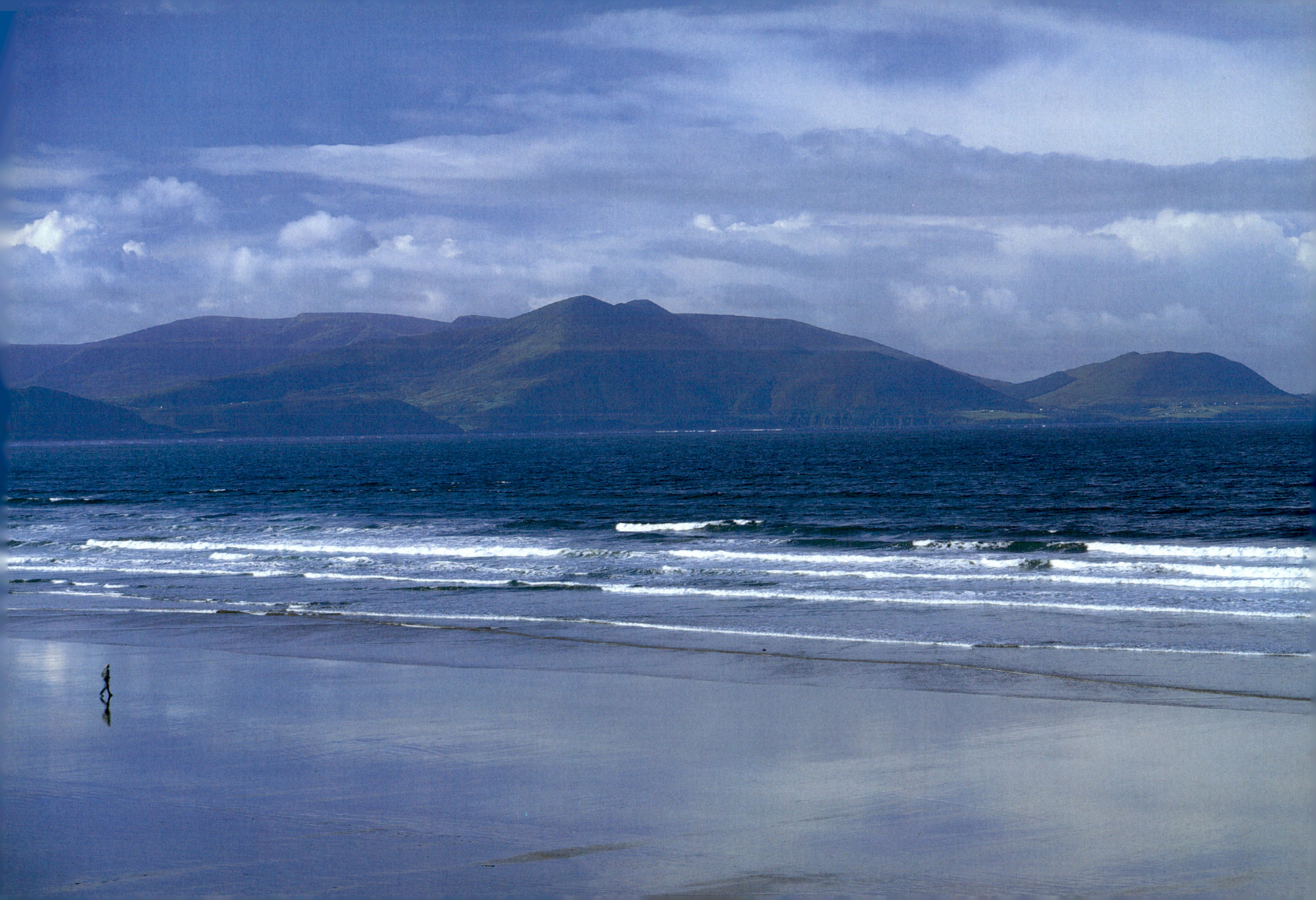

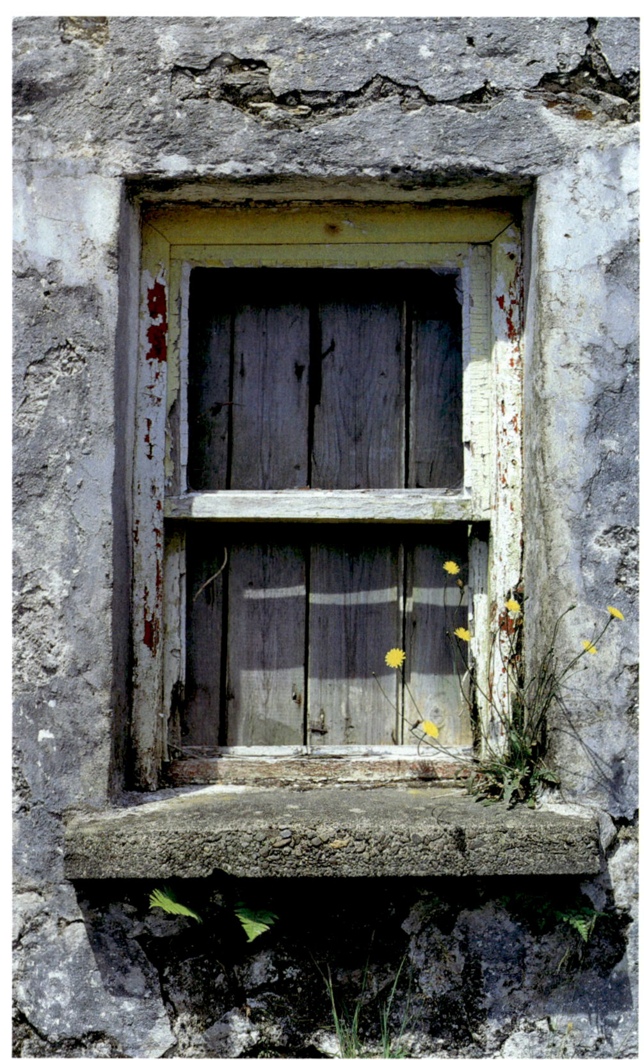

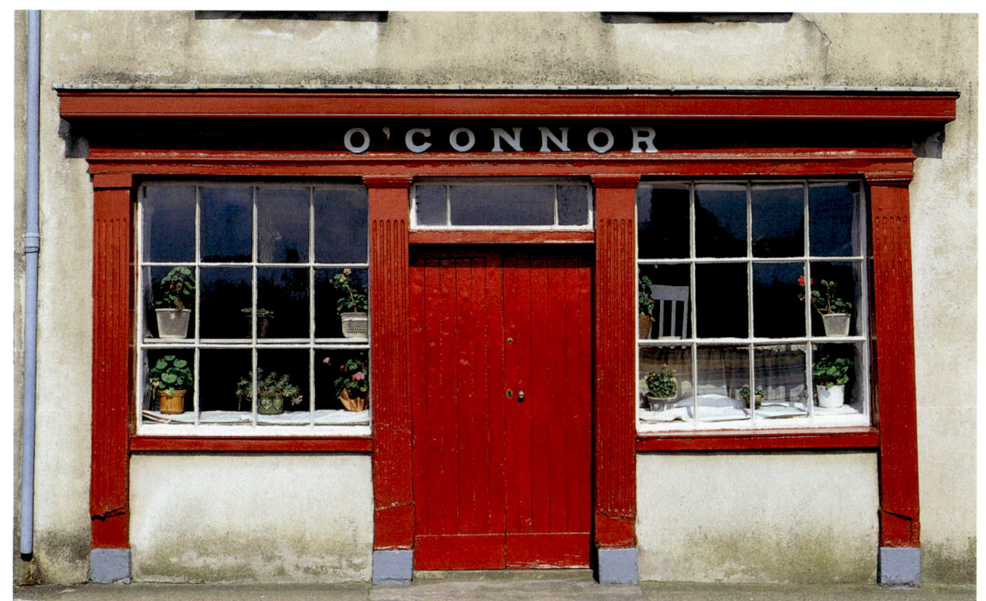

Sneem (left)
Two miles to the south is the beautiful hotel and estate of Parknasilla, on the shore of the Kenmare River. There is a private golf course for hotel residents and good sea fishing in the bay.

Kerry Shop (above)
Typical Irish painted shop front.

Blasket Islands (right)
Thanks to the collapse of the fishing industry in the 1940s, these picturesque islands have not moved in time. In 1953 the government paid the remaining 22 inhabitants to move to the mainland. Now no cars or phones exist on the island.

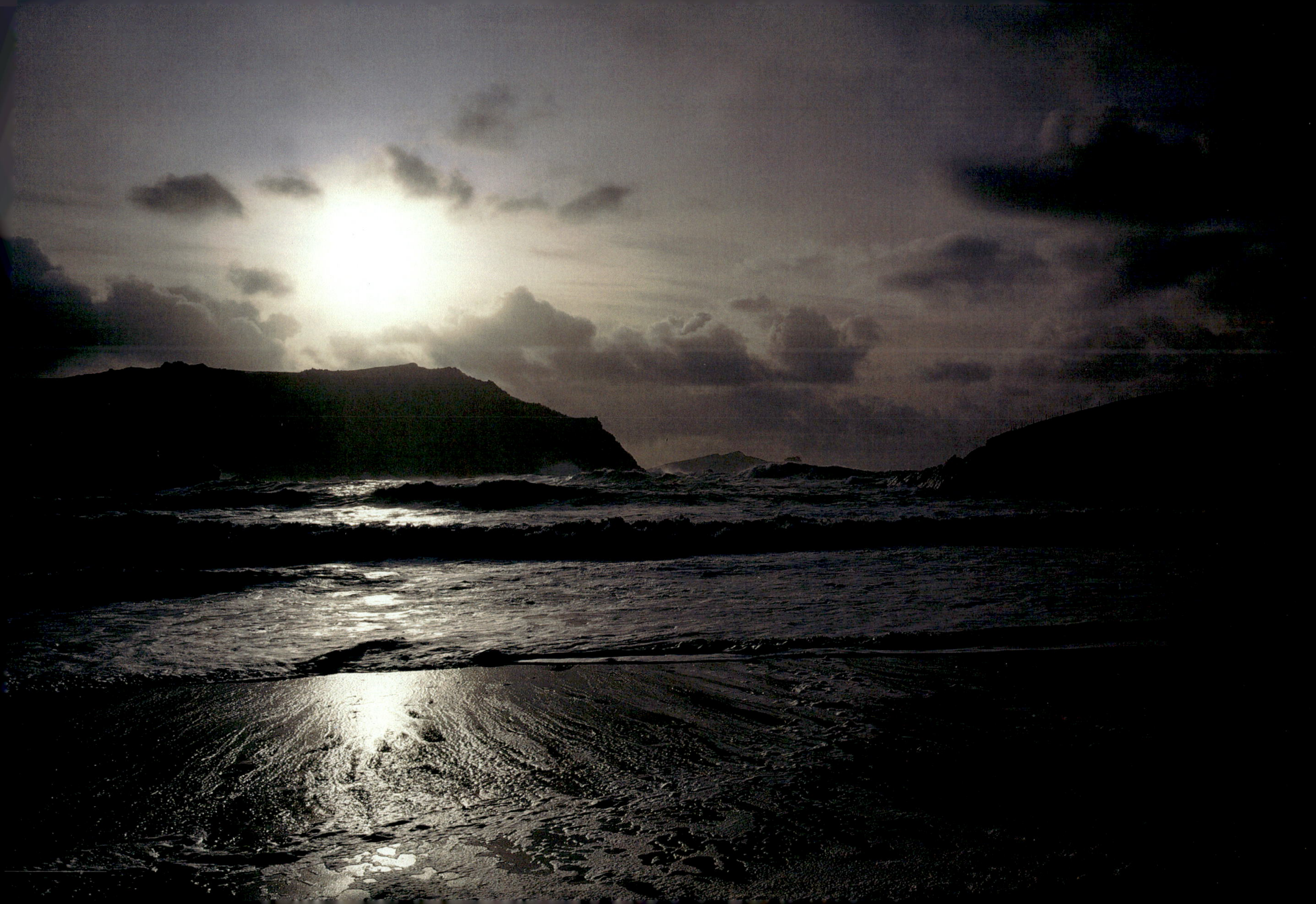

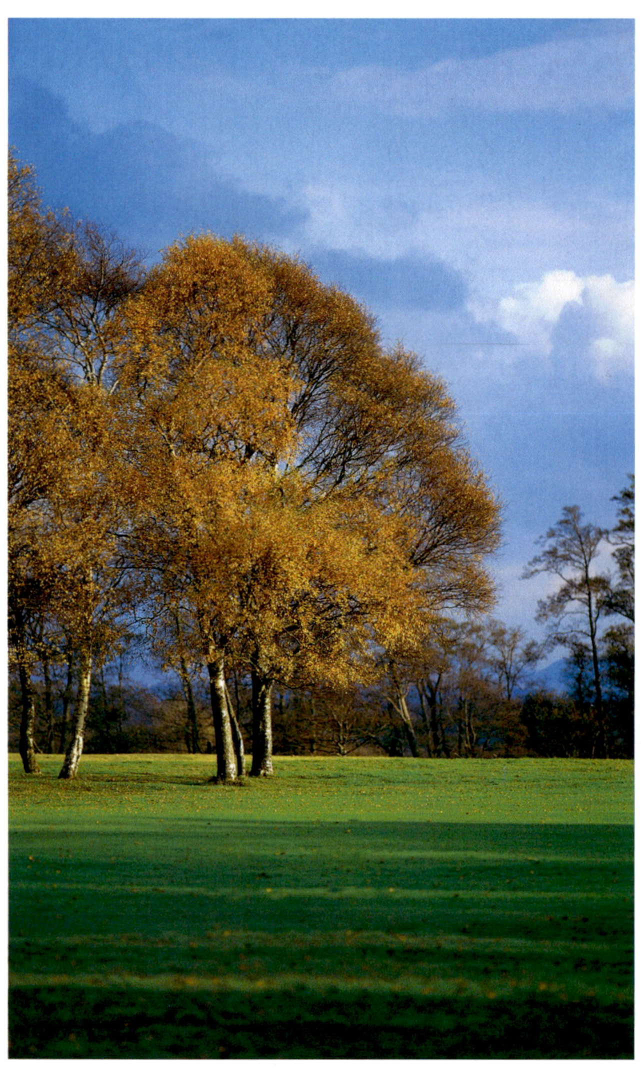

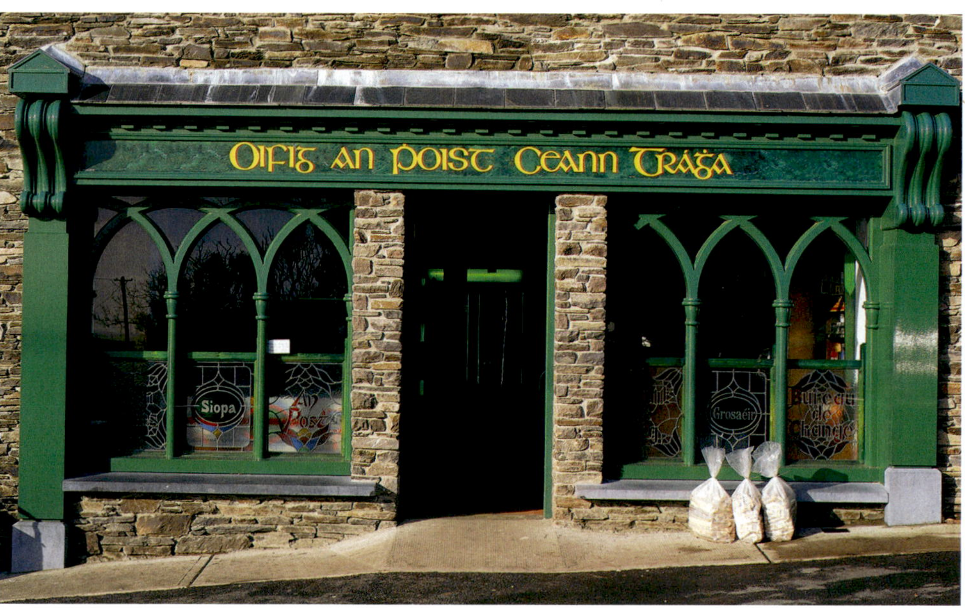

Killarney Golf Course (left)
Golf has been played in Killarney since 1891, originally on a nine-hole inland course. Then in 1930 it was expanded to an 18-hole course. Killeen played host to the Carroll's Irish Open in both 1991 and 1992. Since then, two other courses have been added.

Ventry (above)
This wonderful post office is in Ventry, an area is riddled with forts, souterrains, standing stones and crosses. On nearby hill-sides lie over 400 strange stone huts known as beehives or clochans.

Dingle Peninsula (right)
Stretching westwards for 30 miles from the low-lying country near Tralee, the Dingle Peninsula is a magnet for tourists.

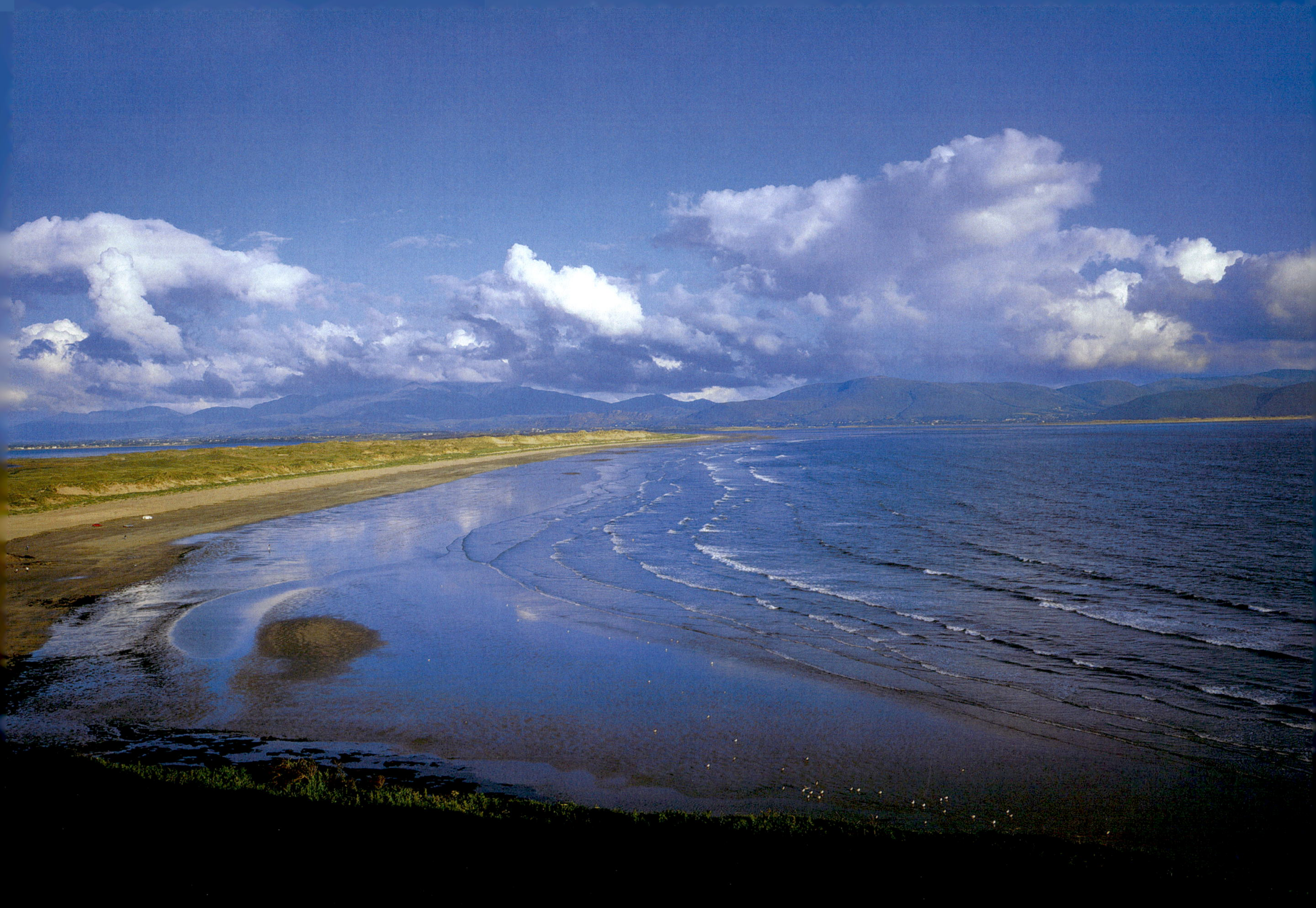

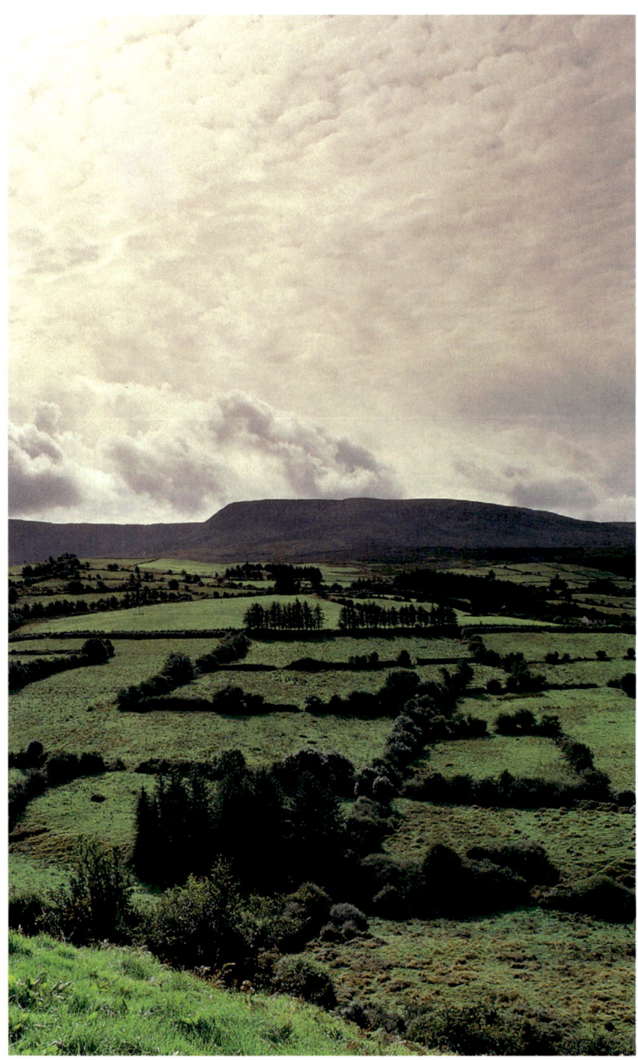

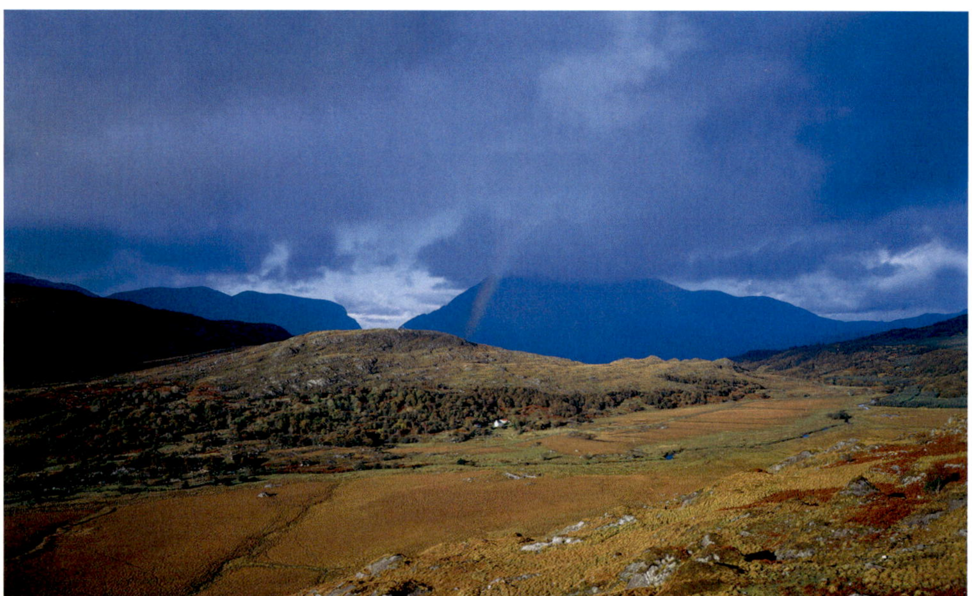

Beara Peninsula (left)
It was from Valentia Island on the western tip of Beara Peninsula that the first transatlantic telephone cable was laid.
Bantry Bay on the southern side is one of the deepest bays in Europe.

Killarney countryside (above)
Killarney (Cill Airne—the Church of Sloes) became a magnificent town about 1750 when the local magnate, Lord Kenmare, developed the tourist business and four major roads were built to the outside world.

Dunloe, Black Valley (right)
The Gap of Dunloe is the six-mile long mountain pass dividing the Purple Mountains from Macgillycuddy's Reeks and is one of the most scenic glaciated valleys in Ireland.

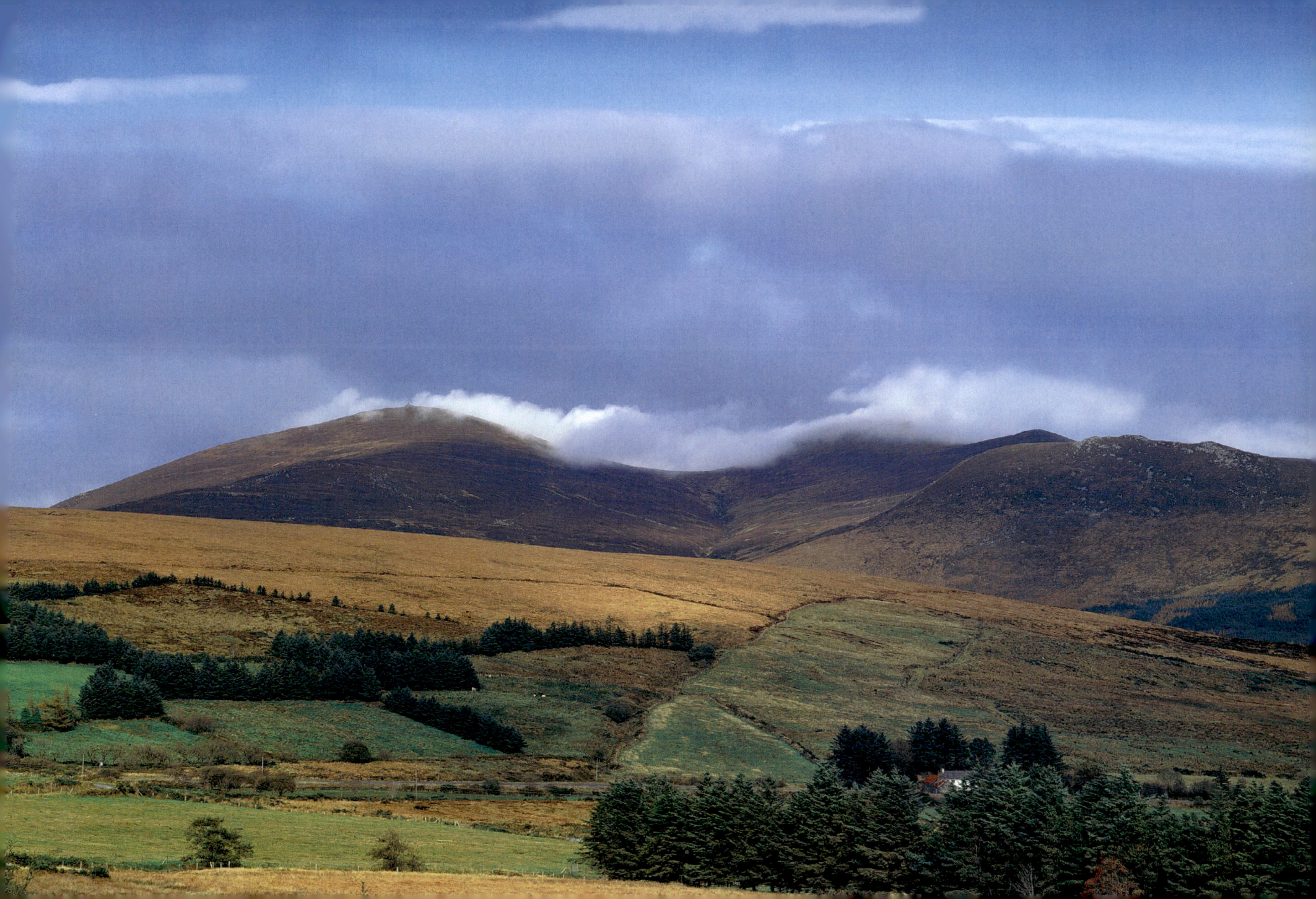

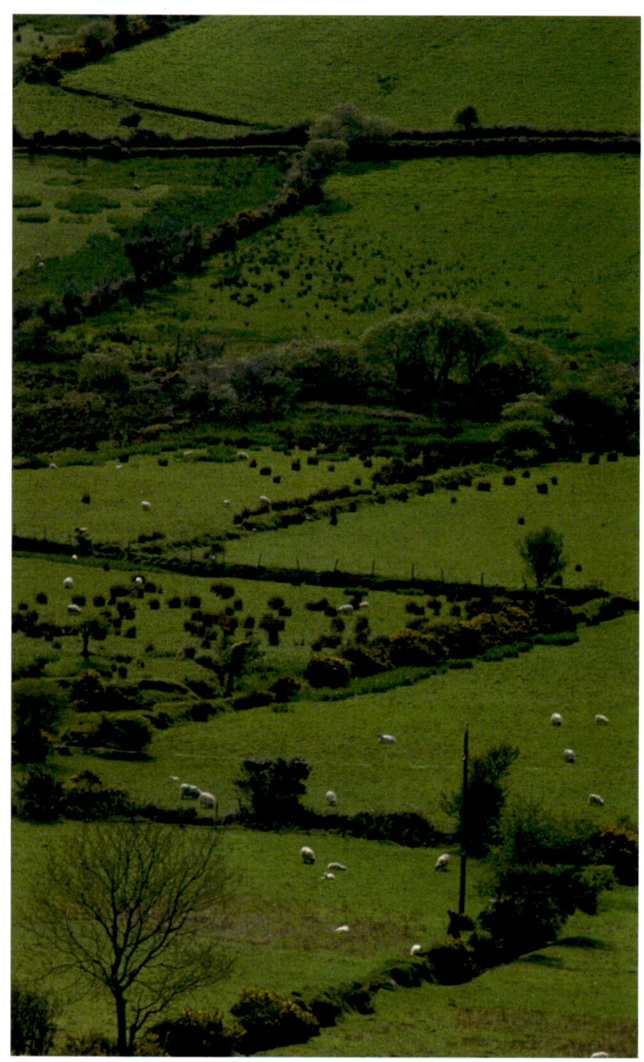

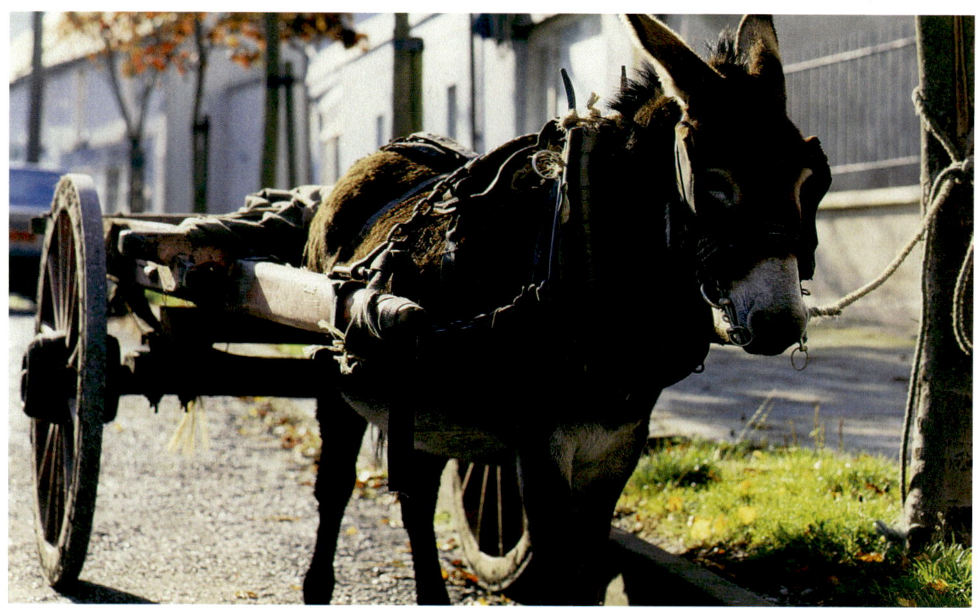

The Green (left)
Ireland's national colour is green and this reflected all over the lush valleys of the verdant countryside. Thanks to its stunning beauty, County Kerry has become a prime tourist attraction.

Donkey and trap (above)
Tourism has a lot to answer for! Donkey power in Dingle.

Dingle Peninsula (right)
The western end of the Dingle peninsula has magnificent coastal scenery, and is an Irish-speaking district where the traditional customs, crafts, and lore are very much alive.

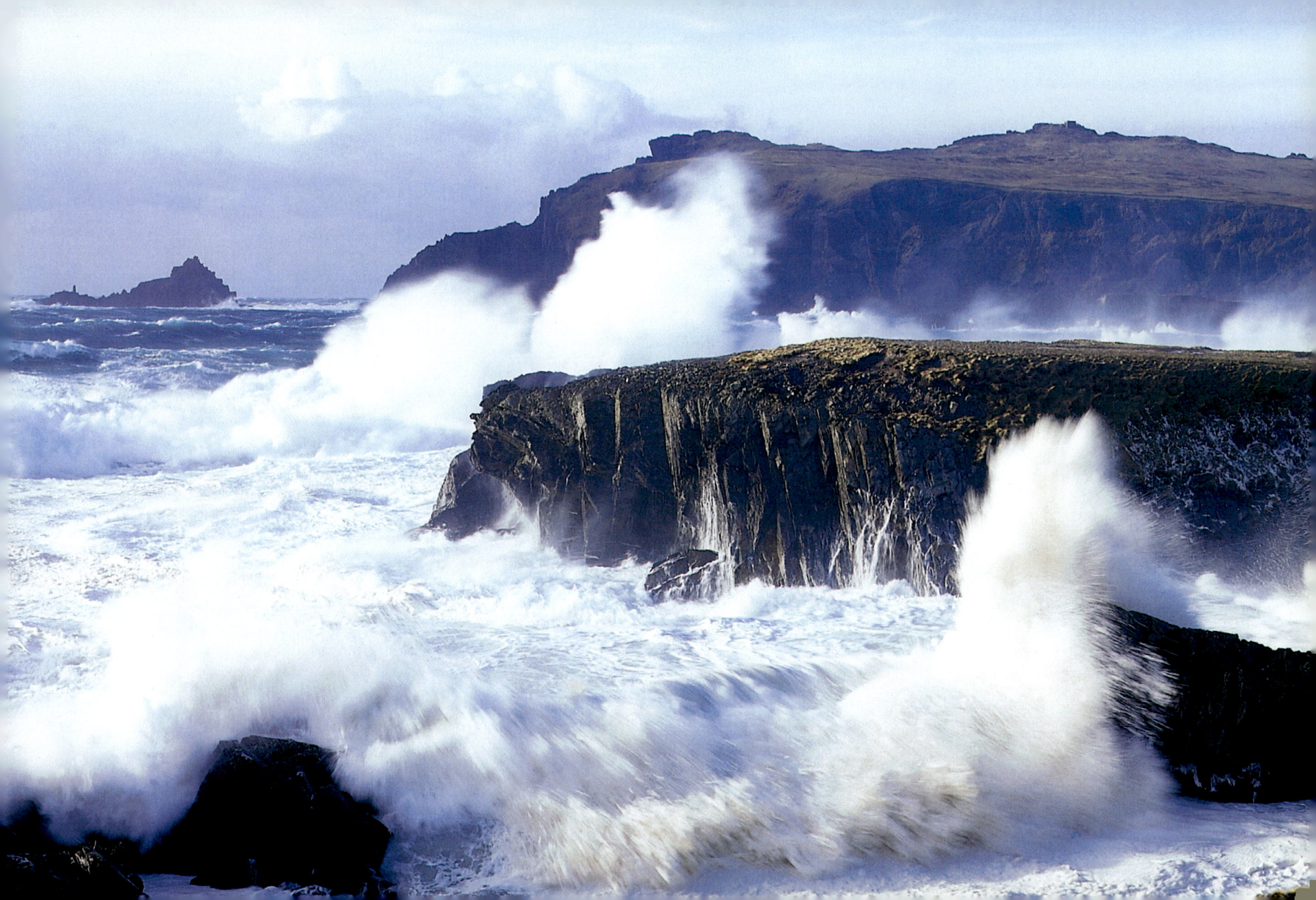

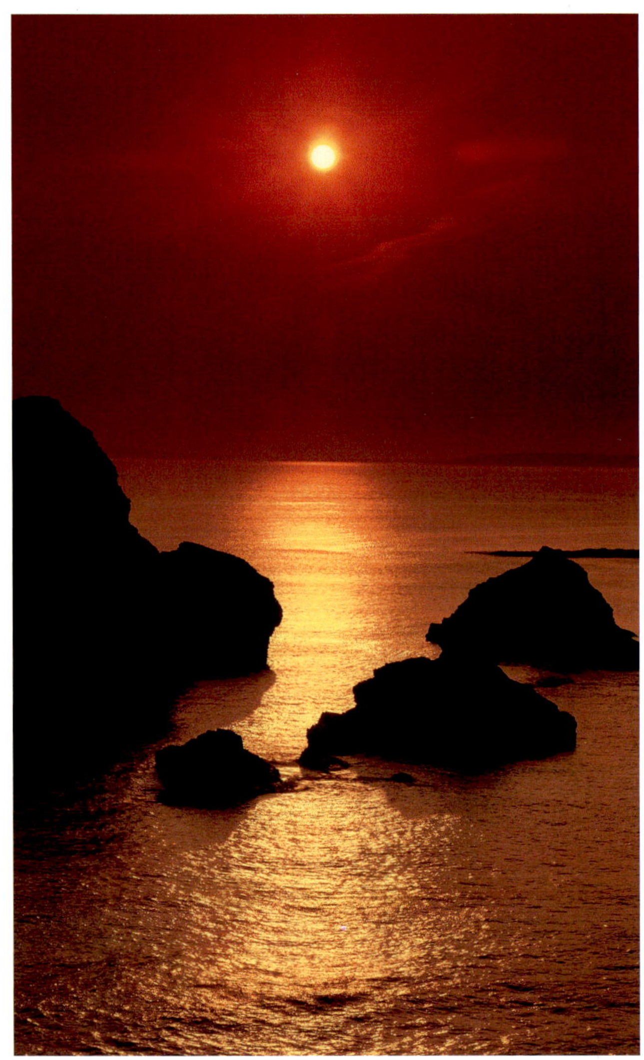

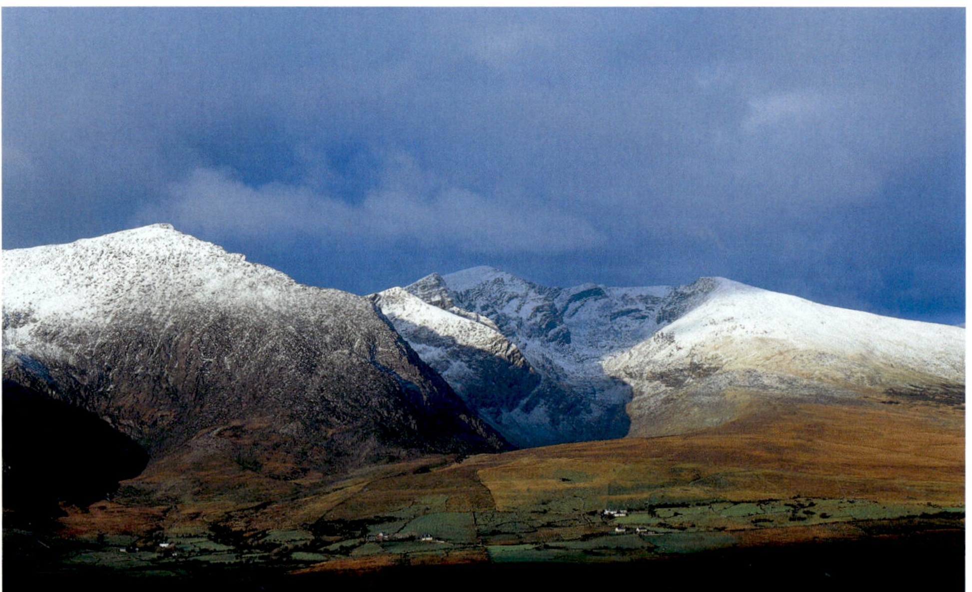

Ballybunion (left)
The coastline at Ballybunion, with its sea caves, rugged cliffs, coves, and beaches, forms a very fine district for seaside holidays. A fine sandy beach fronts the town and continues southwards for two miles.

Brandon Mountains (above)
Set beneath Mount Brandon on the Dingle Peninsula, this remote and beautifully situated village attracts walkers tackling the western approach to the summit.

Eagle's Nest, Kenmare (right)
Situated on the road between Kenmare and Killarney is the Eagle's Nest, a conical hill rising some 1,100ft.

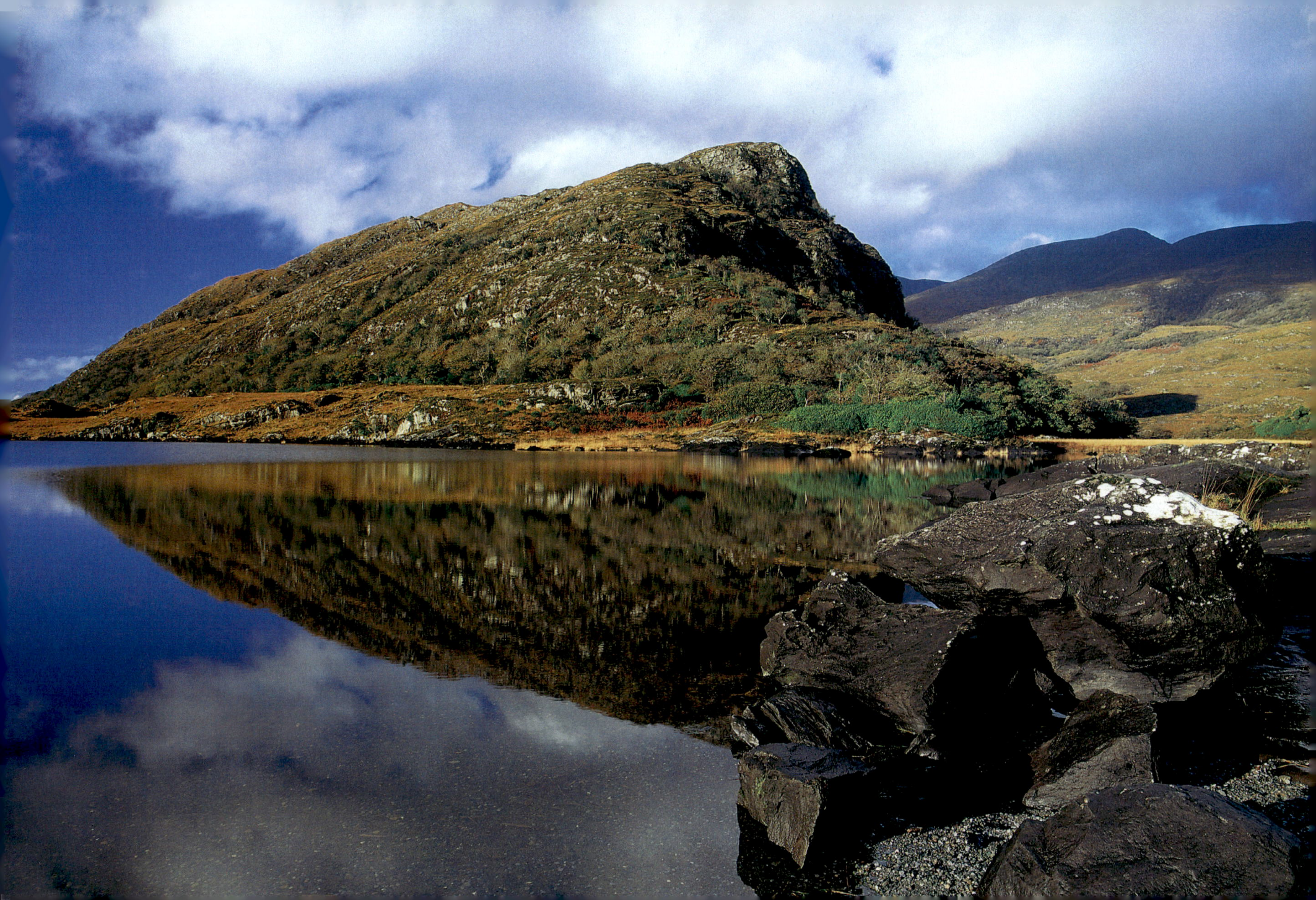

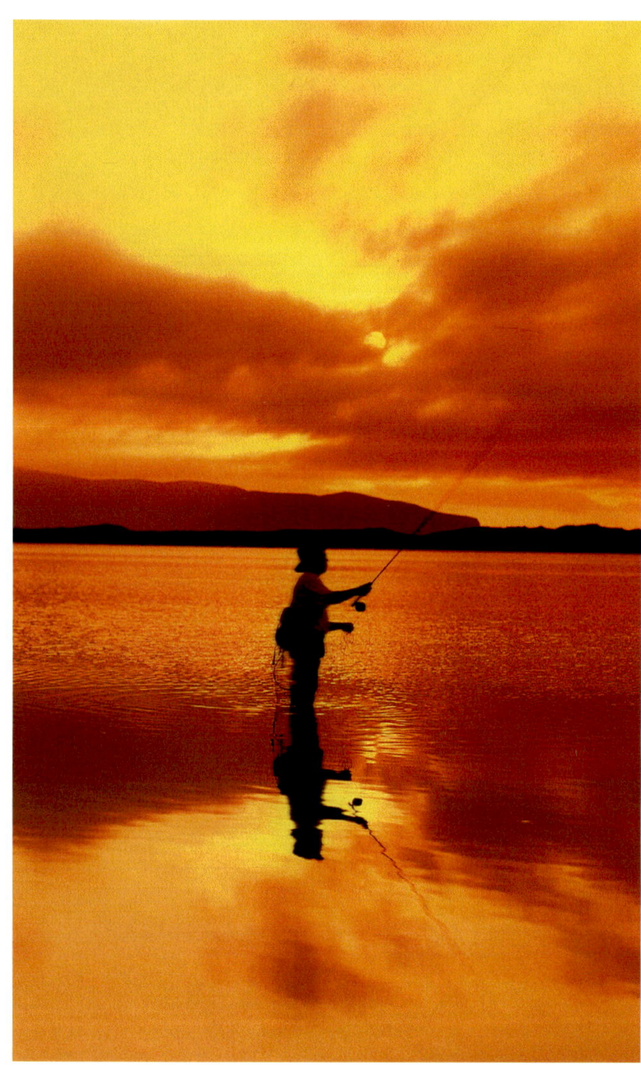

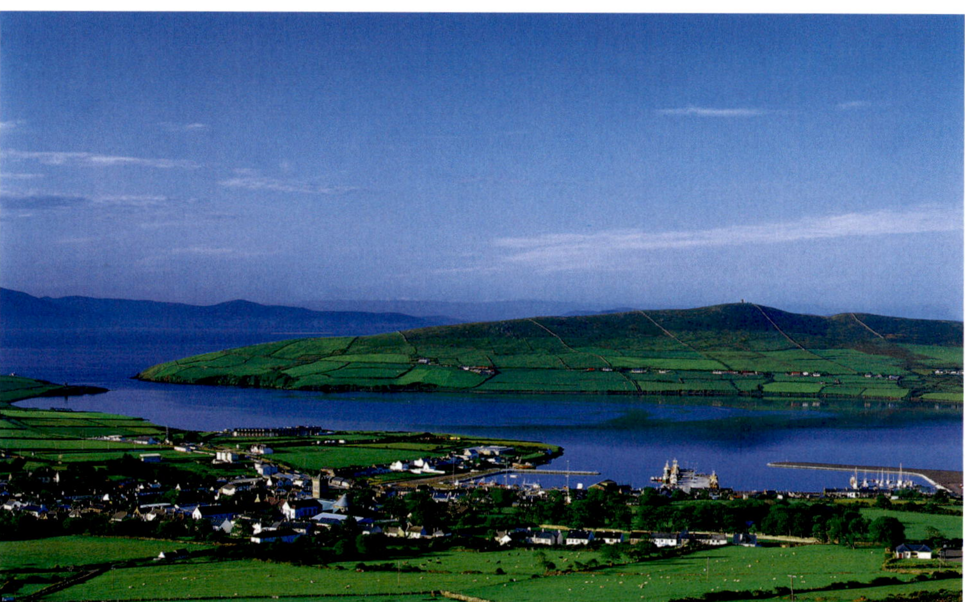

Castlegregory (left)
Sitting in the middle of a veritable animal and bird sanctuary the unspoilt village of Castlegregory has as its back garden an incredible wilderness, including the wonderful valley of Glenteenasig (the valleys of the waterfall).

Dingle Harbour (above)
This market town was built on fishing and farming but nowadays tourism is its main activity. The Dingle Races in August attract many visitors and are a manifestation of Kerry's love affair with the horse.

Dingle Bay (right)
The mountains and rugged seascape of Corca Dhuibhne, the Dingle Peninsula, and the offshore Blasket Islands have long been considered one of the most beautiful areas in Ireland.

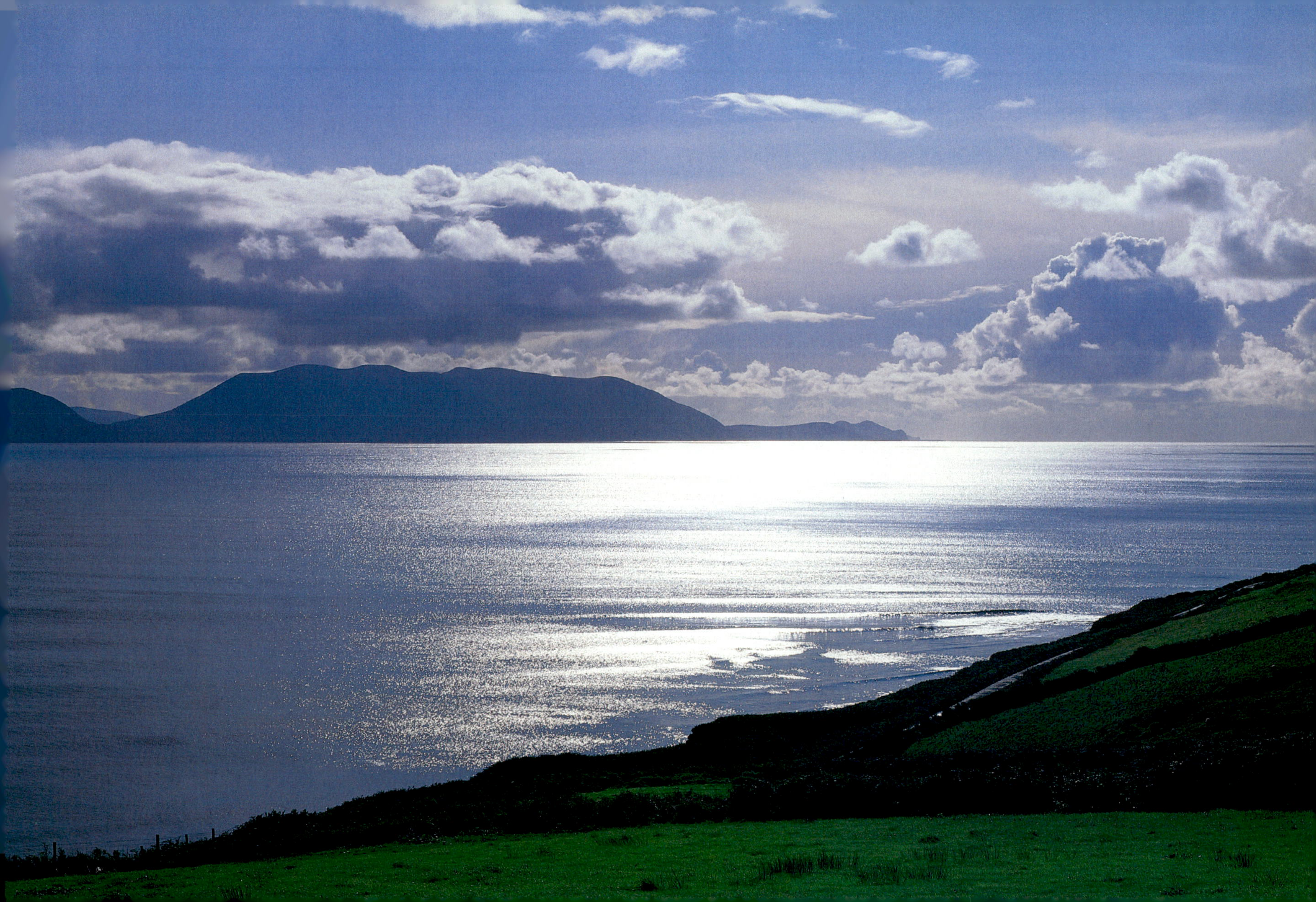

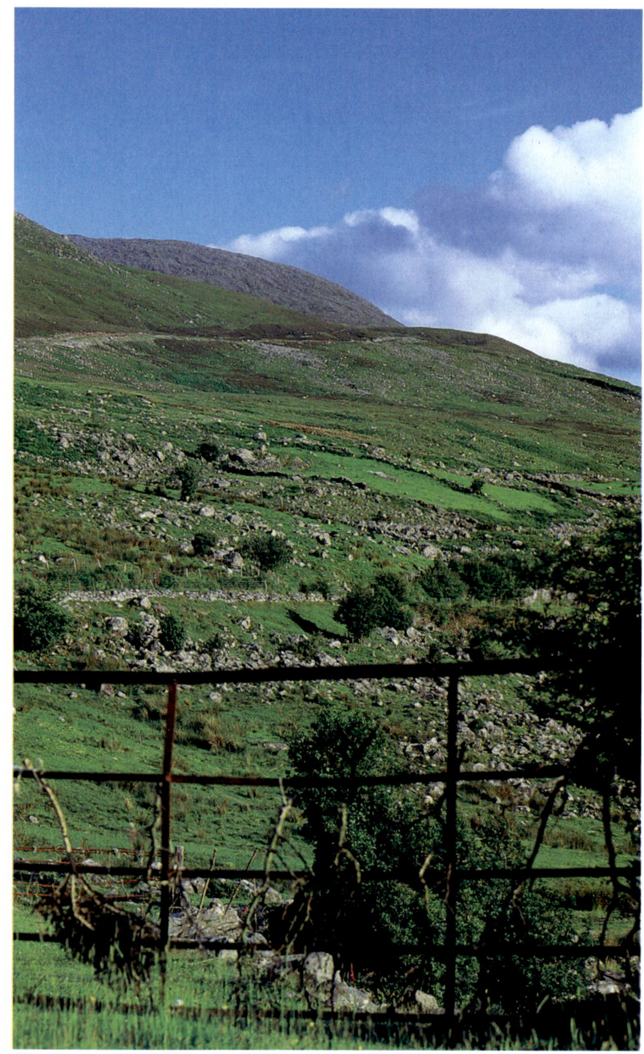

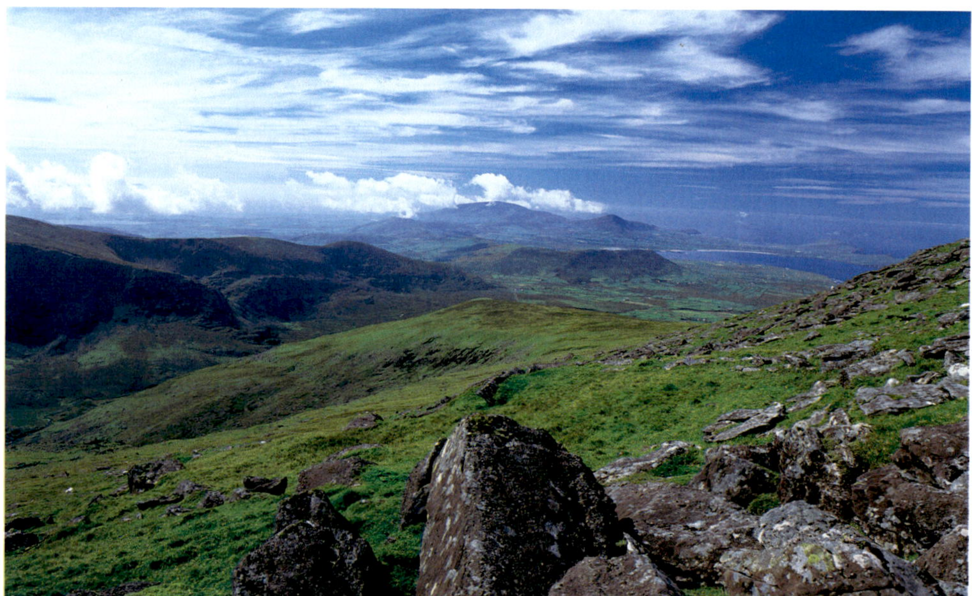

Glencar (left)
A nature lover's paradise, the Glencar area is naturally beautiful with Lickeen Forest, Caragh River, and Caragh Lake, all part of the Ring of Kerry.

Blasket Islands (above)
Another view of the Blasket Islands, separated from Dingle by Blasket Sound.

Glenteenasig (right)
Lough Caum can be found near Glenteenasig Forest, at Aughacashla. Kerry has the three highest mountains in Ireland and numerous mountains which are suitable for climbing, forest walks, and hill walking.

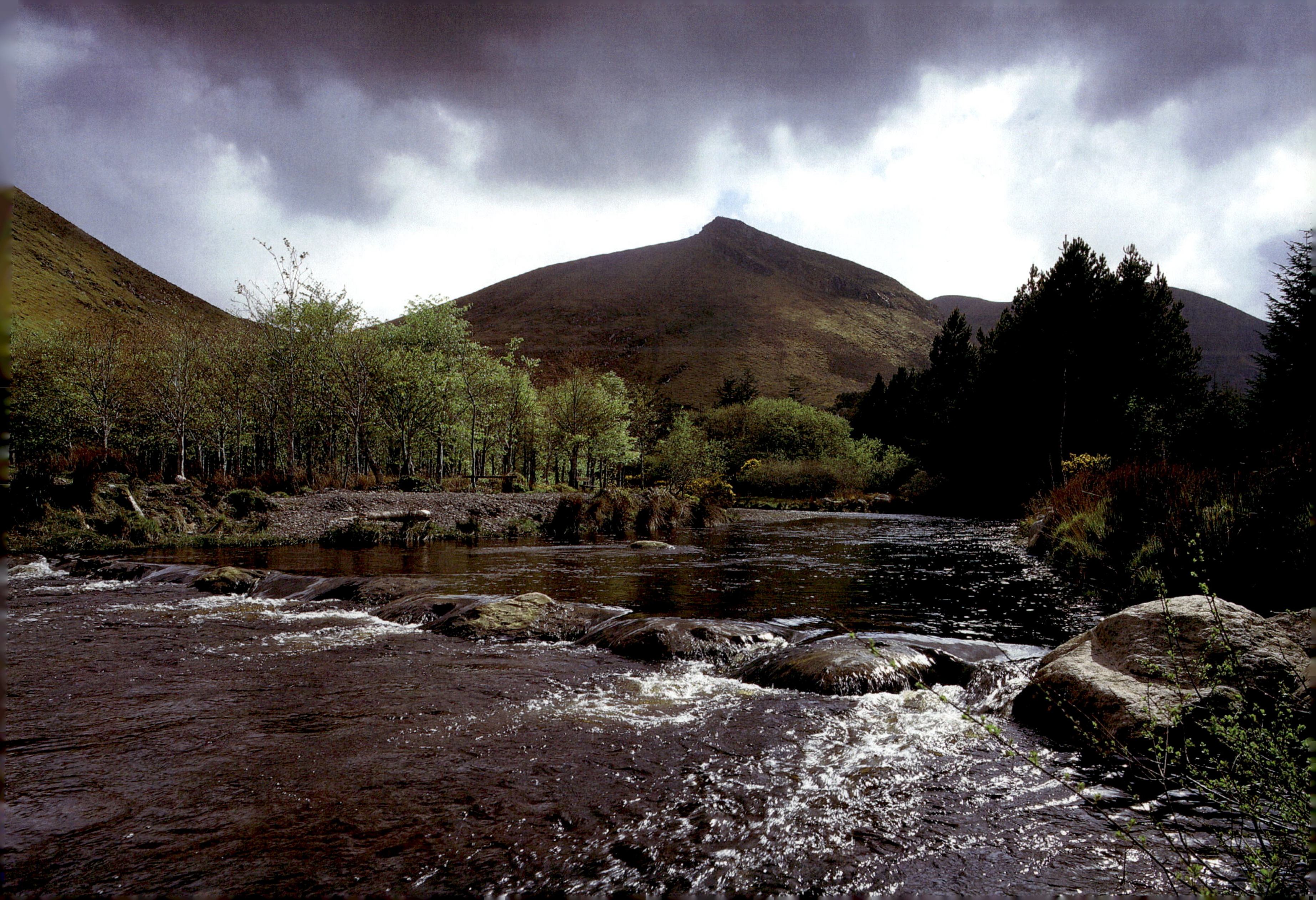

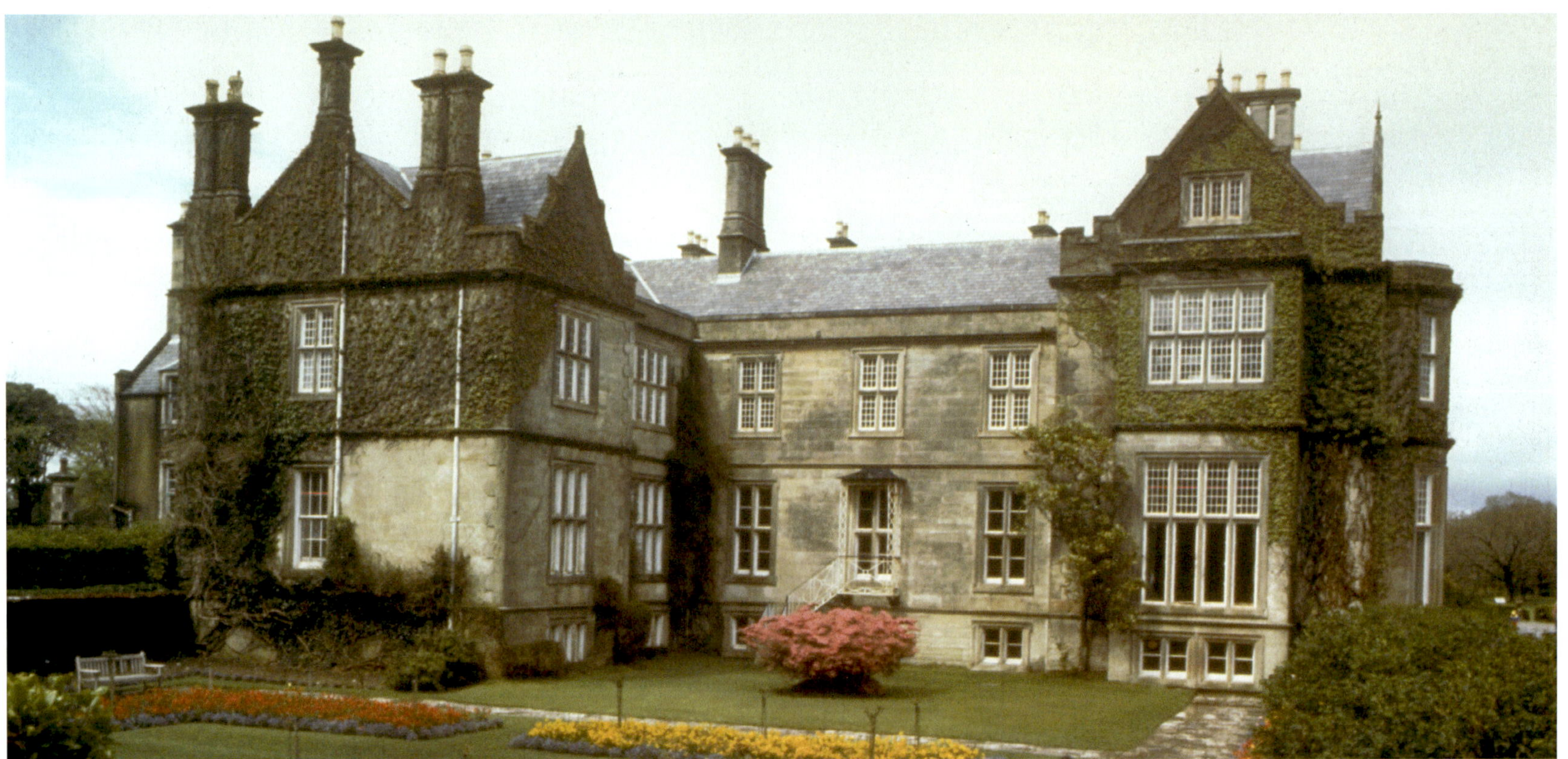

Muckross House
(above and right)
Muckross House was built in 1843, on the edge of Muckross Lake for Henry Arthur Herbert the MP for Kerry. The Herberts entertained many important guests at Muckross, notably Queen Victoria in 1861. Today Muckross House and its Museum of Kerry Life, is set in the Killarney National Park.

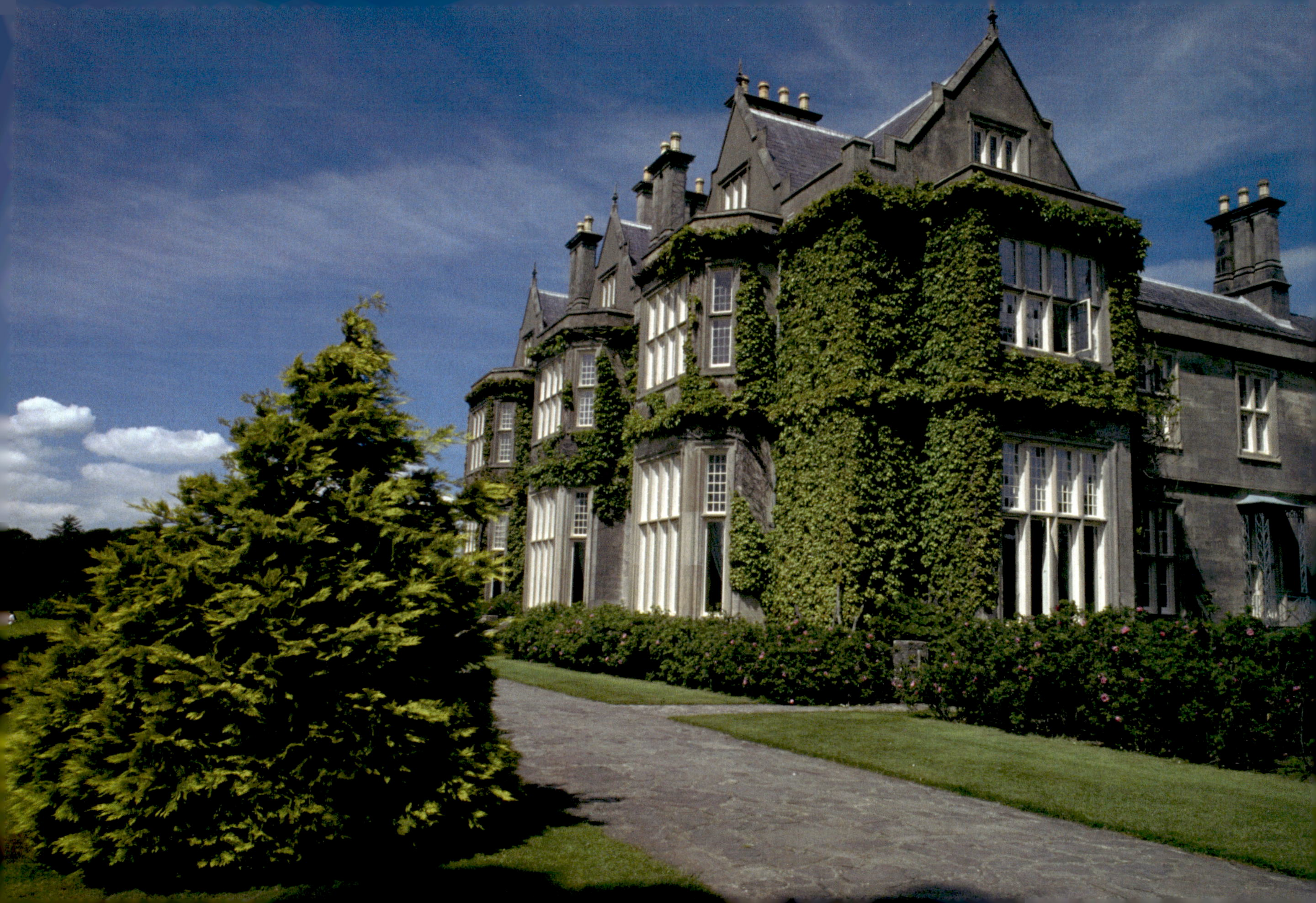

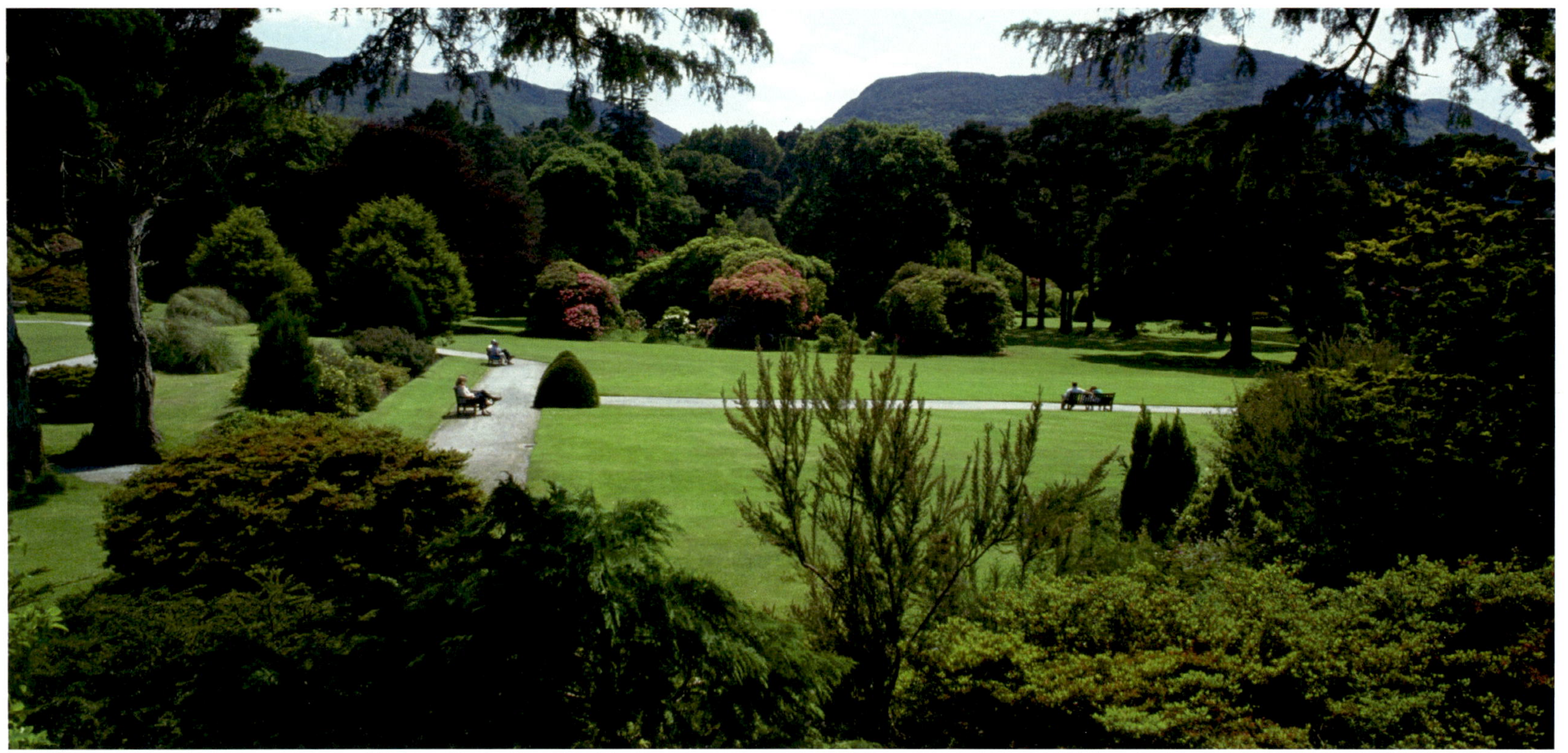

Gardens of Muckross House (above and right)

The gardens were extended in the 1850s in preparation for Queen Victoria's visit in 1861. Early in the 20th century the Sunken Garden, Rock Garden, and Stream Garden were developed. Irish gardeners have created some of the most hauntingly beautiful gardens in the world. There are gardens large and small growing plants from all corners of the globe all over Ireland.

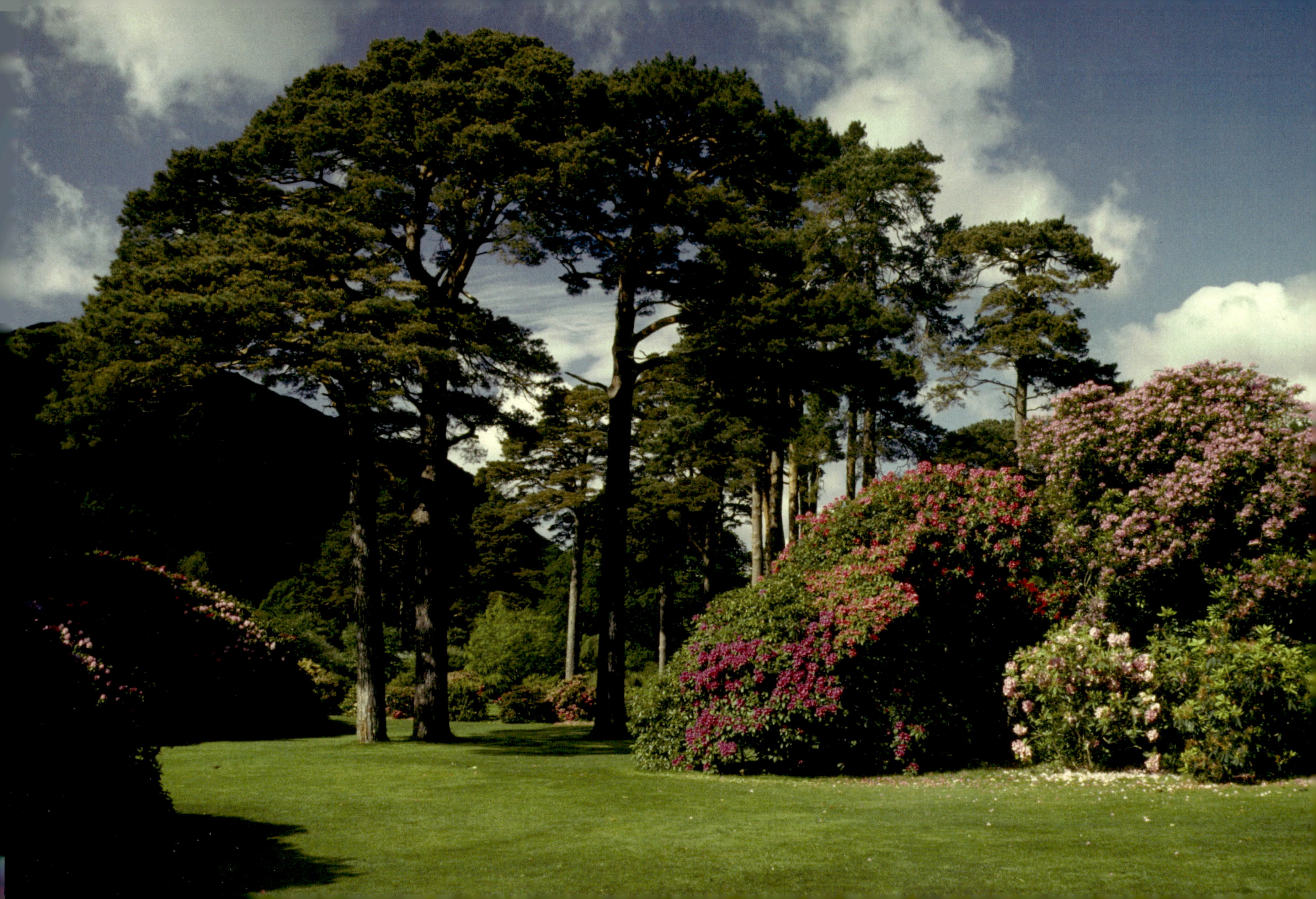

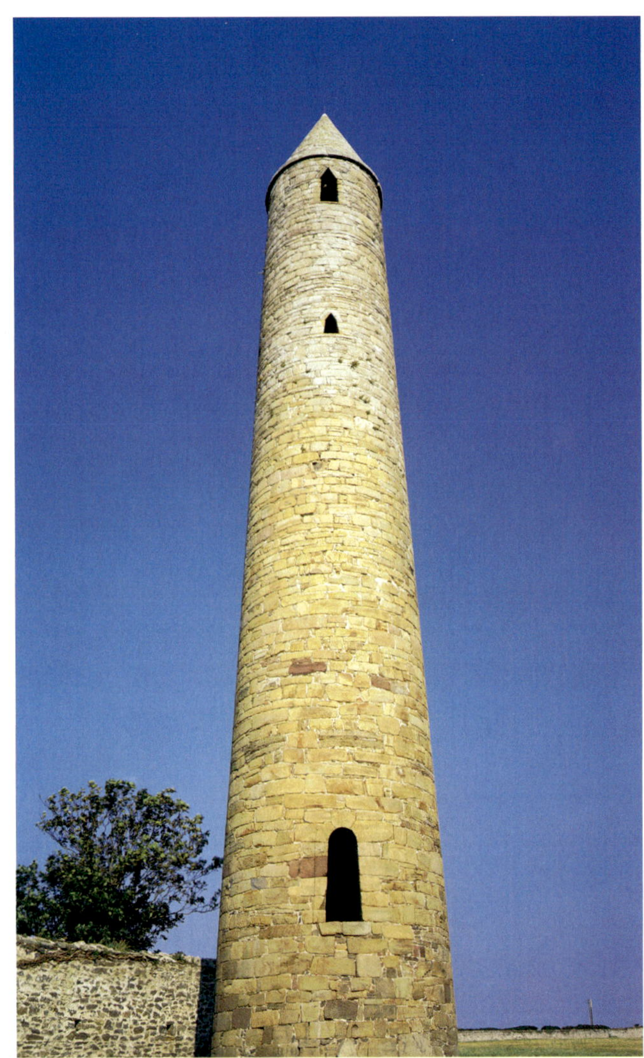

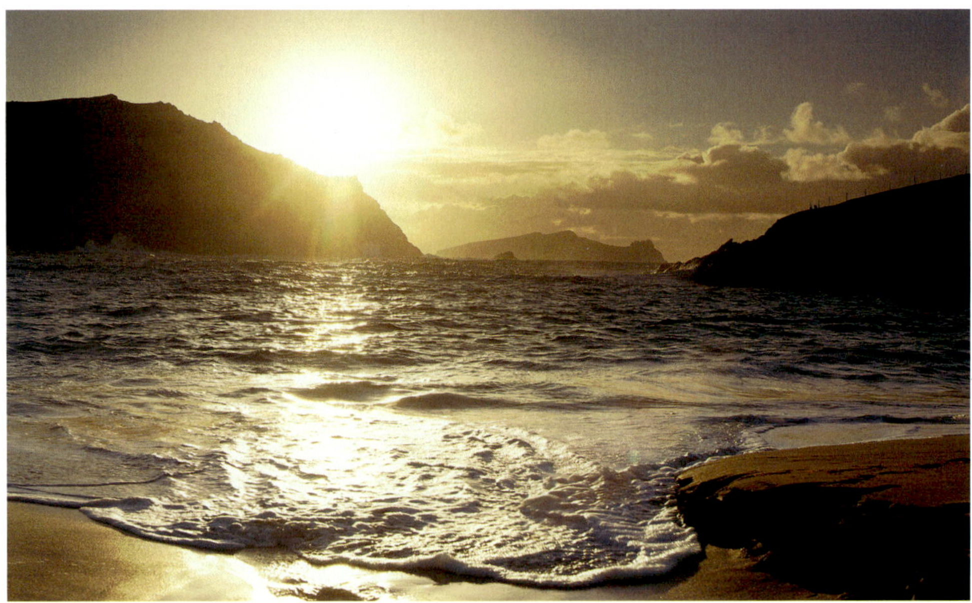

Ratoo Round Tower (left)
An old monastic foundation, ascribed to the early Kerry Saint Lugach, the church in the graveyard was built probably by the Augustinians in the 15th century, though stones from an earlier church are built into its walls.

Cloghane Strand (above)
Cloghane, on an inlet of Brandon Bay beneath the eastern slopes of Brandon Mountain, has a fine beach and is a good base for climbing Brandon (3,127ft).

Slea Head (right)
From Slea Head on a clear day you can see the Blasket Islands which are the last outposts of Europe and are known as the "next parish to America".

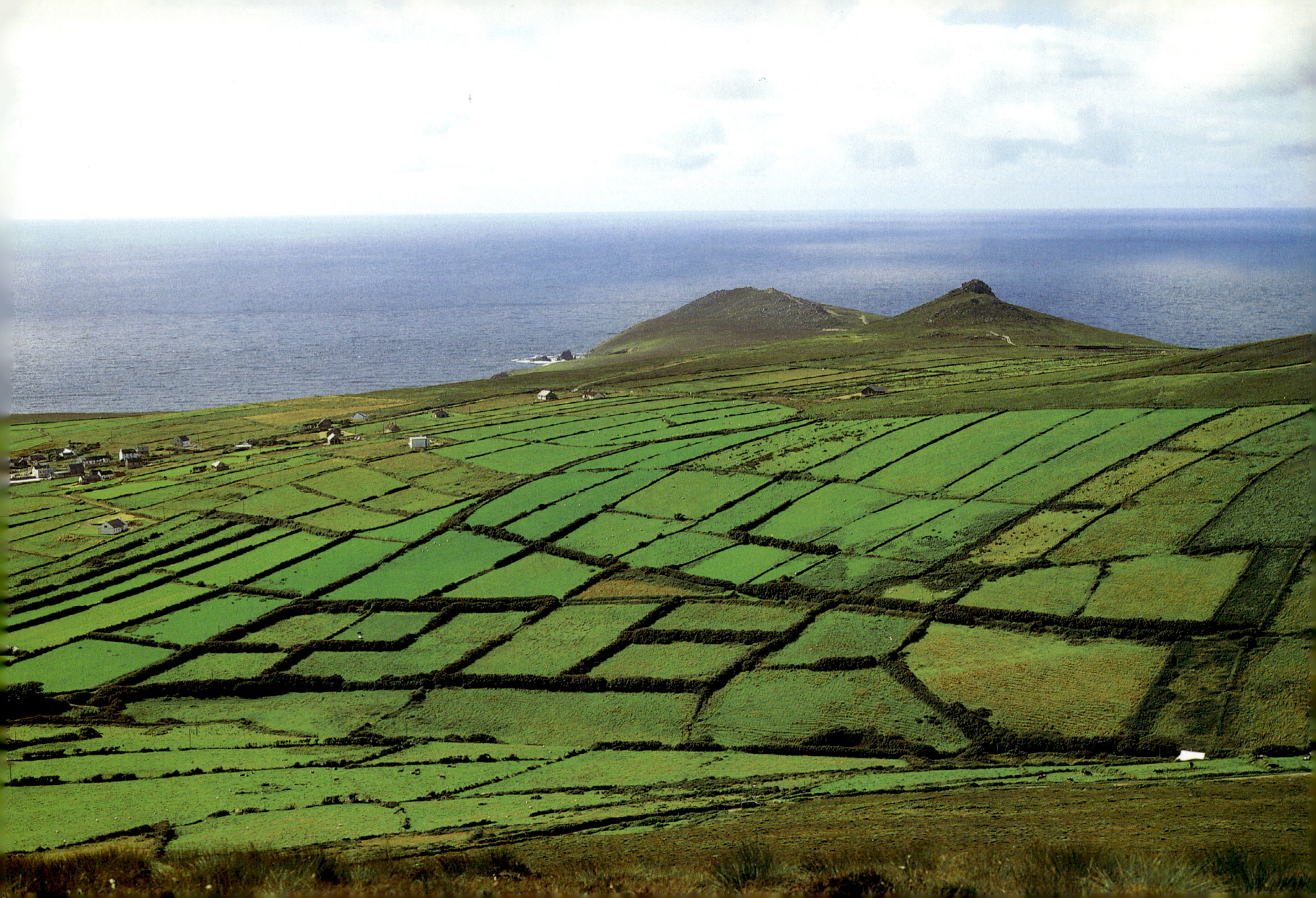

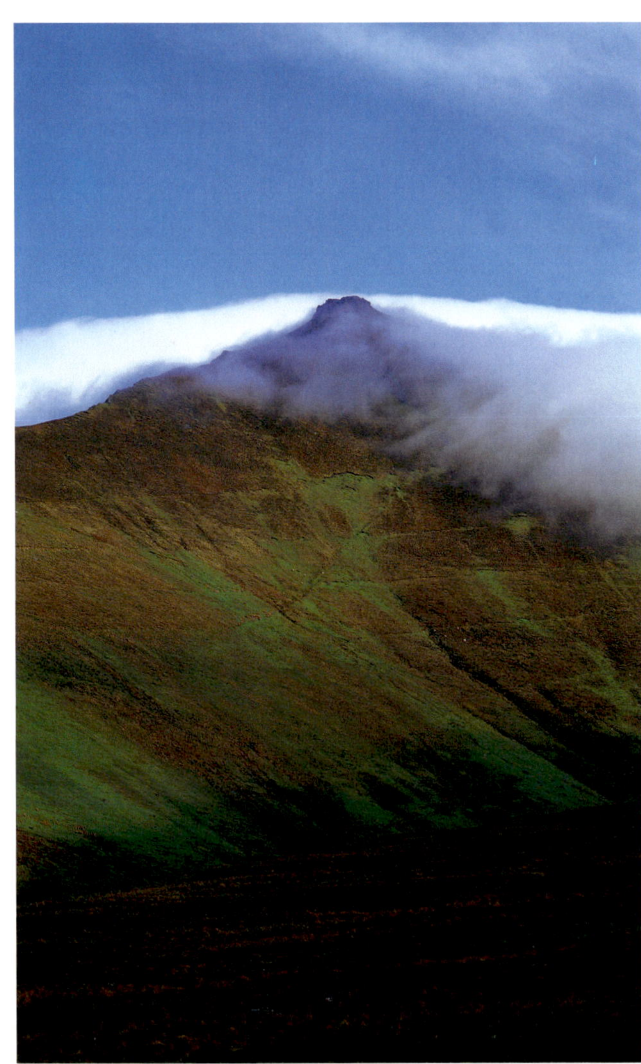

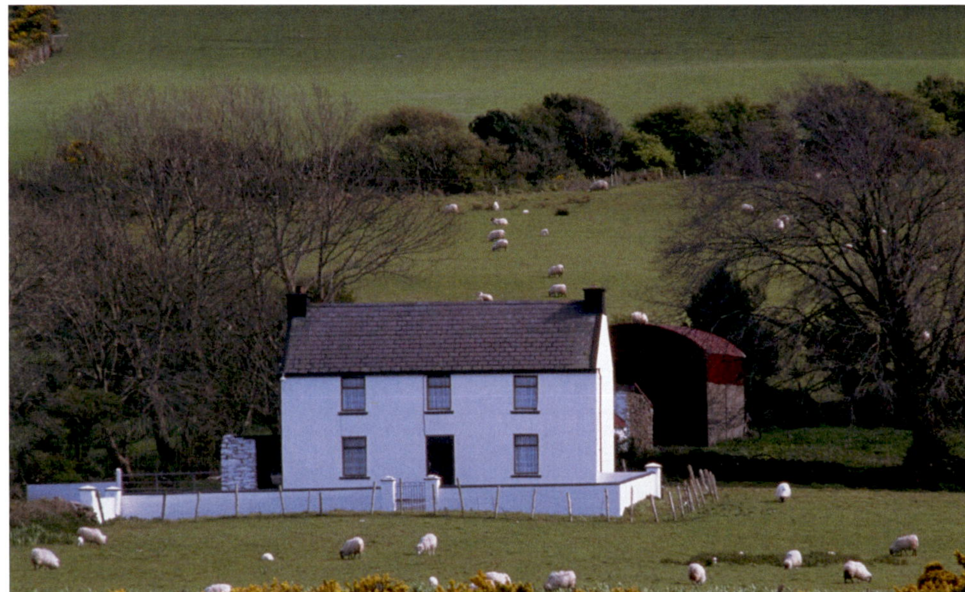

Caherconree (left)
It is said Curoi Mac Daire had his fortress here at Caherconree on the Brandon Peninsula. Legend says that Curoi was able to set the walls of his fortress spinning so nobody could get at the gateway at night.

Ring of Kerry (above)
Remote house in the mountain scenery near Moll's Gap on the ring of Kerry—a tour around the Iveragh Peninsula from the Lakes of Killarney, through Sneem and Ballinskelligs to Killorglin.

Ballybunion Cliffs (right)
Along the breathtaking cliffs lies the legendary nine daughters' blow hole where, it is said, a local chieftain in a wild rage cast all nine of his daughters to their deaths.

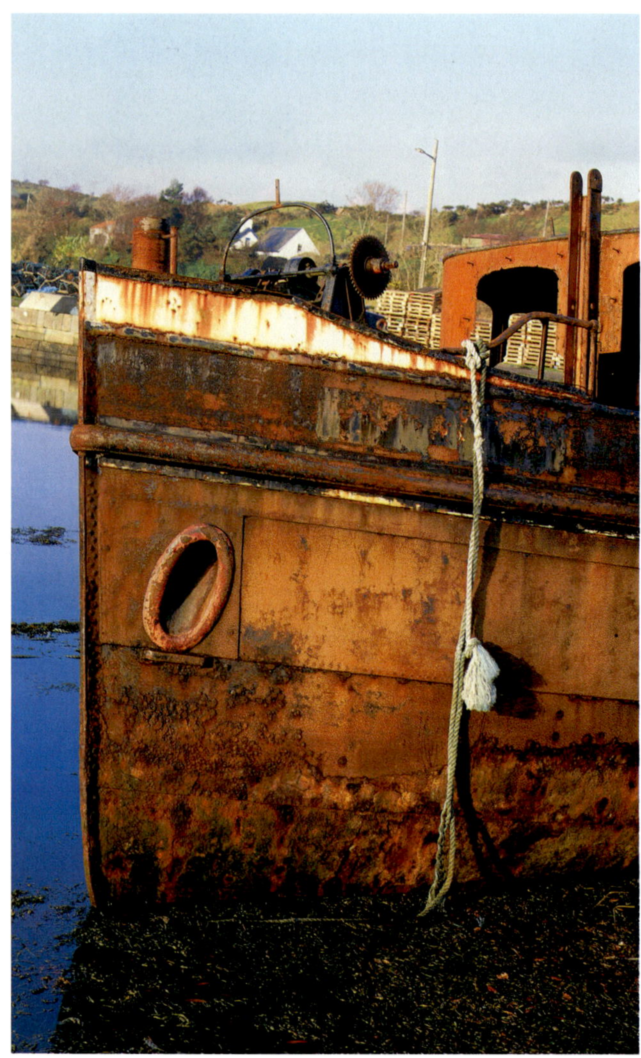

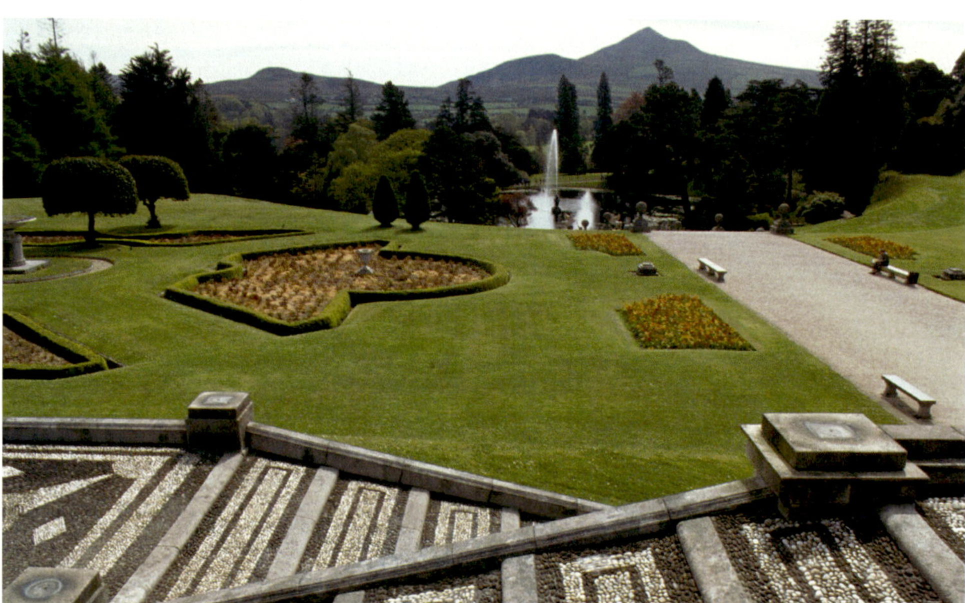

Kilmackillogue (left)
Until 1970 salmon were found in every river and every stream in this area. They were considered a poor man's dish and the local children got very tired of eating salmon all the time.

Powerscourt Estate (above)
Powerscourt is a Palladian house in County Kerry built in 1731. Gardens were added—one to the Italian style in the 19th century and a 20th century Japanese garden. A feature of the gardens are the large number of statues.

Lug Worm Mounds (right)
The Dingle Peninsula is famed for its fishing and the best bait is lug worms because they are full of blood and juices which when hooked lay a fantastic scent trail to attract fish.

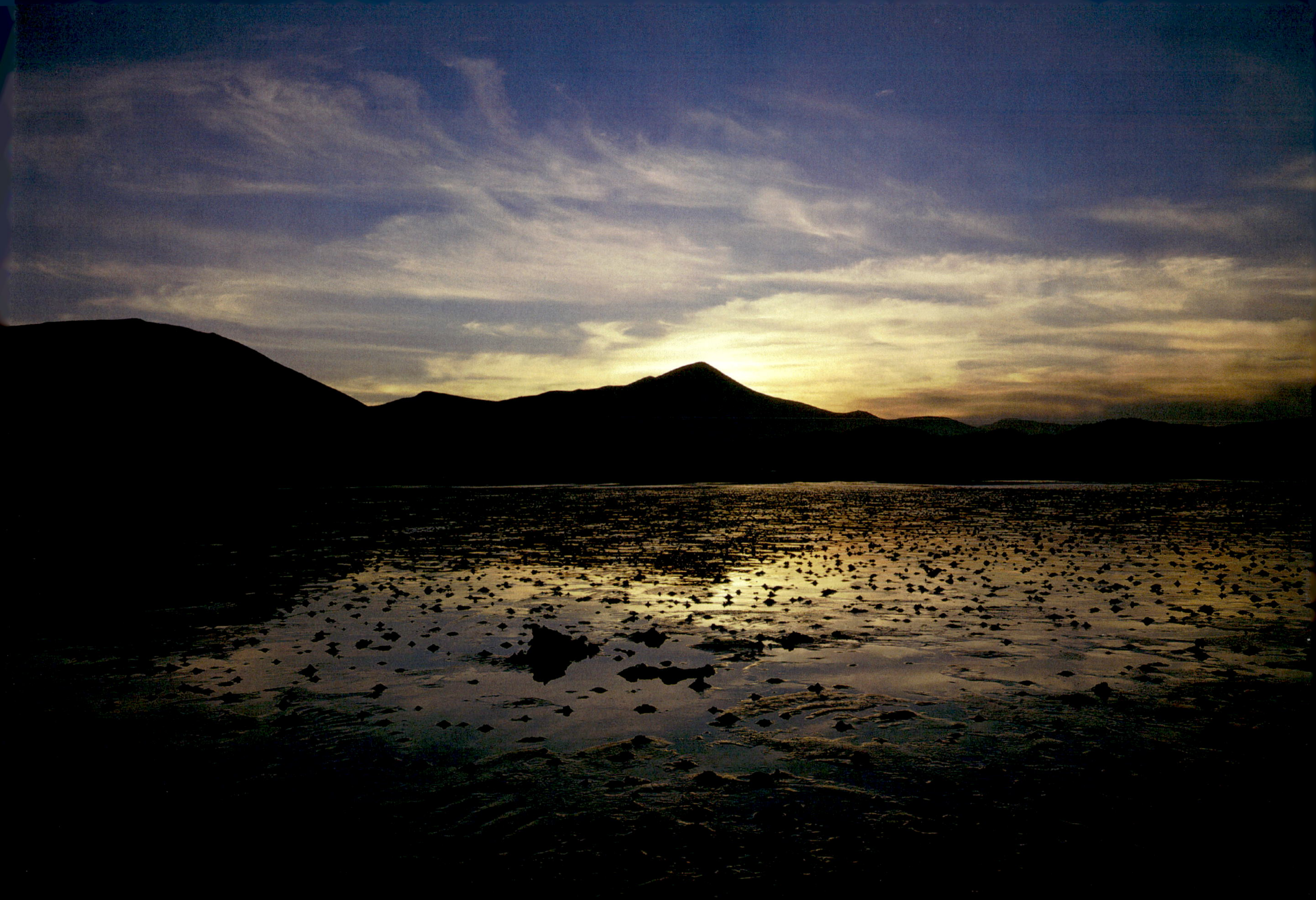

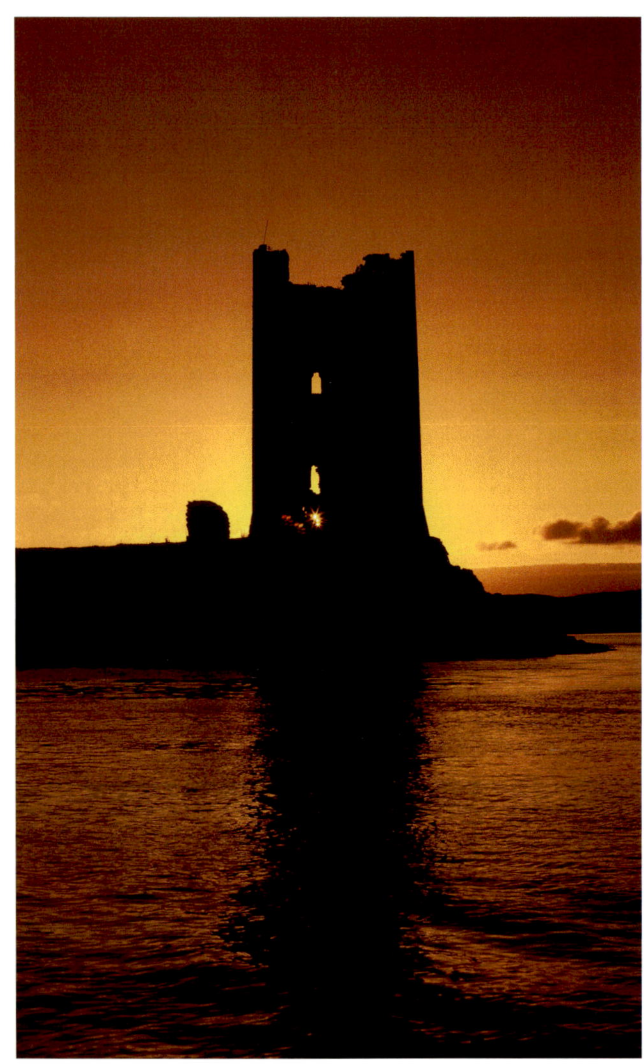

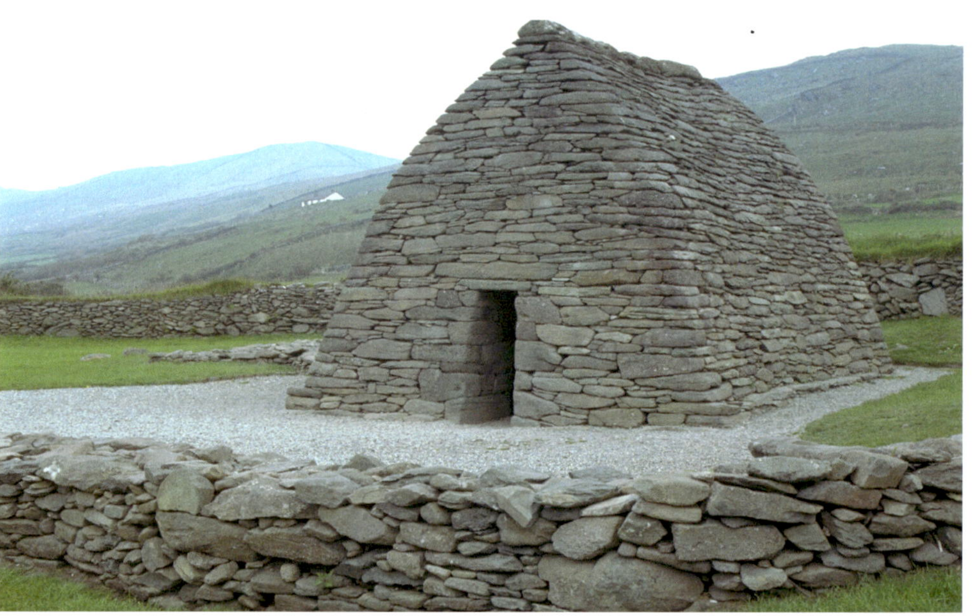

Barrow Castle (left)
The ruins of the castle on Fenit Island date back to the 12th century. From Barrow Harbour Brendan the Navigator is reputed to have set out on his travels to America almost a thousand years before Christopher Columbus

Gallarus Oratory (above)
This small oratory, built without mortar, uses corbel vaulting—a technique developed by Neolithic tomb-makers. Shaped like an upturned boat, Gallarus Oratory overlooks the harbour at Smerwick on the Dingle Peninsula.

Kenmare (right)
Charmingly situated at the head of Kenmare Bay, where the Roughty River meets the sea, Kenmare is an excellent centre for exploring both the Iveragh and Beara peninsulas.

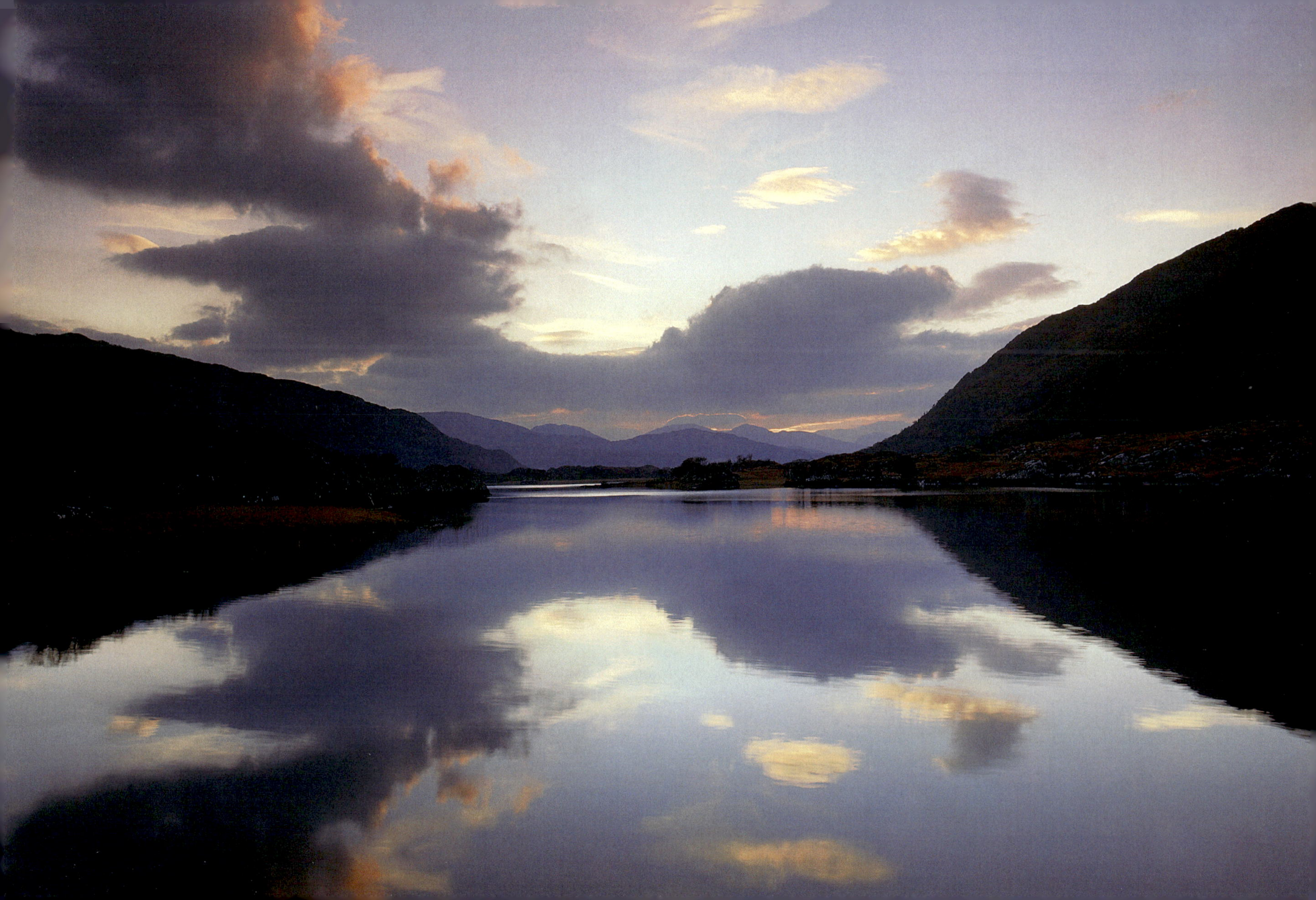

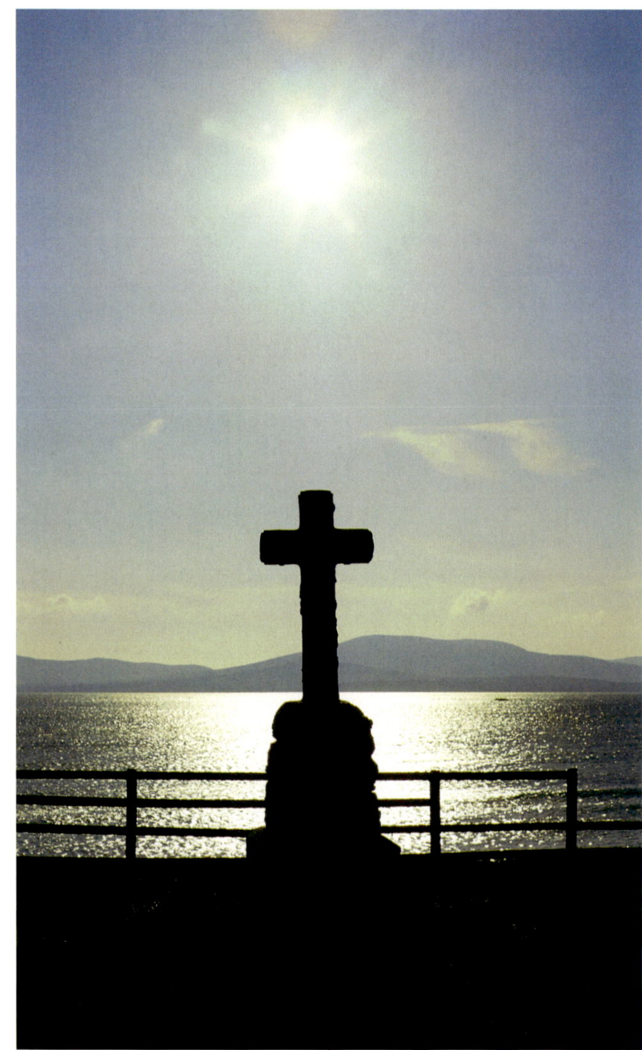

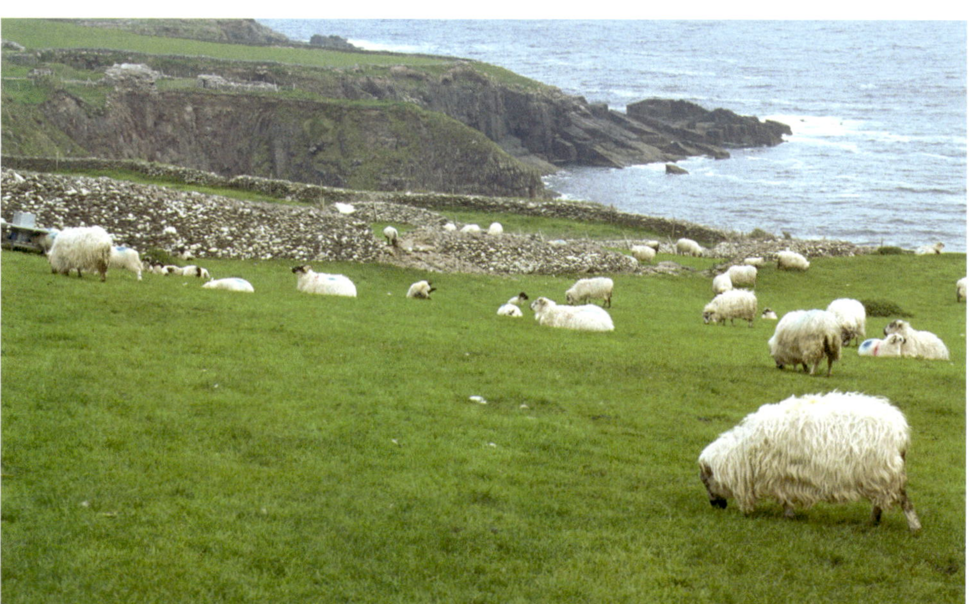

Waterville Cross (left)
Waterville, also known as the "Little Whirlpool" has some of the most breathtaking scenery in Kerry. Forming part of the Ring of Kerry, it lies between Currane and Ballinskelligs Bay.

Sheep, Dingle Peninsula (above)
Grazing near Ballyferriter, where there is a museum of local material culture and a profusion of gaily painted cottages.

Kenmare River (right)
Salmon, sea trout, and small wild brown trout are all found in Kenmare River. Visitors can buy permits and try their luck, the salmon are especially good in spring.

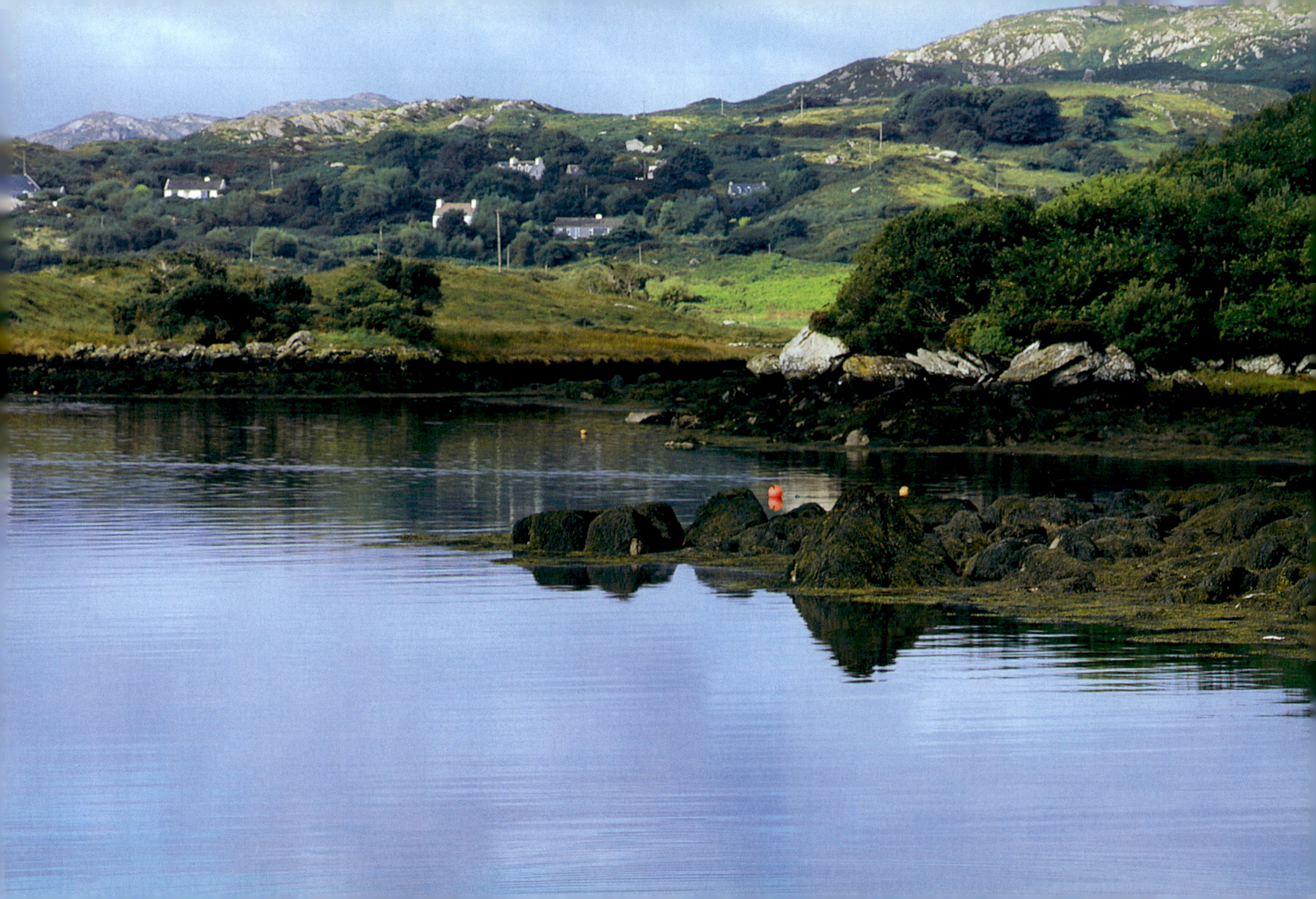

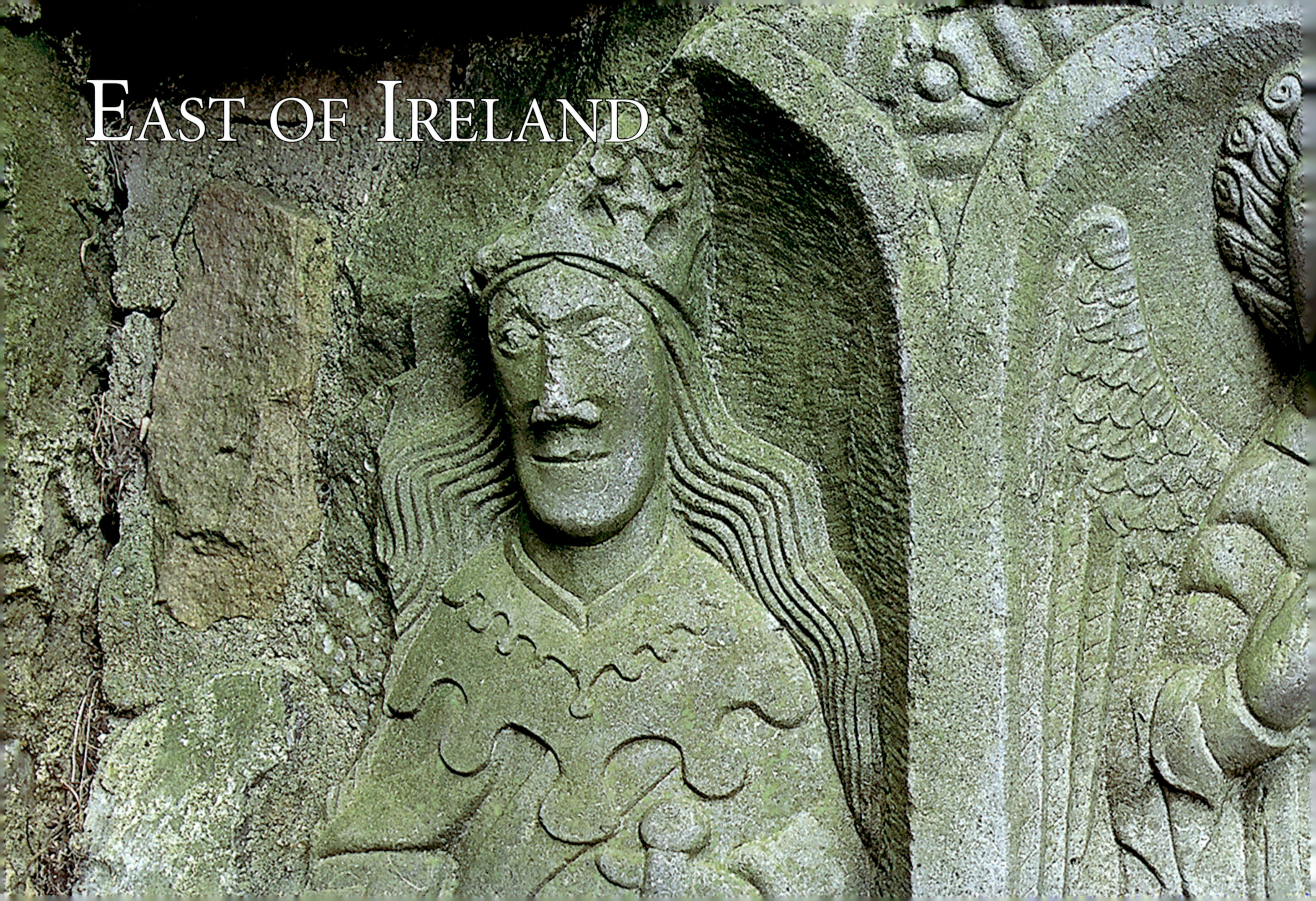
East of Ireland

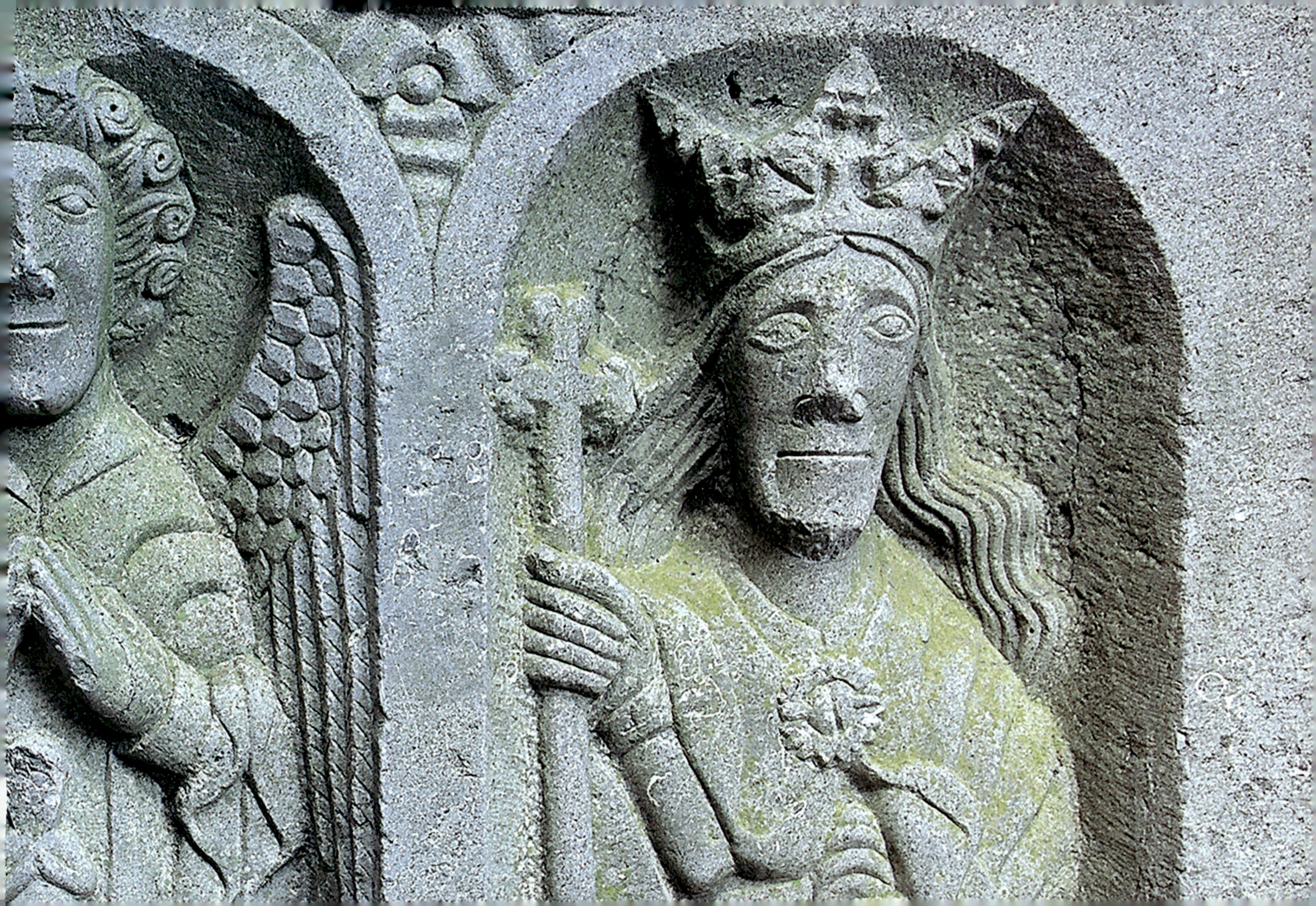

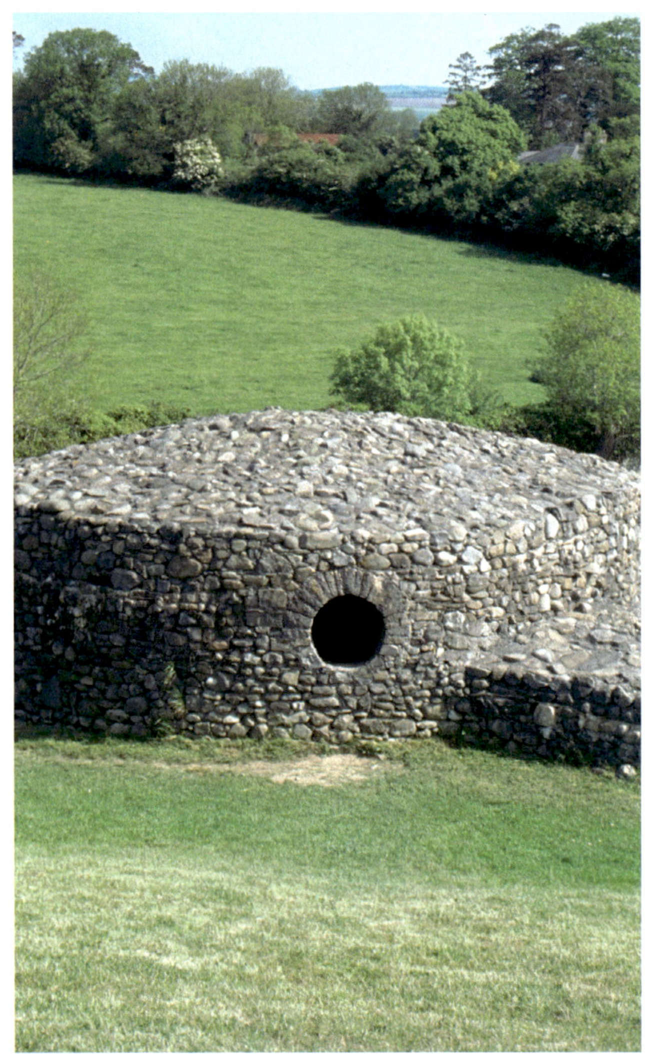

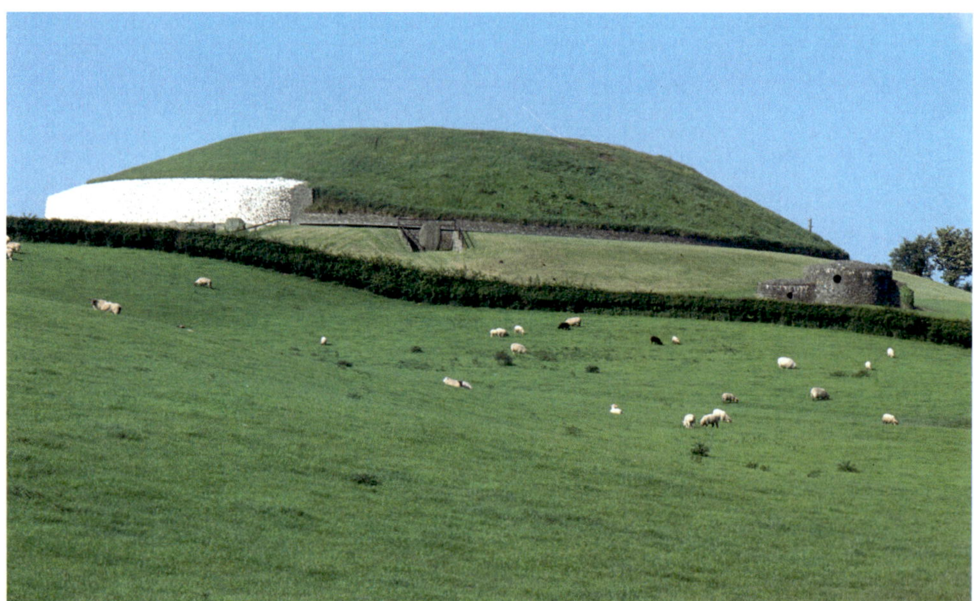

Newgrange
(above and left)
The three neolithic passage tombs at Newgrange, County Meath, were built over 5,000 years ago. The tomb is exactly positioned so that at dawn on Winter Solstice, a shaft of light penetrates the passageway and illuminates the inner chamber. Inside are many etchings, the most significant of which is the tri-spiral design on the entrance stone. Nobody knows exactly what the designs meant to the original artists.

Hill of Slane
(right)
A Franciscan monastery was built on the Hill of Slane in the 6th century to commemorate where St. Patrick announced the arrival of Christianity to pagan Ireland with the lighting of the first Easter fire in 433 AD.

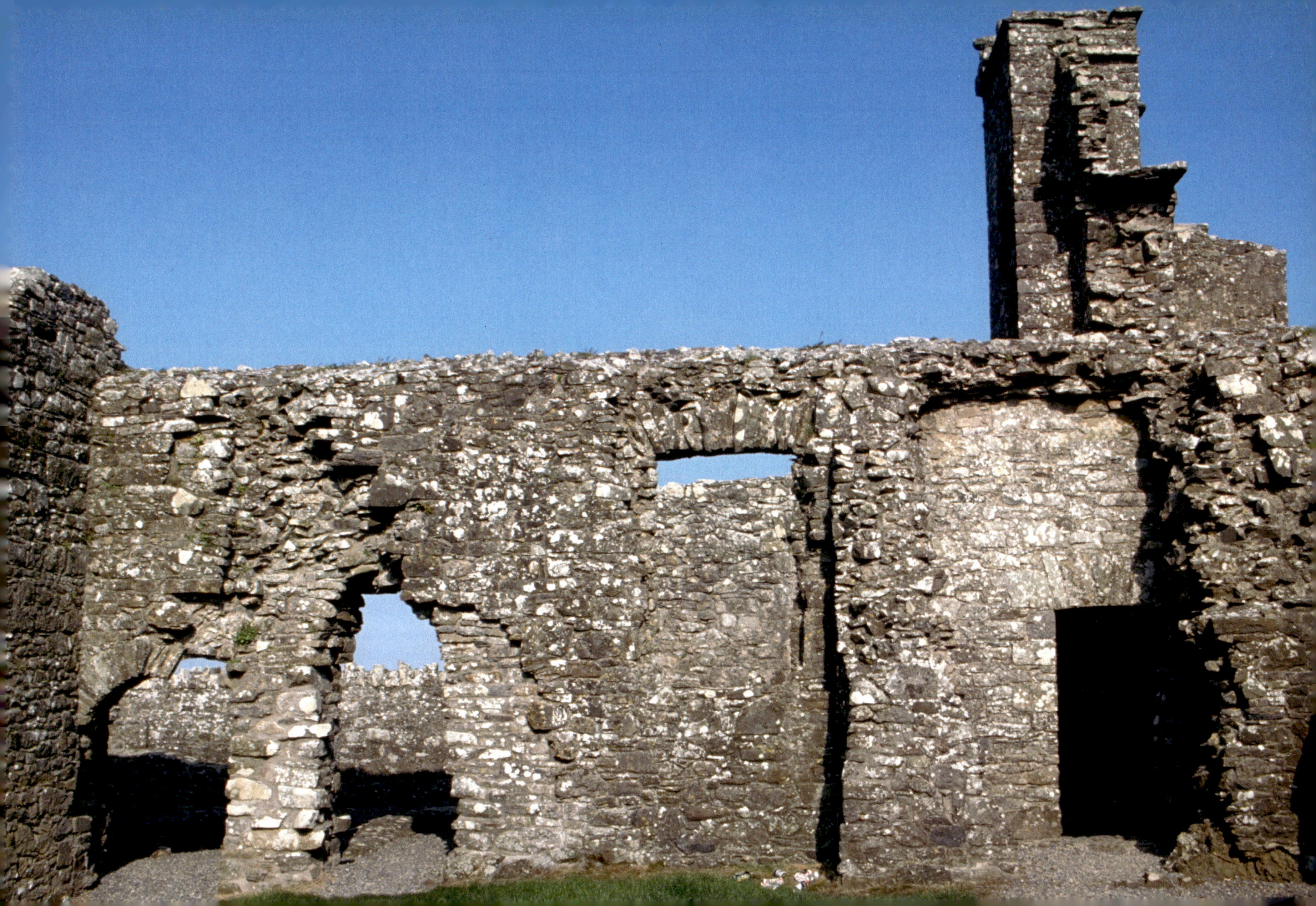

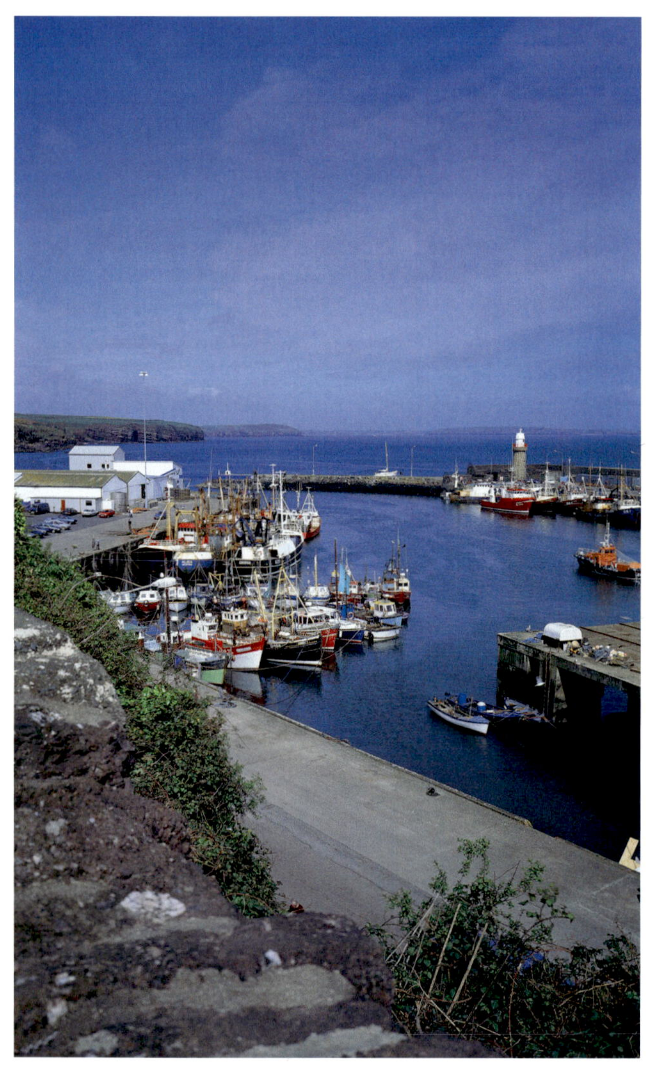

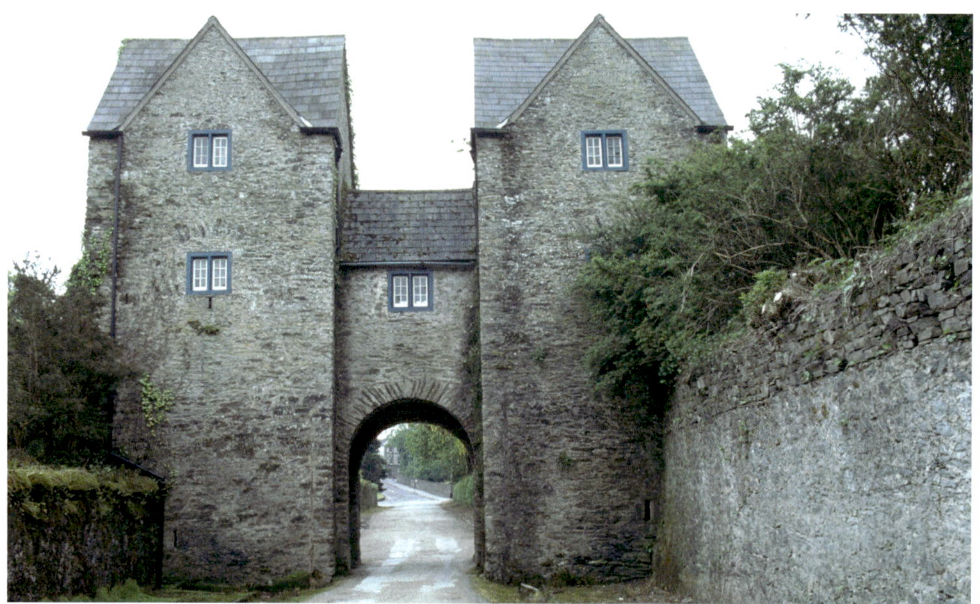

Dunmore East Harbour (left and right)

One-time packet station for mails between England and the south of Ireland, this small fishing port is built in the Breton style, and has several thatched cottages. The sheltered harbour makes Dunmore an important fishing port and is one of the five designated National Fishery Harbours with the second highest figure for fish landings after Killybegs.

Lismore Castle (above)

The Irish home of the Dukes of Devonshire since 1753, Lismore Castle overlooks the Blackwater Valley and the rolling, wooded hills to the Knockmealdown Mountains.

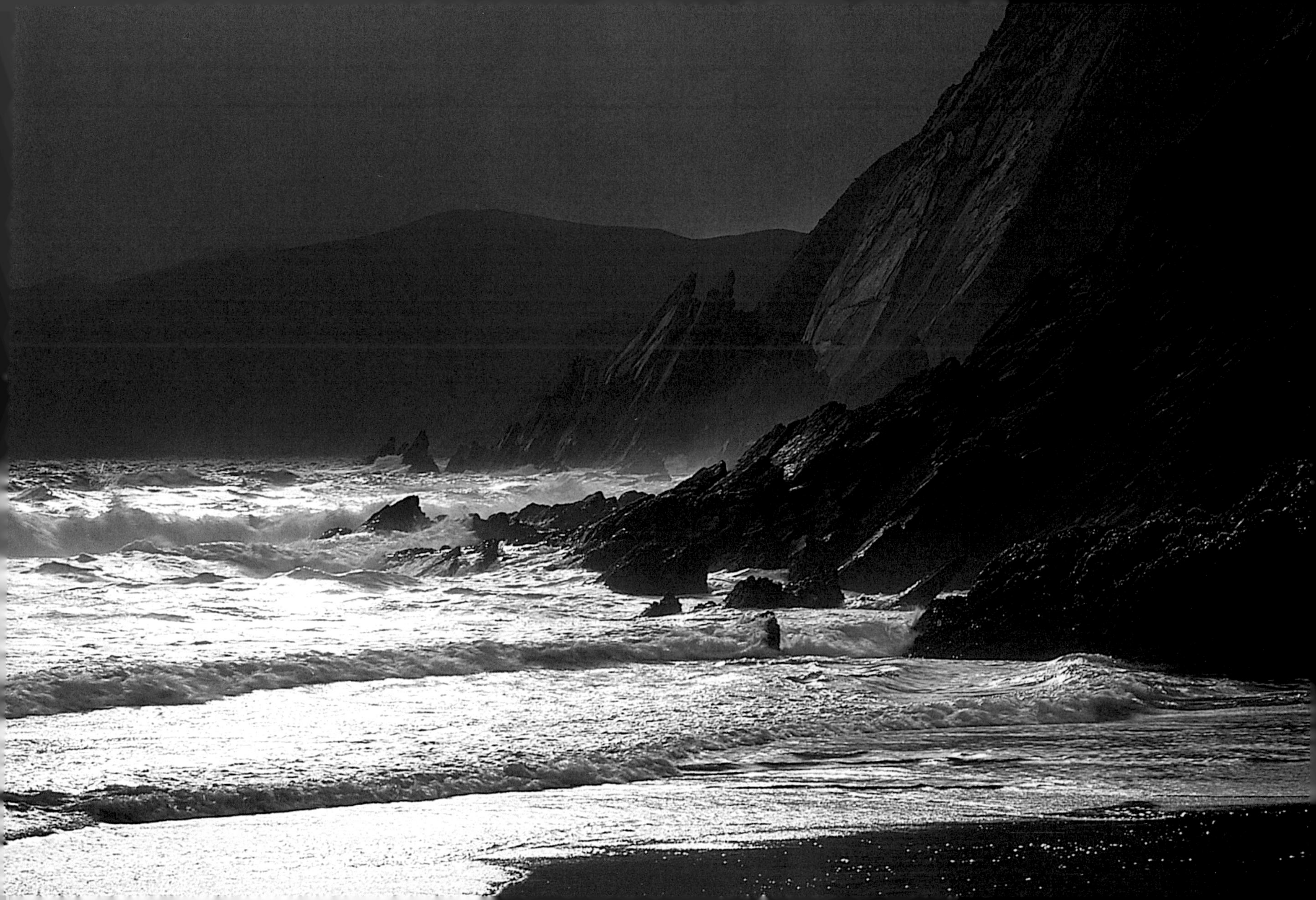

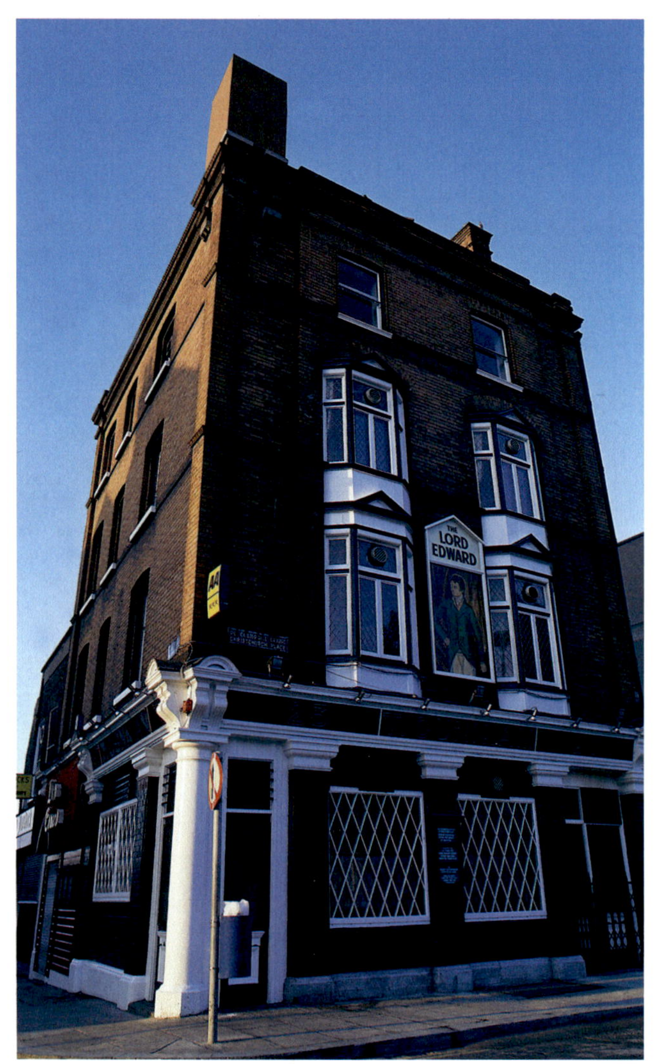

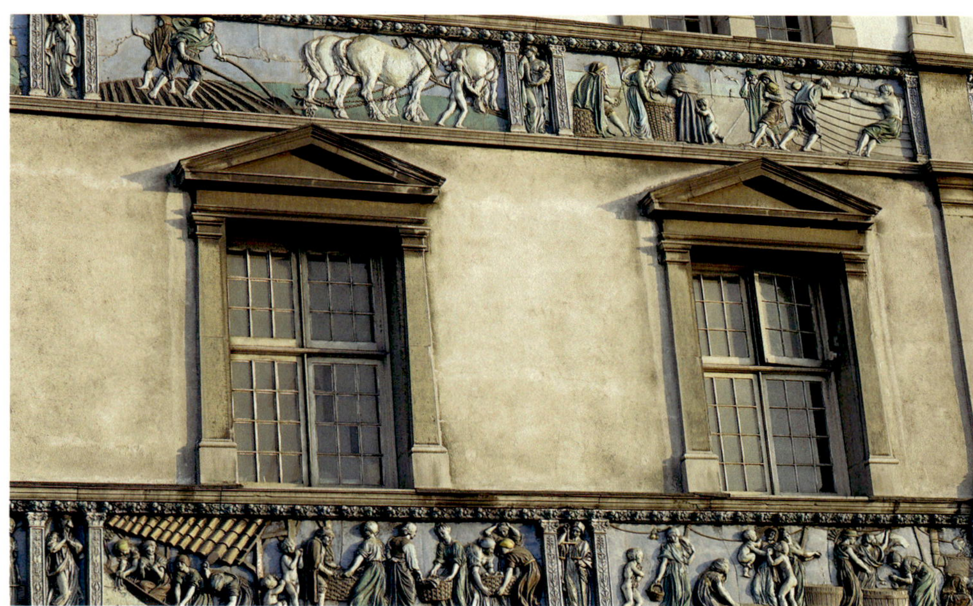

Decoration, Essex Quay (left)
In Medieval Dublin Case's Tower—a small round tower, two storeys high—was situated on Essex Quay nearly opposite Ss. Michael and John's Church.

Lord Edward Restaurant (above)
Established in 1890 the Lord Edward, is Dublin's oldest seafood restaurant and pub, conveniently placed between Christchurch Cathedral, Dublin Castle, and St Patrick's Cathedral.

Thatched Cottage (right)
All over Ireland one comes across vernacular architecture like this, often beautifully restored and maintained.

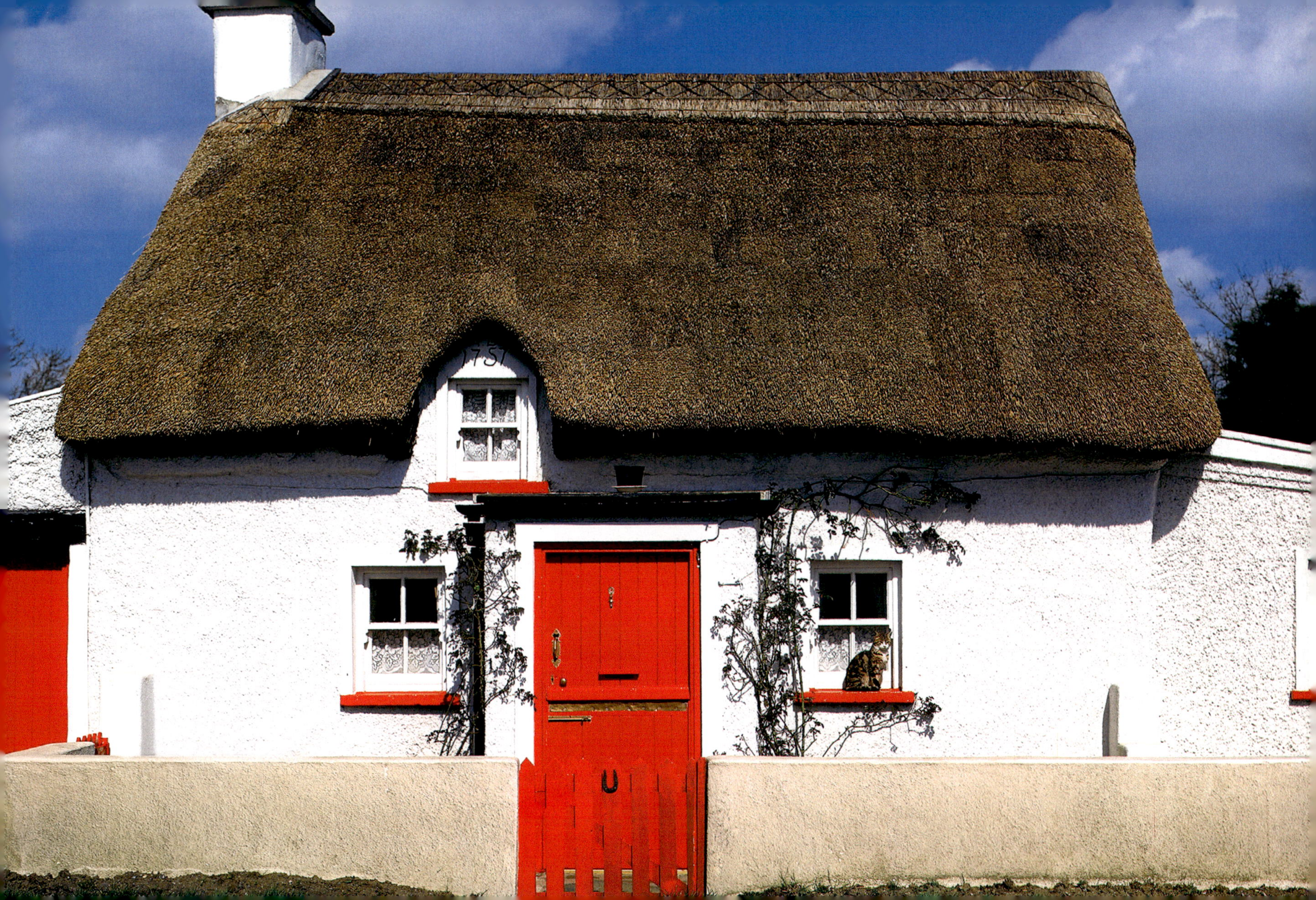
1757

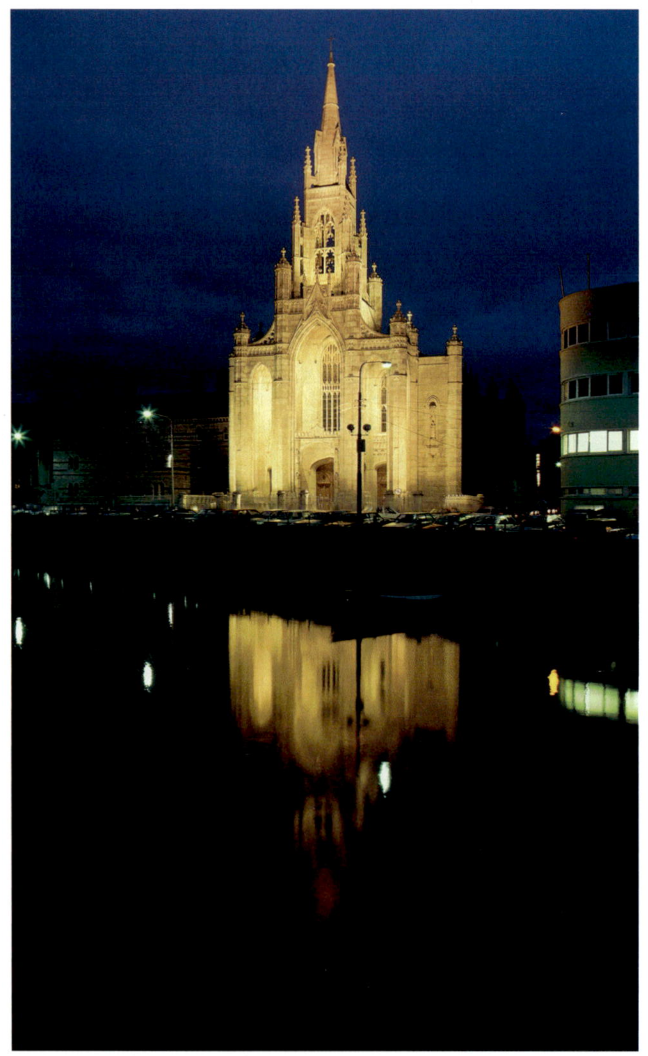

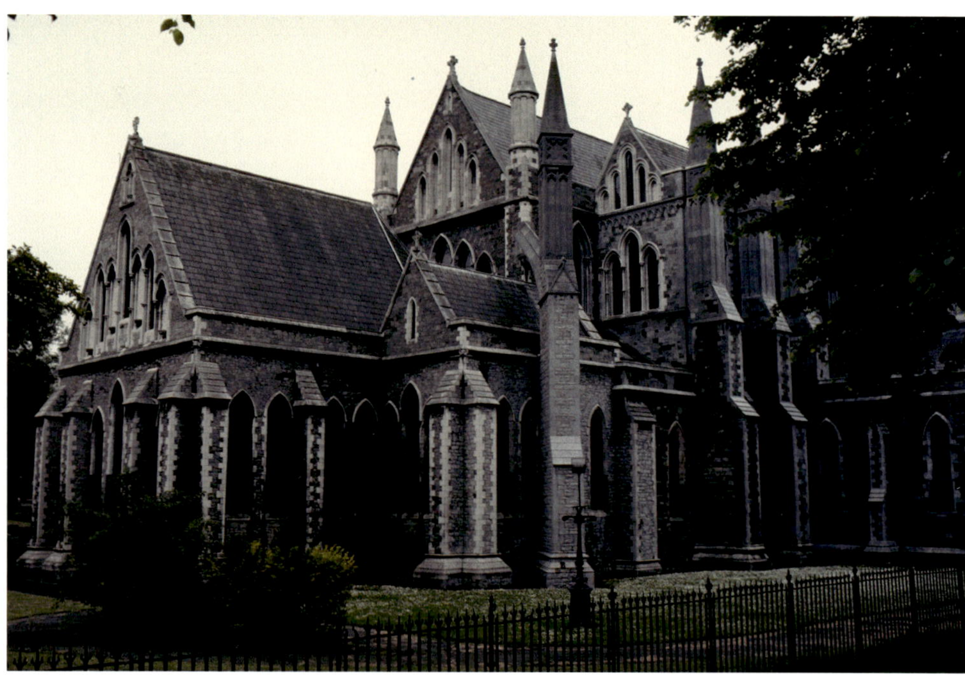

St. Patrick's Cathedral

Traditionally the site of a holy well used by St Patrick for baptisms, a church was established here as early as the late 5th century—a stone marking the site of the well was found in 1901. Founded in 1192 by Archbishop John Comyn, the cathedral and palace were intentionally built outside Dublin's city walls so that the church would not have to submit to the jurisdiction of the City Provosts. St Patrick's is the national cathedral for the Protestant Church of Ireland and is used by the state for ecumenical services.

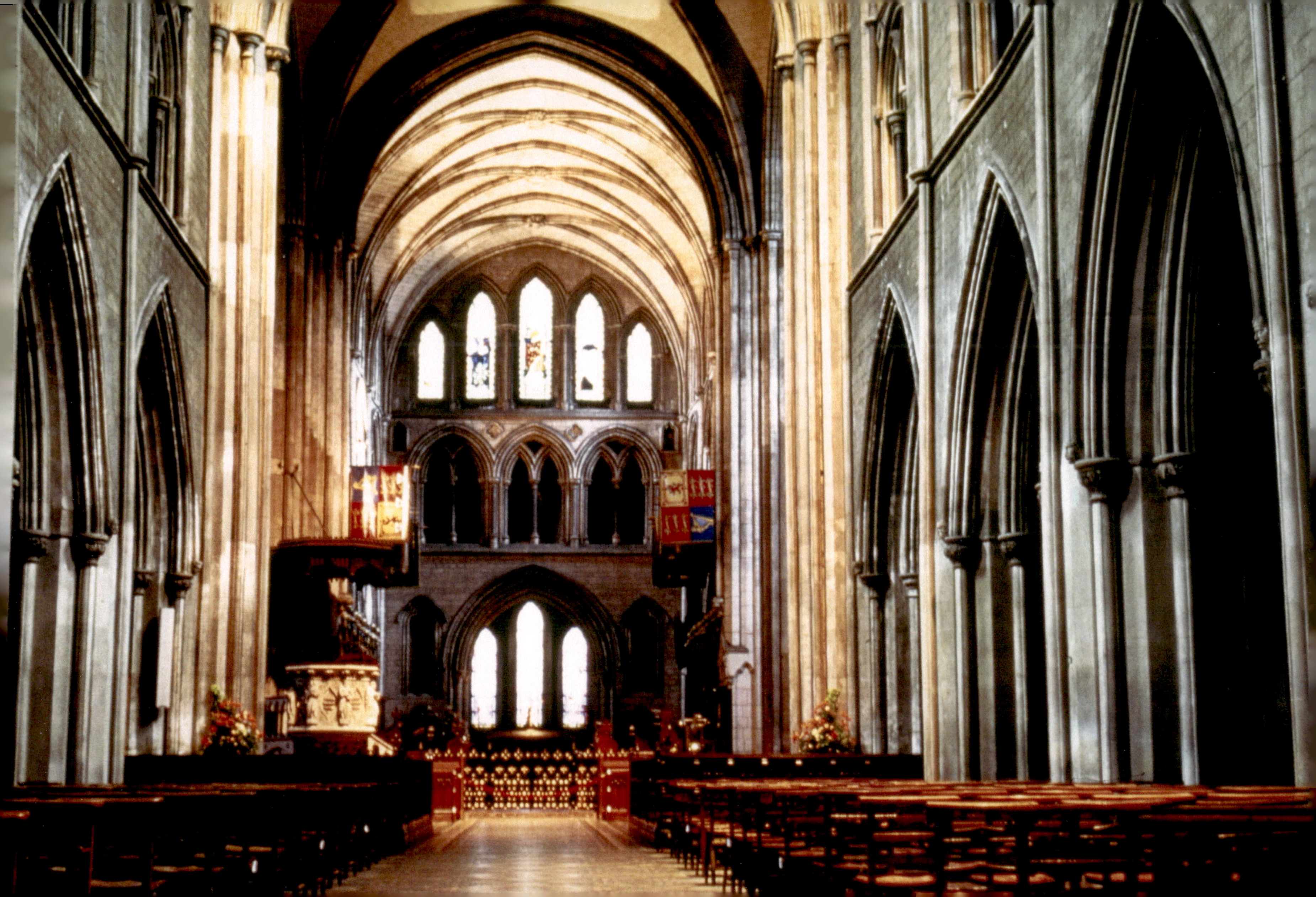

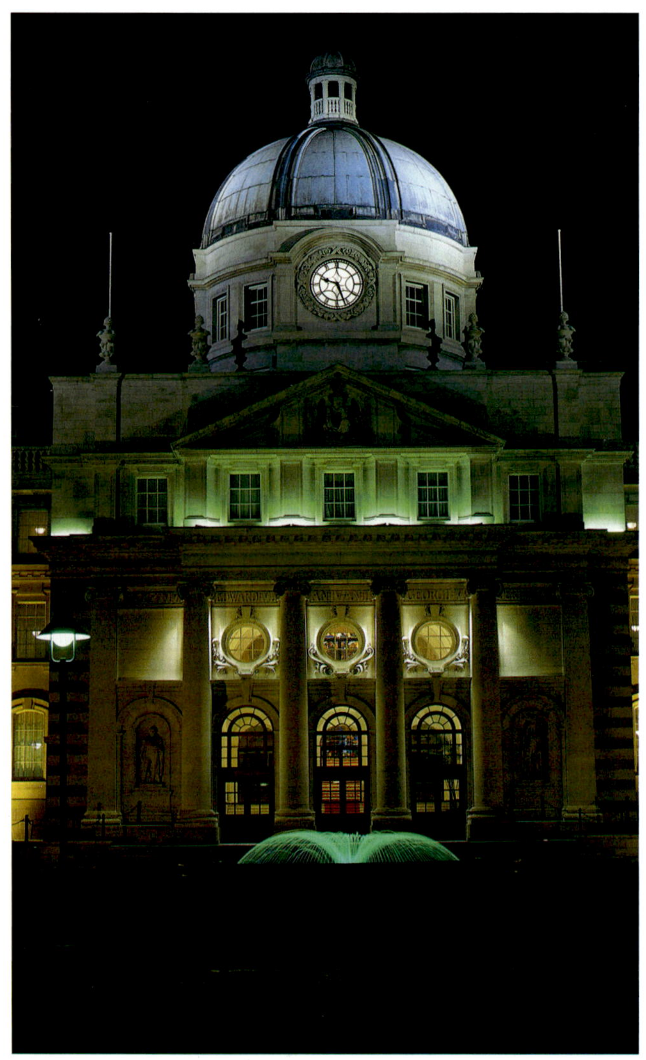

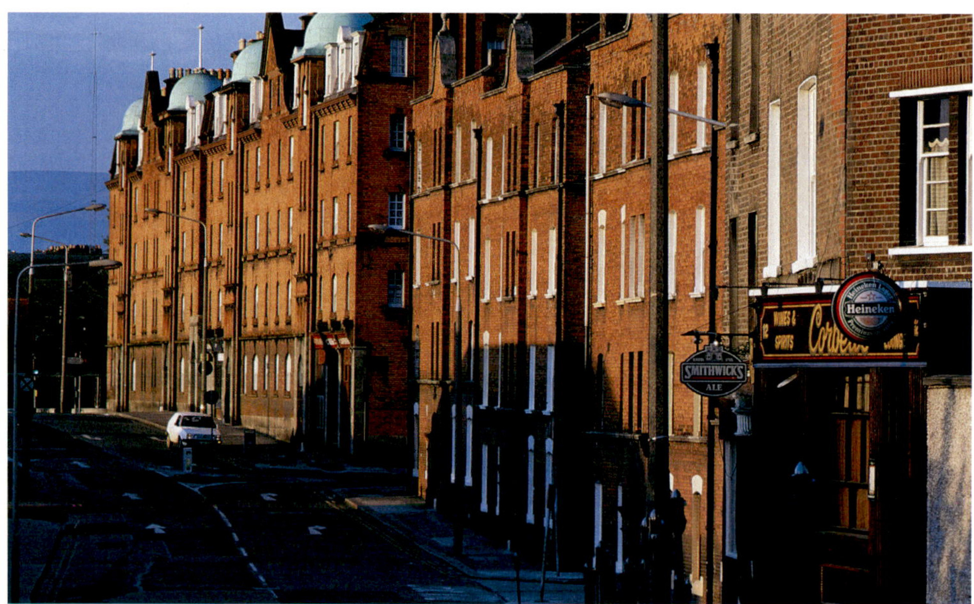

Government Building (left and right)

One of the most impressive of Dublin's buildings and recently restored as Government Office, the building was constructed as a College of Science. It had a long gestation period with the foundation stones was laid by Edward VII in 1904 and final completion only in 1922 after the end of British rule. The architect was Sir Aston Webb although credit is usually also given to Thomas Manly Deane whose offices were demolished for the building but who played little part in the project.

The Liberties Area (above)

One of the oldest parts of Dublin is known as the "Liberties". At one time it was the heart of the city's rich industrial heritage.

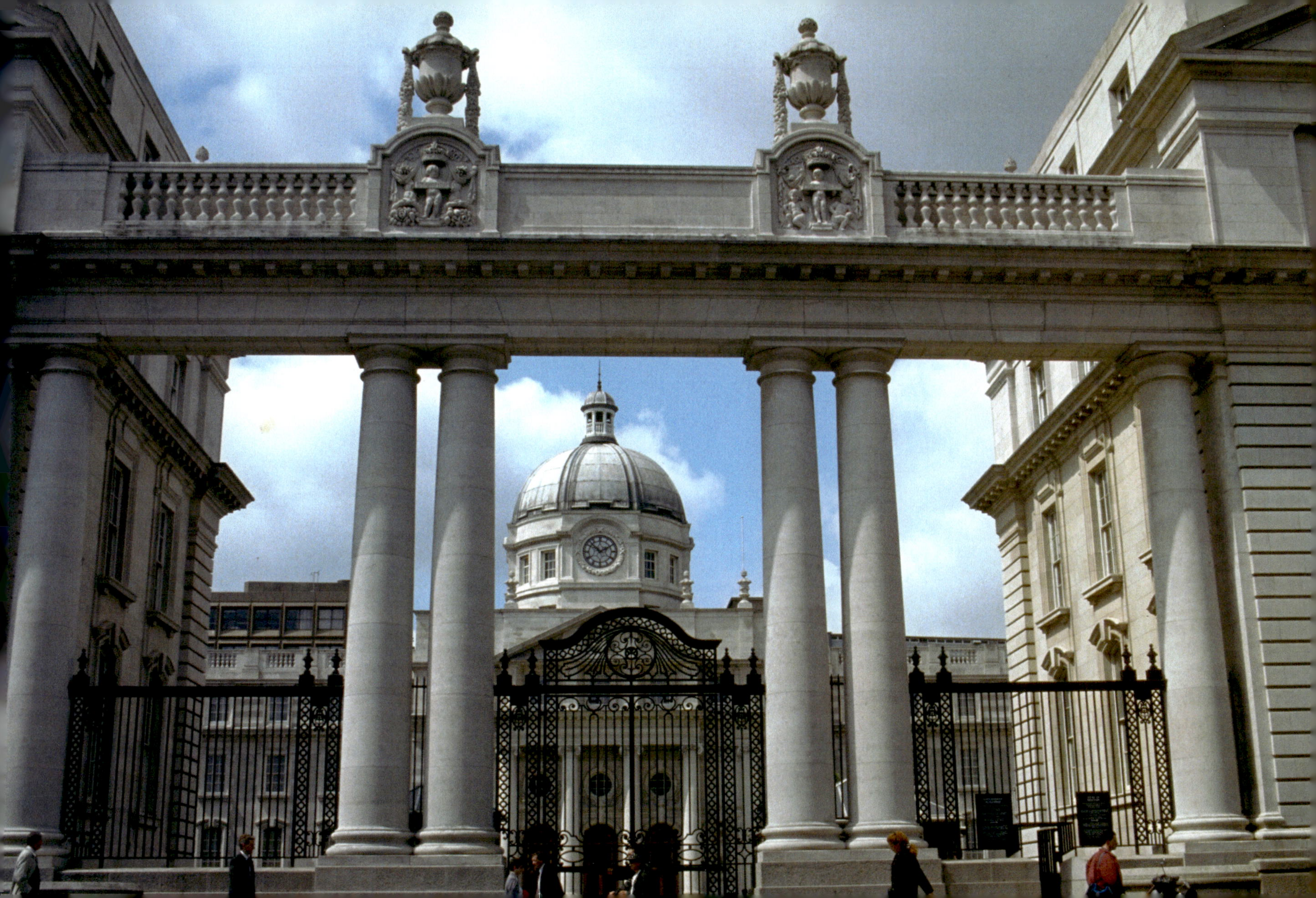

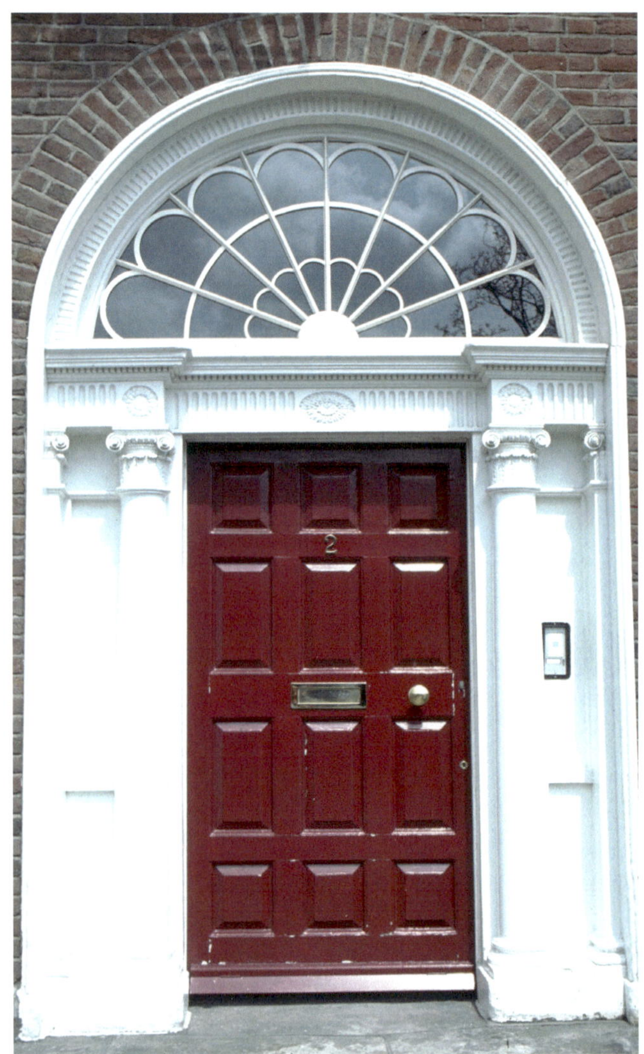

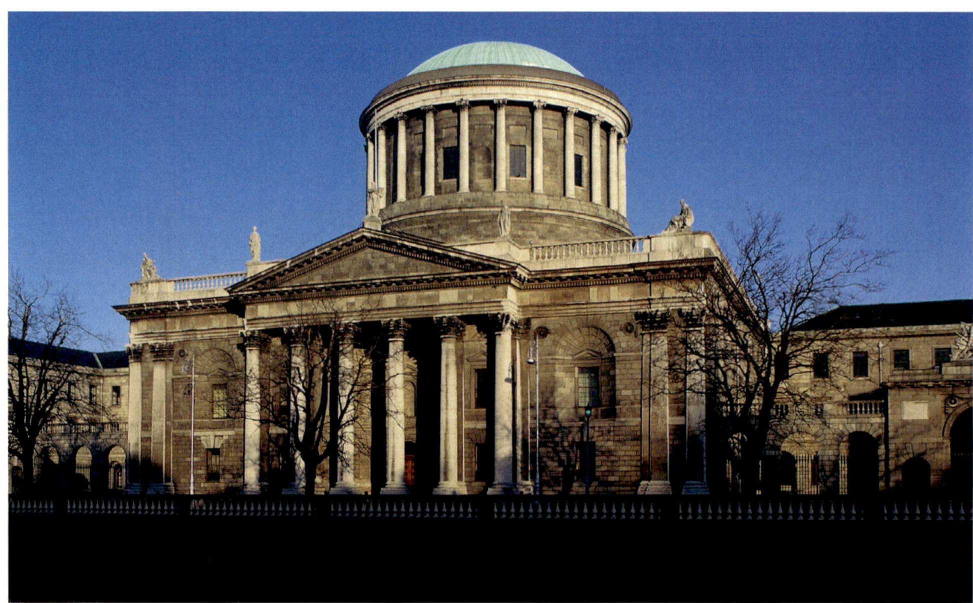

Georgian door, Dublin (left)
The eighteenth century saw a rapid growth in the size and population of Dublin. The city prospered. The mediaeval walls were swept away and new broad streets and squares constructed on either side of the Liffey.

Four Courts (above)
One of the landmarks of Dublin with its large drum and shallow dome, and visible all along the Liffey, Four Courts derives its names from the four divisions of the judicial system in Ireland—Chancery, King's Bench, Exchequer, and Common Pleas.

Trinity College (right)
Founded in 1592 by Elizabeth I Trinity is Ireland's oldest university and the only constituent college of the University of Dublin. This photograph shows Pomodoro's sculpture "Sphere within Sphere" (1982).

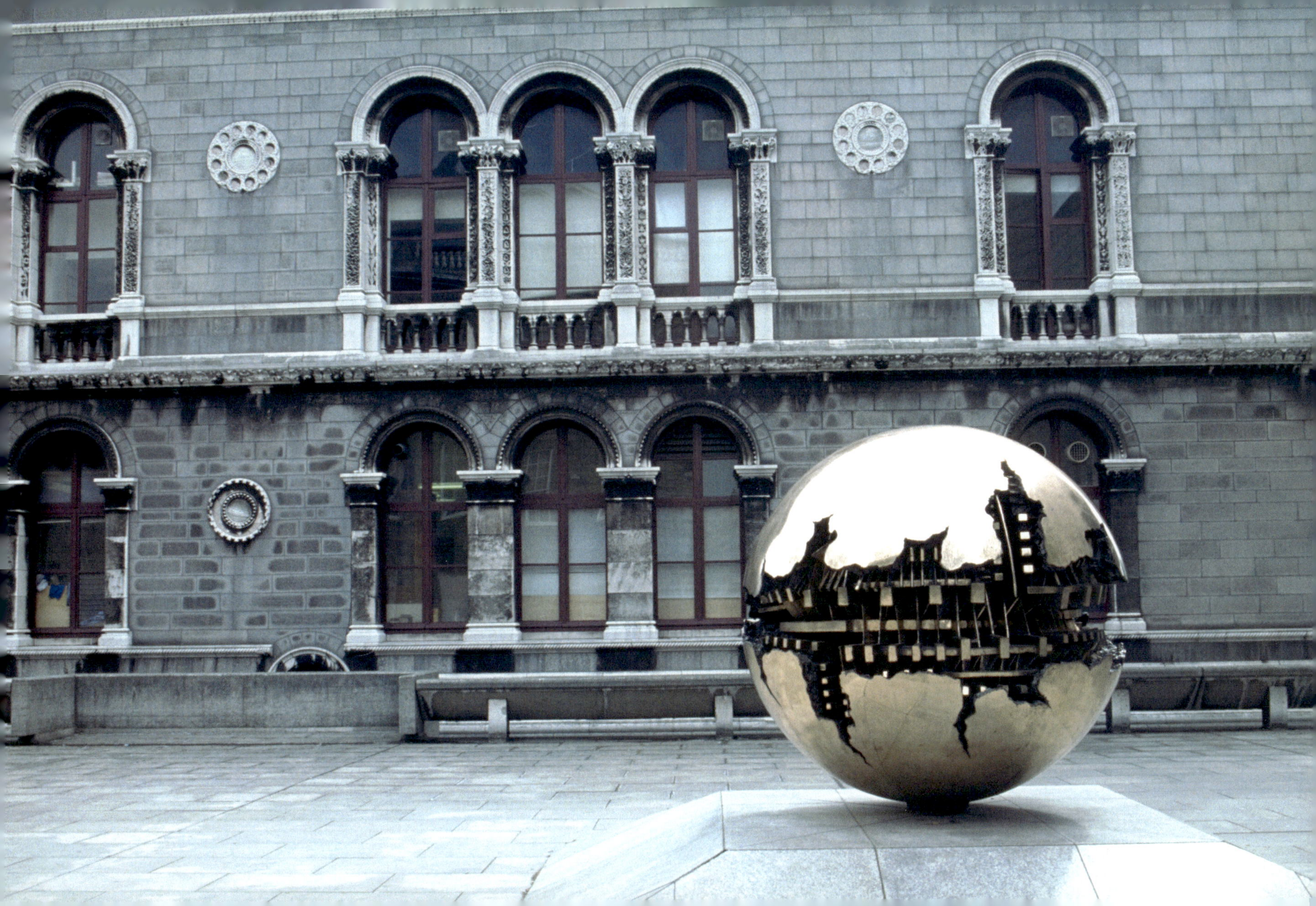

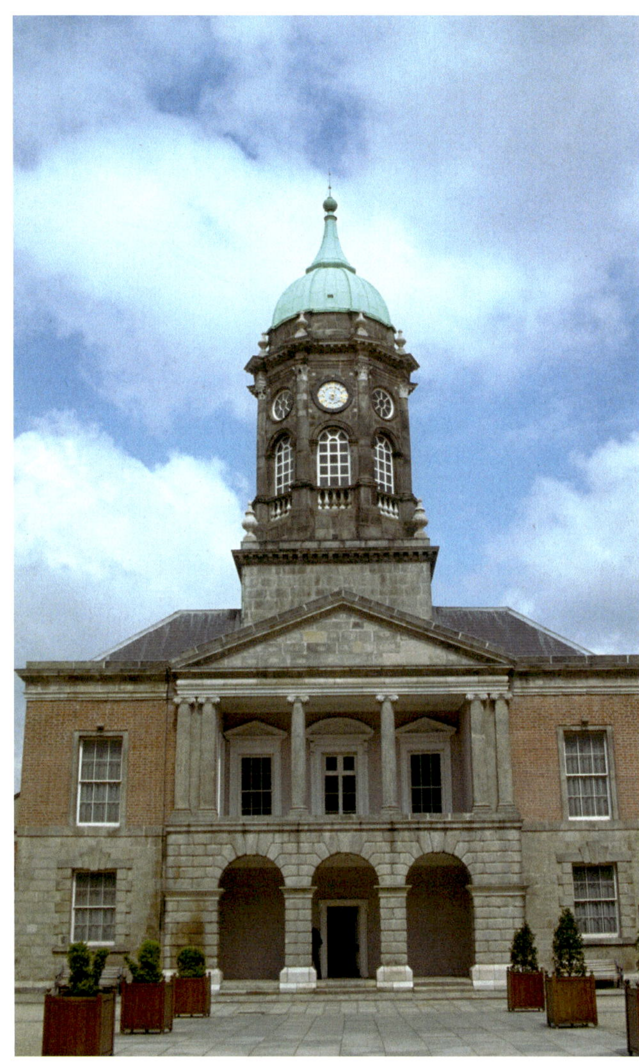

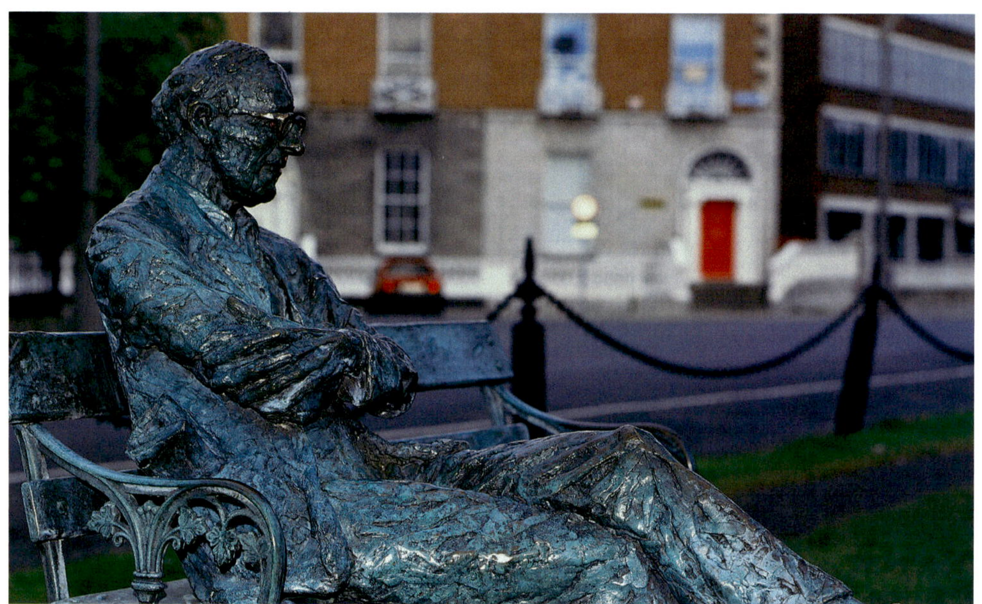

Dublin Castle (left)
More of a palace than a castle and currently used to entertain heads of state, it was originally built on the orders of King John in 1204 although rebuilt extensively after a fire in 1684.

Patrick Kavanagh Statue (above)
Born in Mucker, County Monaghan in 1904, the author moved to Dublin in 1939. This lifelike statue of him seated on a bench is on the bank of the Grand Canal in Dublin—and more than one visitor has unwittingly begged its pardon.

Dun Laoghaire Harbour (right)
Situated near Dublin, Dun Laoghaire began as a fishing village, but since the 19th century, it has become part of the sprawling suburbs of the capital. King George IV officially opened the Harbour in 1823. The Car Ferry Terminal was completed in 1969.

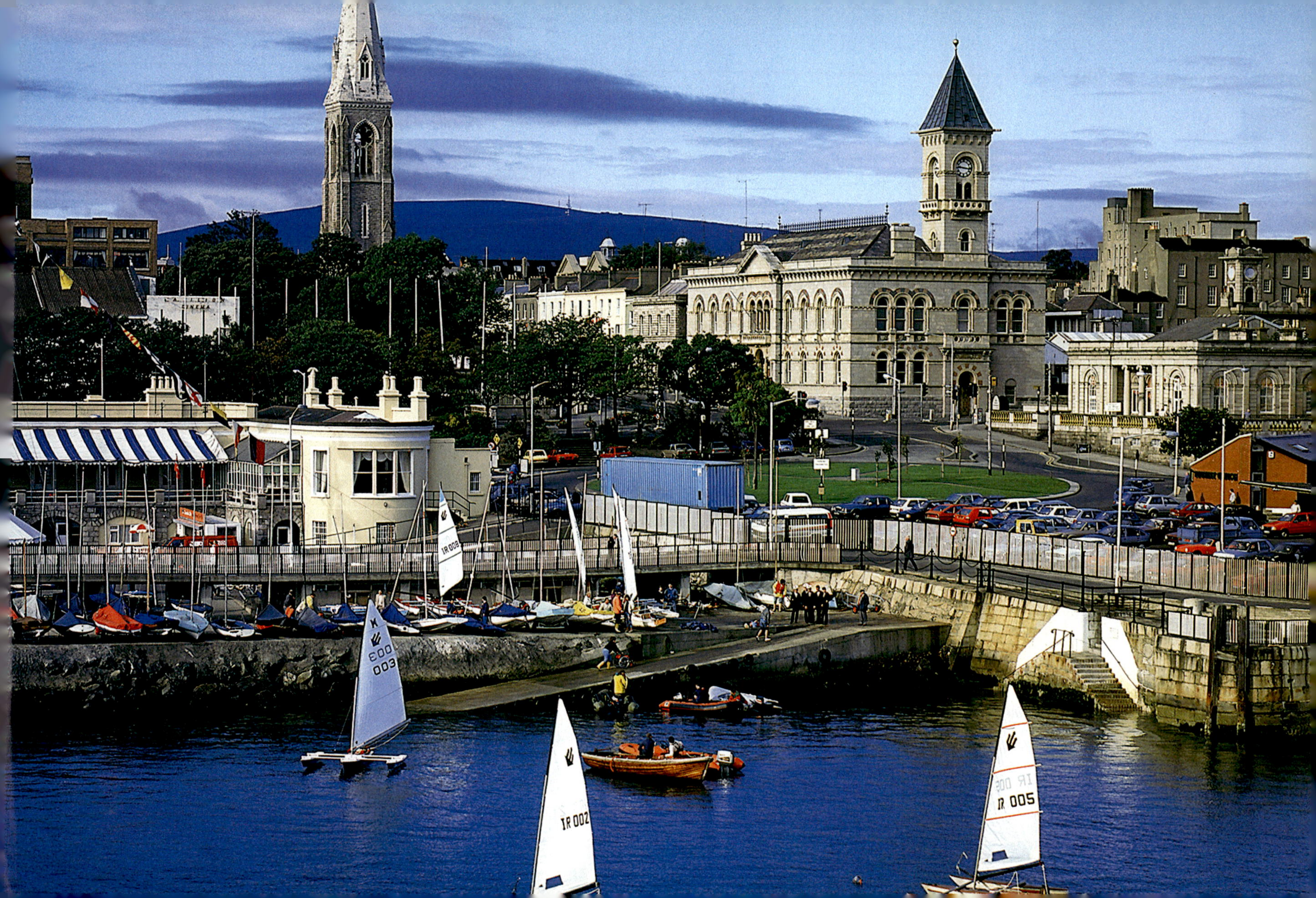
003
IR 002
IR 005

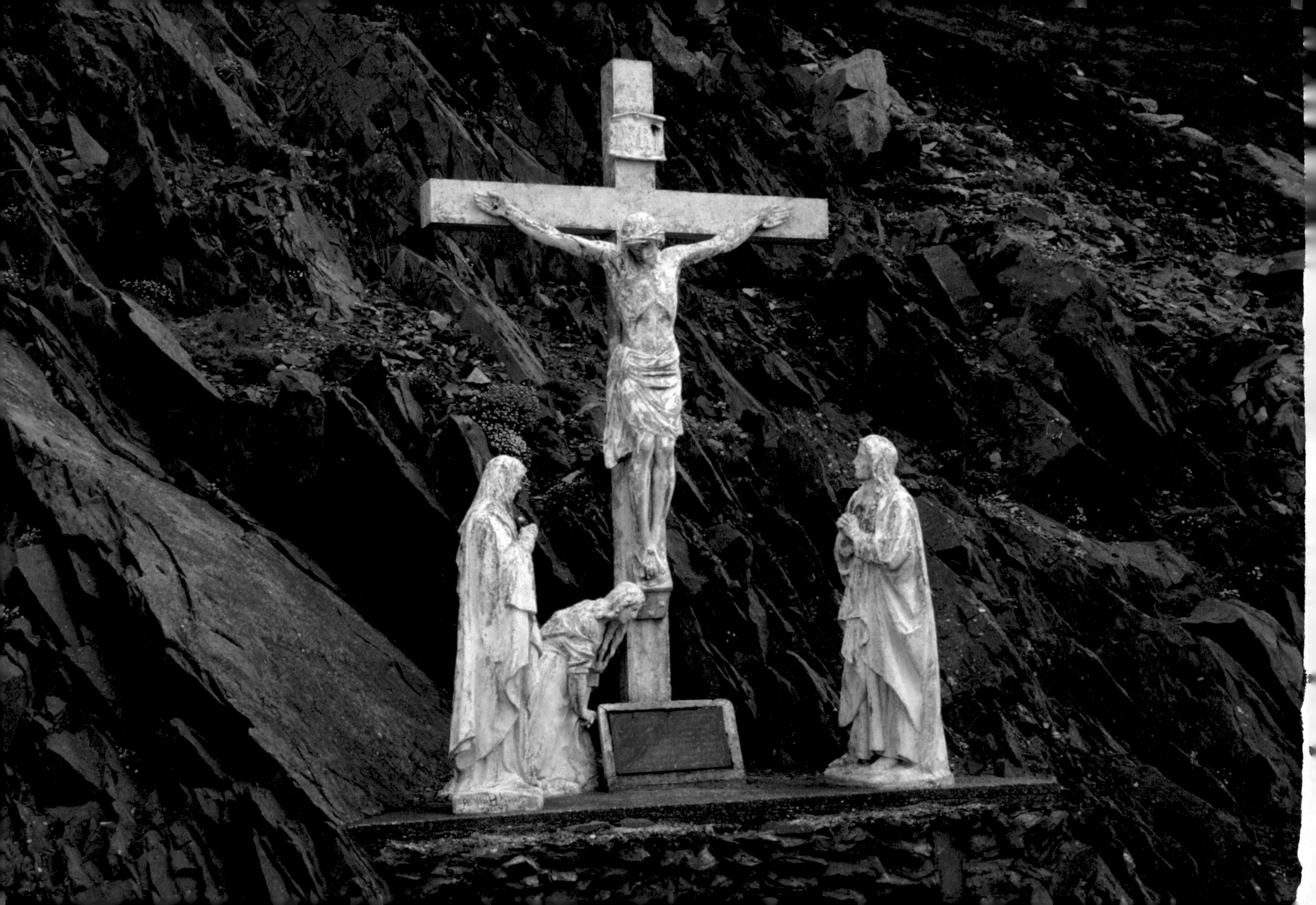

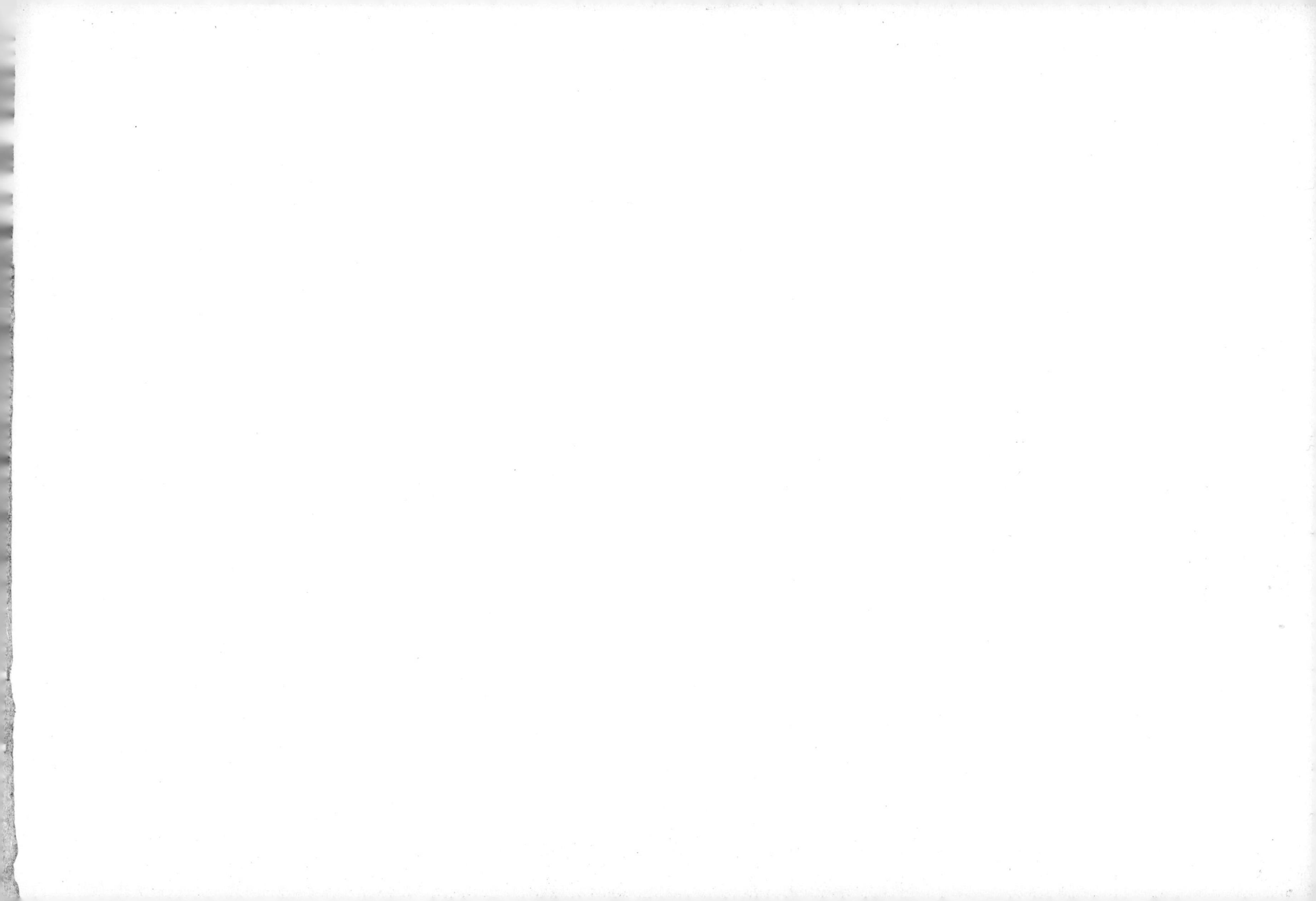